PROVINCIAL AND TERRITORIAL LEGISLATURES IN CANADA

PROVINCIAL AND TERRITORIAL LEGISLATURES IN CANADA

Edited by
Gary Levy and Graham White

UNIVERSITY OF TORONTO PRESS

Toronto Buffalo London

© University of Toronto Press 1989
Toronto Buffalo London
Printed in Canada

ISBN 0-8020-5825-6 (cloth)
ISBN 0-8020-6734-4 (paper)

Canadian Cataloguing in Publication Data

Main entry under title:

Provincial and territorial legislatures in Canada

Papers presented at a conference held in Quebec City in March 1987.
Includes bibliographical references.
ISBN 0-8020-5825-6 (bound) ISBN 0-8020-6734-4 (pbk.)

1. Legislative bodies - Canada - Congresses
2. Provincial governments - Canada - Congresses.*
3. Canada - Politics and government - Congresses.
I. Levy, Gary.   II. White, Graham, 1948-

JL179.P76 1989   328.71   C89-094867-4

CONTENTS

ACKNOWLEDGMENTS

The papers for this book were prepared for a March 1987 conference in Quebec City on the Parliamentary Tradition in Canada. The idea originated in a discussion the editors had with Professor Robert Jackson of Carleton University during a previous conference, also in Quebec. It seemed to us that although many conferences devoted to legislatures take place they usually consist of politicians talking to politicians, or parliamentary staff talking to parliamentary staff, or professors talking to professors. What was needed, we thought, was a forum bringing together everyone interested in parliament and legislatures for the purpose of thoughtful discussion about the state of parliamentary government in this country.

Ideas are free but conferences cost money. The next step was to find a sponsor and by happy coincidence 1986 happened to be the seventy-fifth anniversary of the Commonwealth Parliamentary Association. Each of the regions of the association was encouraged to hold some special event to mark the occasion. We approached the Canadian Region of CPA for funds and they agreed to provide a subsidy to get our project off the ground. The Speaker of the Quebec National Assembly suggested the Quebec legislative building as a most appropriate site for a discussion of parliamentary tradition in Canada.

With further financial support from the Canadian Study of Parliament Group and the Social Sciences and Humanities Research Council of Canada, a three-day conference took place in March 1987. Approximately one hundred delegates, including parliamentarians, academics, students, staff, legislative interns, and interested individuals from across Canada, attended.

We would like to record our appreciation to several persons whose assistance and co-operation were essential to either the conference or the eventual publication of this book. These include Pierre Lorrain, Speaker of the Quebec National Assembly; Ian Imrie, secretary general of the Canadian Region, CPA; André Trudeau and his colleagues from the Members Services Directorate of the National Assembly; James Mallory, past president of the Canadian Study of Parliament Group; Virgil Duff of the University of Toronto Press; Diane Mew who copy-edited the manuscript and Anna LaBallister of the Parliamentary Associations Secretariat in Ottawa, whose involvement in this project from its earliest organizational stages up to publication was always above what we had any reasonable right to expect. We are, of course, particularly grateful to the individual contributors who not only prepared the original papers but updated or revised them in light of recent developments or comments at the conference.

Aside from the articles included in this volume, several other papers were presented at the conference, including one on the Senate by Gary O'Brien, director of the Senate Committees Branch, one on the election of the Speaker of the House of Commons by Deputy Speaker Marcel Danis, and one on the House of Commons by Professor Jackson. The decision to exclude these papers from the present volume is no reflection on their quality but simply an editorial decision to concentrate on provincial and territorial assemblies about which much less has been written.

Gary Levy   Graham White

GRAHAM WHITE AND GARY LEVY

INTRODUCTION

The comparative analysis of Canadian provincial and territorial assemblies

Canada is a veritable laboratory of parliamentary government with no less than fourteen legislative assemblies and over eleven hundred legislators. The Senate, by virtue of its non-elected nature, is somewhat of a nonpareil and there is no dearth of material on the House of Commons. But the other twelve legislative assemblies, ten provincial and two territorial, have received less interest.[1] They are the subject of this collection.

Our aim is twofold: to make available recent information about provincial assemblies for students of individual provincial political systems, and to provide the basis for a comparative analysis of a key set of Canadian political institutions. These institutions are well suited to comparative analysis since their basic structures and operating principles are essentially similar.

The importance of provincial legislatures will increase considerably if and when the 1987 constitutional amendments agreed upon by the prime minister and ten provincial premiers come into effect. The so-called Meech Lake Accord would increase the number of areas where the unanimous consent of all provincial *legislatures*, not just *governments*, is required in order to amend the constitution. For the first time provincial legislators are going to have a role in the governance of the federation. While we can only speculate on the effect of this, we think it has the potential to alter some traditional ideas about Canadian federalism and, indeed, Canadian politics in general. For this reason alone it is worth learning more about how provincial and territorial assemblies operate.

The northern territorial assemblies share, by custom if not by law, most of the features of provincial houses. If the Meech Lake Accord is ratified without change, the territorial assemblies will see a decline in their status vis-à-vis provincial ones. For this and other reasons, political life in the north is focusing on some issues that go to the very heart of what Canada is about and how it is to be governed. We have no hesitation in including northern assemblies in this kind of comparative study.

Institutional Transfer

Provincial assemblies are examples of both the extent and the limitation of the process by which institutions are transplanted from one society to another. All derive their basic structure and fundamental operating procedures from the British House of Commons. The principles of responsible government, cabinet solidarity, and loyal opposition are common to all, as are many less central practices and customs. Yet variations in historical development and in political culture across the provinces have shaped the basic institutional framework significantly. Moreover, the process of institutional transfer was less straightforward than might first be imagined. So far as was practical, the representative institutions which emerged in the older provinces were attempts to adapt to local circumstances the parliamentary institutions then prevailing in Britain. It is thus not surprising that a British observer of the Nova Scotia House of Assembly in the 1970s should find many of its procedures similar to those of the British House of Commons prior to the 1860s.[2] For provinces west of Ontario, Westminster remained the theoretical inspiration but in practice the House of Commons in Ottawa was the practical model. Even today the rules of procedure in several provinces stipulate that in cases where there is no provincial precedent they shall be decided in accordance with rules in force in Ottawa.

Provincial legislatures have adopted few of the major changes that have transformed the British House of Commons since the 1880s. Thus the formal question period established by the provinces over the past two decades owes rather more in form and tactics to question period in the Canadian House of Commons than to British question time. Procedural wrangles are much more likely to be sorted out in provincial assemblies by recourse to the Canadian *Beauchesne's Rules and Forms of the House of Commons*[3] than to the British *Erskine May's Parliamentary Practice*.[4]

The 1985 Report of the Special Committee on Reform of the House of Commons (the McGrath Report) generated far more interest at the provincial level than any recent set of British reform proposals. The principal thrust of the McGrath Report was to restore to parliament its lost importance by providing for individual MPs a meaningful role in the formulation of public policy. Among the reforms proposed by the McGrath committee, and for the most part implemented early in 1986, were the following: changes to the rules for private members' bills, which substantially increased their influence over government policy; expansion of committee powers; and the election of the Speaker by secret ballot to enhance the independence of parliament from government.

Institutional transfer between provinces appears to be quite limited. Members of provincial legislatures tend to know very little about one another's institutions, whereas they often know a good deal about the House of Commons, no doubt in part because of their contact with their counterparts in Ottawa, as well as the sprinkling of former MPs in provincial houses. Such institutional transfer as does occur among provinces is usually in the sphere of services, perhaps because these are more readily transplanted piecemeal into varying local contexts than are procedures, which are more likely to be rooted in the unique traditions and circumstances of each provincial house. By way of illustration, Ontario and several other assemblies granted representation to the opposition parties on the body responsible for the administration of their legislature before the House of Commons adopted the principle.

On occasion institutional transfer occurs less because a province finds an idea attractive than because it is shamed into following suit with its fellows. Two developments in the realm of public accounts committees illustrate the point. Until recently, Nova Scotia and Prince Edward Island were the only provinces whose public accounts committees were chaired by government members. Without question, a major element in the decision by both provinces to appoint opposition chairmen was pressure to conform to the practice followed everywhere else in the country. A similar dynamic explains the Saskatchewan Public Accounts Committee's move a few years ago to abandon its practice of *in camera* hearings in favour of public meetings, as is the norm for other such committees.

Considerations of Political Culture

One theme to emerge clearly from the papers in this book is the importance of understanding provincial legislatures in their local context. Ian Stewart sets out the general relationship of political culture to legislative institutions. His analysis demonstrates the strength of this relationship in PEI, but it is evident in other papers as well. The traditionalism of Nova Scotia, the polarization of Manitoba and British Columbia society, Saskatchewan's social democratic tradition, the pragmatism of Ontario, and the sense of community in the Northwest Territories all powerfully affect their legislatures.

Political culture is a very broad concept, but it loses its explanatory power if treated simply as a residual category, encompassing everything which cannot be accounted for by other variables. This point comes through clearly in Louis Massicotte's treatment of the Quebec National Assembly. Quebec is often thought to differ markedly from all other provinces in its political culture but in most ways the National Assembly, though 'embedded in Quebec history,' to use Massicotte's phrase, is not particularly distinct from other provincial parliaments.

The Legislative Assembly of the Northwest Territories differs in a very basic way in that it has no political parties. As pointed out in the article by Kevin O'Keefe, this reflects a different way of approaching politics which derives from a population predominantly drawn from a cultural tradition different from the rest of Canada. This is not to suggest that the Assembly does not operate within the traditions of British parliamentarism; indeed, it recalls for us the often overlooked fact that in Britain the principles of responsible government developed prior to the emergence of disciplined political parties. Nevertheless, the procedures of the legislature of the Northwest Territories, the influence of MLAs, individually and collectively, and the overall role of the legislature in governance vary markedly from legislatures structured in terms of political parties, where members are first and foremost party representatives. Whether the Assembly is best understood as a consensual house, or simply a non-partisan one,[5] there can be no doubt that some of the generalizations set out below are of limited applicability to it, not because of its size, not because responsible government is still so new there, but because of the absence of parties.

Not all local peculiarities should be construed as manifestations of political culture; some are 'historical accidents.' This can mean a good deal more than the fact that in Prince Edward Island the government sits to the Speaker's left because in the early days that side of the Chamber was better heated. Frederick Engelmann's paper demonstrates the importance for the Alberta House of the province's tendency to go 'from one overwhelming majority to another.' Certainly part of this tendency is rooted in Albertan political culture and in social and economic conditions, but the gross distortions of the electoral system in transforming votes into legislative seats have exacerbated the scale of the majorities. Similarly, the 1975-81 minority government in Ontario, which so profoundly affected its legislature, arose from a unique confluence of unusual political events and was certainly not preordained by the nature of the province's society or political culture.[6] Even making allowances for quirks of history, provincial legislatures offer an unusually promising setting for examining the relative importance of structure and culture as explanations for differences in political institutions.

Size

Size is perhaps the most important variable in comparing the operation and effectiveness of provincial houses. The provinces cover the entire spectrum, with Ontario and Quebec having the largest houses (130 and 122 members). Of course, large is a relative term; by comparison with the national legislatures in Canada, the United Kingdom, and the United States these are small houses. By almost any standard, the legislatures of Prince Edward Island (32 members), Yukon (16), and the NWT (24) are small, but, as Patrick Michael's paper on the Yukon shows, the ability of even very small houses to function as parliaments depends much less on their size than on the attitudes of their members. The other seven provincial houses have from 52 to 83 members, five lying within the 52 to 64 range.

Several important consequences flow from this variation in size. First, in smaller houses, cabinets make up a much larger proportion of the membership. For reasons that need not detain us here, but which frequently strike visitors as bizarre, most provinces have cabinets of twenty or more. Thus often one-third or more of members in the House are ministers, who not surprisingly are more concerned with their ministerial than their legislative responsibilities. By comparison, in Ontario the cabinet represents only about one-fifth of the House and in Ottawa the proportion is even lower. Moreover, absolute numbers may be as important as proportions: in a house of fifty to sixty members, even for governments with comfortable majorities, there may only be about a dozen private members on the government side. A small government back bench might be expected to be in a better position to influence the cabinet than a large one, since each individual would count for a good deal more. In practice, however, the reverse seems to characterize provincial houses: the fewer the government private members, the less clout they possess. Of course, an important qualification to this proposition is that where the government holds only a slim majority over the opposition, as has been typical of Manitoba in recent years, individual government private members may count for a good deal despite limited numbers. The defeat of the NDP government in Manitoba by a single maverick back-bencher in March 1988 is an extreme but instructive case. More generally, though, it is hardly coincidental that the two provincial legislatures where members enjoy the greatest degree of independence are also the largest.

One way size affects the member's independence lies in the way that it can severely limit the scope and effectiveness of the committee system. A commonplace observation is that committees offer the greatest potential for members to influence government activity and to contribute to the policy process, yet if there are only thirty or forty private members available to serve on committees, the possibilities of their development are sharply curtailed. This problem is exacerbated when, as frequently happens, the private members on one side substantially outnumber those on the other side. In Nova Scotia, prior to the 1988 election there were only nine opposition members, split between two parties. Manitoba has a similar number of government private members;

this is simply too few for an effective committee system. What constitutes an effective committee system may be open to debate, but most certainly it is not a committee structure which exists mainly on paper. Several of the provincial legislative assemblies regularly establish elaborate committee systems which seem quite impressive until it is recognized that many of the committees rarely meet.

Specialization and role differentiation are also affected by size. While traditionalists might mourn the passing of the 'member-for-all-seasons,' capable of holding forth authoritatively on all manner of issues, government has become so complex that only by specialization can members hope to understand it or to influence it. But an effective division of responsibilities among opposition critics or official party spokesmen requires at the very least a dozen members, whereas opposition parties, even those enjoying the status of official opposition, commonly have caucuses well below this number.

Size can be an important determinant of procedure. To take but one illustration, smaller houses seldom refer legislation or estimates to standing committees; instead, Committee of the Whole is used much more extensively for these purposes. This is more than a technical distinction since the atmosphere in Committee of the Whole (which is in essence the House operating under slightly relaxed rules) tends to be more partisan than in standing committees. Moreover, witnesses – civil servants, interest groups, or private citizens – proscribed from Committee of the Whole, are permitted, indeed encouraged, to speak before standing committees. Conversely, smaller chambers can afford the luxury of more straightforward procedures. Michael Ryle, a British clerk who served for a time at the Table in the Nova Scotia legislature, has suggested that 'much of the complexity of Westminster and Ottawa procedures ... is a direct response to the problem posed by a large number of increasingly active Members. [Procedural] simplicity may be both more desirable and more possible in a smaller House.'[7]

Finally, size might reasonably be expected to have an effect on the atmosphere of a house: the interpersonal relations in a house of 55 would surely be different from those characterizing houses of 130 or 282 members. It would be equally plausible to argue that for smaller legislatures, 'familiarity breeds contempt' – that the personalization of hostility intensifies conflict – or conversely that 'to know one is to love one' – that members who know one another better are more likely to recognize their qualities as people, thereby leading to more harmonious relationships among members. Paradoxically, it may well be that the generally good interparty relations which characterize the larger houses – Quebec and Ontario – arise because of their size. A larger membership permits more cross-party contact through committee work, and it is when members spend extended periods in committees, away from the political pressure-cooker of the Chamber, working together on common problems, and especially travelling together, that they come to appreciate the human dimension of their opponents.

Political Parties

The size and number of parties within the legislature is of critical importance. Legislatures with more than two significant parties are qualitatively different from two-party houses. As Engelmann points out, the impressive accomplishments of Grant Notley as leader of a one-man (later two-man) party in Alberta caution against dismissing parties with minimal representation. Yet it is not unfair to characterize the Saskatchewan and Manitoba houses in mid 1987 as two-party legislatures, notwithstanding the single-member third parties in each. Aside from the ability of third-party members, perhaps the most important factor lies in the relative size of the opposition parties. One of the reasons that the New Democrats, with only three MLAs, were a significant force in the 1984-88 Nova Scotia House was that official (Liberal) opposition consisted of only six members. Now that the Liberals outnumber them twenty-one to two, their influence will likely diminish. Even under a very generous interpretation, only four provincial legislatures in 1988 can be considered three-party houses: Ontario, Nova Scotia, Manitoba, and Alberta. Over the past two or three decades, most other provinces have had some experience with more than two parties enjoying significant representation in the legislature, if only for a few years.

With three parties in the House, the possibility arises of minority government. Leaving aside the overriding question as to whether minority or majority makes for better government, it cannot be disputed that the legislature collectively and members individually exercise substantially greater power and influence under minority government. Historically, however, minority government has been very much the exception at the provincial level. Alberta, Quebec, Nova Scotia, Prince Edward Island, and New Brunswick have never experienced minorities; Manitoba in 1920-22, 1958-59, 1969, and since early 1988, and Newfoundland in 1971, had brushes with minorities, but the fate of the government often lay in the hands of independents rather than with parties. Saskatchewan had a minority between 1929 and 1934, as did British Columbia in 1952-53 and Yukon in 1985-86. In short, Ontario is the only provincial jurisdiction which, like Ottawa, has had prolonged recent experience with minorities: in 1943-45, 1975-81, and 1985-87. Several provinces have experienced coalition governments but these do not normally enhance the role of the legislature in the way that minority government does.

The presence of three parties creates an interesting question as to whether the fundamental division within the legislature is ideological – the NDP versus the old-line parties – or structural – government versus opposition. The Ontario paper points out that the presence of three parties greatly complicates the political calculus in the House, principally through the competition between the opposition parties.

It does not just matter how many parties are represented in the House; the nature of those parties, in particular their ideology, counts for a good deal. In legislatures where the NDP is a significant force more attention is generally devoted to fundamental questions about the role of the state in the economy, the distribution of wealth and power in society, and kindred concerns than in legislatures where the NDP is not a presence. In these legislatures, debate centres more on issues of governmental competence, probity, and the like.[8]

Conditions of Service

The availability of the annual publication *Canadian Legislatures*, which contains comprehensive comparative data on services and resources available to members in all Canadian legislatures, renders a detailed discussion of this topic unnecessary. It is worth emphasizing, however, the tremendous variation in resources which Canadian provincial legislators can call upon. In Ontario and Quebec members are very well served, both on an individual level, with respect to personal staff, constituency offices, and the like, and collectively, with caucus research facilities and professional non-partisan committee support staff. In some of the smaller houses, particularly in the Maritimes, members find themselves with precious few services and resources. The easy equation of better resources with a better legislature should be avoided, not least because of the extent to which resources tend to be devoted not to improving members' performance as legislators but to enhancing their re-election prospects. Still, it could reasonably be argued that whether members are serving their constituents, contributing to the policy process, or simply debating the issues, without some minimal level of services they cannot perform their duties effectively. Clearly, several Canadian legislatures have yet to attain such minimum standards.

In Quebec and Ontario certain economies of scale – in libraries, computer facilities, committee staff arrangements, and so on – give larger houses a certain advantage in providing their members with resources. Probably of greater significance is another dimension where these two legislatures differ markedly from most other provincial houses. An Ontario MPP has on average about 70,000 constituents, and the Quebec MNA roughly 52,000; in contrast, members in Atlantic Canada and in Manitoba and Saskatchewan all average fewer than 18,000 constituents and in Alberta the figure is about 29,000.[9] Thus pressure for constituency service has been much greater in Ontario and Quebec; in turn, members there have pushed more vigorously for additional resources (and have been able to mount a more convincing case for them). When members come to realize the possibilities open to them through personal staff and other resources, their appetite is whetted rather than sated.

Provision of enhanced services creates demands for further services. An essentially unexplored area of legislative studies in Canada is the role of legislative bureaucrats – who naturally tend to be more numerous and more professionalized in the legislatures with better services – in pushing for further expansion of facilities. As with most aspects of life, motives are mixed here: not only is there the inherent tendency of bureaucrats to attempt to expand their empires, but the new breed of legislative bureaucrat believes that for members to perform their roles effectively, they need substantial, high-quality resources.

Social Characteristics

Many of the papers in this book contain data reiterating the most common finding of studies of federal legislators: in terms of social characteristics, they are not representative of their electors. Members typically are older, better educated, and of higher socio-economic status than their constituents; by comparison with the general population, relatively few of them are women or of ethnic backgrounds other than Anglo-Celtic or European. The demographics of elected members vary from the populace in other ways as well, but the fundamental question is whether these differences matter. After all, both sense of duty and political self-interest dictate that members strive to represent all their constituents. Severe underrepresentation of social groups in legislatures is of substantial consequence, for two very different reasons. First, we need not accept the contentious premise that a member must belong to a group in order to fully understand its problems and perspectives to recognize that most members lack the time and inclination to immerse themselves in the experiences of a wide range of unfamiliar groups. It is not so much that members are hostile or uncaring about such groups, though this is a possibility, but they naturally are guided by and their priorities are largely determined by their own backgrounds and experiences. Accordingly a legislature with few, if any, women, or handicapped will not be as attentive to the problems of these groups. Secondly, politically salient groups that perceive their members to be excluded from such visible and supposedly representative governmental bodies as legislatures may not place much faith in the political system, thereby reducing its legitimacy.

The Independence of Members

Another possible point of comparison among provincial legislatures is the degree of independence from the government or the cabinet. One of the principal themes in the literature on parliamentary reform, evident in this collection, is the question of independence. As the various papers illustrate, legislative independence has many dimensions, only a few of which can be touched upon here. Within broad limits, the autonomy of provincial legislatures varies substantially across the country, but party discipline is essentially invariable. With the notable exception of the Northwest Territories, where the absence of parties renders the notion meaningless, party discipline is strong and pervasive in provincial assemblies. In no Canadian legislature are members nearly as willing to defy the party whip as are British MPs.[10]

Three particularly important aspects of legislative independence are the position of the Speaker, the financial and managerial autonomy of the House, and the ability of committees to determine their own agendas. The Speaker must be neutral and non-partisan in presiding over the House; this entails not only fair and even-handed decisions, but avoidance of the perception of partisan favouritism. Louis Massicotte's account of the Quebec speakership of thirty years ago illustrates the problem. On balance, the prestige of the speakership and the faith of the members in Speakers' neutrality have increased significantly in recent years throughout Canada. Yet a strong residue persists that the speakership is essentially a consolation prize for government private members who fail to make cabinet. This outlook is reinforced by the strong sense that the appointment of the Speaker is the premier's prerogative rather than the choice of the House; it seems unlikely that any province will soon follow Ottawa's lead in electing the Speaker by secret ballot. Furthermore, the practice of appointing Speakers to the cabinet, which would be an anathema in Britain and at best improbable in Ottawa, remains common at the provincial level. Much, however, depends on the personality of the Speaker and his determination to act independently on behalf of all members, as Agar Adamson's discussion of Speaker Donahoe's work to improve the Nova Scotia House of Assembly attests.[11]

Even the most independent-minded Speaker will be hamstrung without an autonomous administrative structure. More generally, to the extent that a legislature is dependent on the government for the provision of important administrative services, or more significantly, for the determination and approval of its financial requirements, that legislature lacks a basic prerequisite for independence. A key element is a Board of Internal Economy or Members' Services Committee to set administrative policy and to establish legislative budgets on which the opposition is represented and is taken seriously. In all provinces the government can control this body should it wish to do so, but in several provinces it acts with considerable independence from the government. As of early 1988 Newfoundland was the only legislature where the opposition was excluded from even nominal participation in the running of the legislature.

Autonomous administrative bodies with some measure of opposition involvement were all but unknown in provincial parliaments a decade ago; their spread is an important indication of the growth of legislative independence in Canada.

Committees represent perhaps the most effective means for private members to influence public policy and can powerfully enhance government accountability. These functions are far more readily performed by committees which do not need authorization to embark on policy studies or to hold investigations. Aside from public accounts committees, which typically enjoy free rein to look into any item of past government spending,[12] most legislative committees lack the power to initiate any activity without approval from the government. In jurisdictions where committees are not constrained in this way, such as the Northwest Territories, Quebec, and Ontario, committees tend to be more effective in enabling private members to influence the policy agenda. (As long as there were overwhelming majorities in Alberta, private members on the government side seemed to have worked out quite an adequate system of caucus committees but, as indicated in the Engelmann paper, it is not certain yet if strong caucus committees can coexist with strong legislative committees.) Not surprisingly, as committees become more independent and effective, they push more strongly for the removal of procedural shackles, and as they are given their own head to determine their own courses of action, they become still more independent and effective.

The Evolution of Parliamentary Government

One final point to emerge from the essays in this book is the magnitude of change in Canadian provincial legislatures over the past two decades. A collection of papers on provincial assemblies written in the 1960s probably would not have been much different from one produced in the 1940s or even the 1920s. We must be wary about equating change with progress or reform, but with few exceptions the authors of these papers are cautiously optimistic about the state of parliamentary government in provincial legislatures. To be sure, the cabinet still dominates the legislature, private members are essentially without power over public policy, and extensive scope exists for further reform. In most if not all legislatures, however, members are in a far better position than were their counterparts in the 1960s to influence policy, to hold the government accountable, and to represent their constituents. This is true in terms of both the services available to members and the procedures at their disposal. Equally as important, the idea seems to be gaining acceptance that members should be more than mindless voting machines – that they can and should contribute to policy development; that the Speaker and the apparatus of the legislature should be independent of government; that adequate services are essential if legislatures are to work effectively.

Recent reforms may be less important for their substance than for the potential they have created for truly substantial improvements. That changes will continue to transform our provincial and territorial legislatures seems indisputable; whether they will strengthen our provincial parliaments is an open question. Perhaps this book can contribute to the reform process.

IAN STEWART

PRINCE EDWARD ISLAND

'A damned queer parliament'

The first election on Prince Edward Island occurred in 1773. Surveying the elected members, the sergeant-at-arms remarked: 'This is a damned queer parliament.' For his outburst, he was fined and fired.[1] Today many Canadians might echo the ill-advised opinion of that unfortunate gentleman, as the Prince Edward Island Legislative Assembly has retained a variety of idiosyncratic characteristics. Nevertheless, this chapter will demonstrate that the PEI legislature operates in a fashion entirely consistent with the fundamental orientations of the provincial political culture.

Approaches to the Study of Legislatures

Prominent in the explanatory battery of any political scientist are the concepts of political culture and political institutions. To account for political phenomena as diverse as voting behaviour and public policy, a full understanding of the surrounding cultural and institutional context is all but indispensable. Yet this begs a prior question. Specifically, what is the nature of the relationship between these two critical concepts? It is, of course, self-evident that a society's political culture and political institutions are not hermetically sealed from each other. At its genesis, some aspects of the institutional framework will reflect at least some social values; subsequently, certain social values (although not necessarily the same ones) will come to be shaped by some aspects of the institutional framework.

Students of Canadian federalism have long recognized the essentially dialectical nature of this process. Partially because of the cultural pluralism that characterized the provinces of British North America in 1867, the Fathers of Confederation opted for a federal, rather than a unitary, constitution. Yet by so doing, they created a set of institutions which has subsequently strengthened, not merely sustained, the initial forces of cultural pluralism. Can we apply this understanding to a study of legislatures? By scrutinizing the evolution of the Prince Edward Island Legislative Assembly, this chapter will explore not only the nature of politics in Canada's smallest province, but also the linkages which can exist between the political culture and legislative institutions of any given society.

In general terms, then, what is the nature of the relationship between orientations and institutions? The intellectual godfathers of the modern concept of political culture, Gabriel Almond and Sidney Verba, were somewhat cautious on this question. Political cultures, they observed, 'may or may not be congruent with the structures of the political system.' Nevertheless, Almond and Verba did assert that where mixed political cultures emerge, 'there are inevitable strains between culture and structure, and a characteristic tendency toward structural instability.'[2] Moreover, like Carl Friedrich, but unlike J.S. Mill, Almond and Verba were at pains to highlight the limitations of constitutional engineering, of transplanting institutional frameworks (whatever their intellectual merit) into an unreceptive political culture.[3] More recent analysts have echoed these sentiments. Hence, John Redekop has observed that if political institutions 'are to function successfully, they must be in fundamental alignment with the central values of our political culture,' while Michael Whittington has claimed that 'the political structures must reflect the dominant values of ... (the) political culture if they are to be effective. If political structures serve to enshrine political values that are not congruent with the values of ... society, then either the people's attitudes must change to conform to the institutionalized values, or the institutions must change to reflect societal values better.'[4]

Such formulations as these raise as many questions as they answer. In particular, what aspects of the legislature must be 'congruent' with the surrounding political culture? There are at least three potential answers to this question. At the most basic level, it might be argued that no legislature can function effectively without widespread popular backing for its *existence*. Loewenberg and Patterson have noted in such successful liberal-democracies as Great Britain, West Germany, and the United States the presence of diffuse social support for the legislature that is unrelated to specific systemic performance. Such support, they conclude, greatly increases the probability of voluntary compliance with state initiatives.[5] While some research in the developing world raises doubts about this thesis, its application to Prince Edward Island is not particularly illuminating. It is true that there is widespread, and in some instances unconscious, support on PEI for the institutions of representative government. It is also true that this backing serves to legitimize the activities of the provincial state. Such observations, however, do little to advance our understanding of the relationship between culture and institutions.

A second, and potentially more fruitful, implication of the 'congruence' thesis would focus on legislative *output*. That which emerges from the legislative hopper, it might well be argued, must be within the mainstream of the surrounding political culture. From this perspective, we could deduce much about the dominant values of eighteenth- and nineteenth-century Prince Edward Island from the fact that at various times the provincial assembly enacted statutes which not only prohibited the 'disorderly riding of horses' and the practice of nude bathing in Charlottetown, but also decreed that the baptism of slaves did not free them from bondage and that the sending of threatening letters was a capital offence.[6] Admittedly, there are several weaknesses with this line of argument. Most notably, political culture and legislative output exist on different planes of generality. No political culture is likely to be policy-specific; at most, a political culture might outline a range of acceptable legislative responses to any particular policy problem. Hence, to understand the specific shape of legislative output would require a move beyond political culture to consider the interests and powers of a myriad of social actors. Hence, while not minimizing the importance of such a project, it is not a central concern here.

Instead, this chapter focuses on a third feature of the congruence theory – legislative rules, roles, and norms. The manner in which legislators approach their tasks, the expectations which govern their interpersonal relations, and the legislative procedures and precedents that have slowly accumulated over time might all be strongly influenced by the cultural context in which they have occurred. While intuitively plausible, such a thesis requires close scrutiny. First, the vast majority of the world's legislatures were established as a by-product of elite, rather than mass, activity. While it may be argued that elites have either unconsciously reflected or consciously affirmed the dominant political orientations of their society, the characteristically unrepresentative backgrounds of political elites prevent any easy assumptions about the representativeness of their values. Secondly, most non-European legislatures were initially modelled on a foreign example (customarily that of the colonizing power). Hence, because societies with such widely divergent political cultures as Kenya, India, Australia, and Canada all shared a common tie to the British Empire, they all adopted the British parliamentary system upon achieving independence. Admittedly, lengthy exposure to some of the same agencies of socialization would have produced a degree of cultural overlap between colonizer and colony (with the values of the latter moving towards those of the former). Nevertheless, if indigenous political orientations have found clear expression in the legislatures of former colonies (including, of course, Prince Edward Island), it is likely to have occurred subsequent to, and within the constraints of, the initial establishment of these legislatures.

A Traditionist Political Culture

Have other observers been able to detect the presence of dominant political values in legislative rules, roles, and norms? Given the highly abstract nature of political culture, no unqualified answer is possible. Nevertheless, analysts of Western European legislative institutions have cautiously advanced affirmative responses. Hence, it has been claimed that Dutch legislative norms have been 'strongly affected by ancient legal traditions which emphasize trustee concepts of representation.'[7] In a similar vein, one observer has claimed that Sweden's consensual political orientations underlie both the absence of provisions for non-confidence votes in the Riksdag, and the seating of legislators alphabetically (rather than according to party affiliation),[8] while another has uncovered the impact of political culture in the importance accorded to the role of the co-ordinator of the Vienna City Council.[9]

For analysts of the New World, however, the linkage between political culture and legislative rules, roles and norms is more problematic. Ronald Hedlund, for example, has argued that despite apparent cultural differences, the legislative norms which operated in Canada, the United States and Chile are remarkably similar.[10] Yet other observers, either more prescient or more fanciful, have disputed Hedlund's thesis. In his analysis of American state legislatures, Alan Rosenthal concluded that, 'how the legislative process works depends to a considerable degree on the ethical climate within the states.' While legislators in states such as Louisiana and Texas openly subscribe to the norm that 'someone is making money off the state and it might as well be me,' their counterparts in the Midwest are constrained by a more 'prudish' state culture.[11]

Can similar observations be made with respect to Prince Edward Island? Before their impact on the Legislative Assembly can be traced, it is necessary to highlight the dominant political orientations of the Islanders. The political culture of PEI has been remarkably stable over the past century, and its leading characteristics are easy to enumerate. Most prominent among these is a pervasive sense of traditionalism, an often unconscious acceptance of established practices. Indeed, in the eyes of one analyst, the most interesting features of Island politics 'are connected with the operation of a full-dress constitution in a small, traditional society.'[12] In comparison to other Canadians, residents of all four Atlantic provinces are more hostile to an expanded role for the state, more intent on retaining links with Great Britain and the monarchy, less permissive on moral issues, and so on.[13] In a recent survey of Islanders, a startling 29 per cent acknowledged being "too much of a traditionalist" ever to vote for the New Democratic Party. The corresponding figures for Nova Scotia and New Brunswick (provinces which have also proved to be unreceptive to NDP appeals) were only 24 per cent and 19 per cent, respectively.[14] In short, traditionalist values constitute the most visible outcropping of the Island's political culture; if they have not found expression in the province's Legislative Assembly, it is unlikely that any other orientations will have been more successful.

In reality, traditionalist values do seem to have affected the type of people who have become legislators on PEI. First, only those candidates who have been nominated by one of the two long-established parties (the Liberals and Conservatives) have had any realistic hopes of becoming MLAs. Although the Conservative Peter Pope briefly crossed the floor to sit as an independent in 1985, J.A. Dewar (in 1919) remains the only example of an independent candidate successfully seeking election to the provincial assembly. Minor party nominees routinely lose their deposits and, in some recent instances, have been outpolled by the spoiled ballot category.

Secondly, most MLAs conform to what might be regarded as a traditionalist image of a leader. Admittedly, it has become a cliché to observe that legislatures have rarely been demographic microcosms of the societies in which they are situated. As numerous studies have painstakingly detailed, the typical legislator has many qualities which distinguish him or her from the typical citizen. What is particularly interesting in the present context is the situation with respect to age and gender. As befits a traditionalist political culture, Islanders have apparently perceived elderly males to be best suited for leadership. The first female MLA in PEI (Jean Canfield) was not elected until 1970, and while the proportion of women in the legislature is no longer markedly atypical by North American standards, it does not remotely approximate the level achieved in the Scandinavian countries. Similarly, while Island politicians at both levels of government are no longer easily distinguishable by their geriatric qualities,[15] the age profile of the provincial legislature has been only perceptibly declining. The MLAs elected in 1982, for example, averaged 48.6 years. In short, the traditionalist predispositions of Prince Edward Islanders do seem to have found expression in the composition of the Assembly.

Such orientations have also been apparent in the widespread reluctance to professionalize the job of the legislator on PEI. High rates of legislative turnover, short lengths of legislative sessions, low salaries, and small staffs are all hallmarks of a non-professionalized legislature and all of these attributes are apparent on Prince Edward Island. In most liberal democracies in the western world, politics has become a full-time vocation. As a result, and notwithstanding some recent dramatic instances to the contrary, legislative turnover has been slowly declining. In the British House of Commons, the American House of Representatives, and the Canadian House of Commons, turnover rates in the nineteenth century often approached 50 per cent; in the late twentieth century, this figure has dropped in all three instances to approximately 20 per cent.[16] Yet the proportion of legislative neophytes returned after each of the last seven provincial elections on PEI has remained in the 25 to 50 per cent range. As in the American state legislatures, enjoying a career in the provincial assembly is not the norm for Island politicians.

The brief legislative sessions which are held every spring on the Island also bespeak of a non-professionalized legislature. In 1984 the legislature sat for thirty-five days; rarely does it sit for more than six to ten weeks a year.[17] It is clear, therefore, that the Legislative Assembly on Prince Edward Island is not suffering from overload. While it may be persuasively argued that the press of public business is sufficient to overwhelm parliamentarians in Ottawa, such has manifestly not been the case in Charlottetown.

Nor have MLAs been highly paid for their services. In comparison to their counterparts in the rest of Canada, Prince Edward Island legislators have consistently received the lowest annual salaries. In the 1950s, for example, private members in the other nine provinces earned anywhere from a low of $2,500 per year in Manitoba to a high of $7,000 in Quebec. For Prince Edward Island, the corresponding figure was $1,000.[18] Of course, thirty years of inflation have expanded these figures almost beyond recognition, but the relative rankings have changed only marginally. In 1986 Quebec MNAs were still the most generously remunerated in the country (at $50,290), while Prince Edward Island legislators were still at the bottom of the scale (at $23,800, almost $8,000 below the next most poorly paid group of MLAs from Saskatchewan). Even if the 1987 pay recommendations of PEI's chief justice are implemented, provincial MLAs will receive an annual total of only $27,000 in indemnity and expense allowance – a figure far below the regional, as well as the national, average.[19]

Finally, Island MLAs have historically received relatively little material or staff assistance in the performance of their legislative duties. Only in recent years have back-bench members been provided with office space; previously, MLAs were obliged during sessions to meet constituents down behind the stairs of the legislature.[20] And Island legislators still do not have any access to the sorts of resources which are routinely available to members of the US House of Representatives, or even of the larger Canadian provincial legislatures. Admittedly, there is a deceptive allure to such a non-technocratic approach. As Mike Breaugh, an Ontario MPP, once opined, 'members of the House and the Senate (in the United States) are basically pawns of the huge staff and bureaucracies which abound. At least Members of the Ontario Legislature can still identify who is supposed to be running the show and retain the ability to make fools of themselves on their own initiative.[21] Yet whatever the charms of public self-debasement, it is clear that a reluctance to provide adequate support for legislators reflects, in part, a pre-modern approach to managing the public's business.

In essence, therefore, the Prince Edward Island Legislative Assembly has yet to be professionalized: turnover rates remain high, annual sessions remain short, salaries remain small, and assistance remains inadequate. Small wonder, then, that most back-benchers consider their jobs to be part-time, rather than full-time responsibilities. Especially for those MLAs who are farmers, the combination of a six-week session in the early spring and the customary constituent contacts about roads, jobs, schools, and the like has not interfered excessively with their usual means of employment.

This norm of the part-time legislator further underscores the uniqueness of Prince Edward Island. It has been observed that Canada's political party system has become increasingly specialized, that with the professionalization of most provincial legislatures, political careers at more than one governmental level are becoming increasingly uncommon. In 1974, for example, fewer than 5 per cent of the members of the federal House of Commons had once held office at the provincial level.[22] Yet for Prince Edward Island legislators, election to the national parliament is, understandably, still considered to be a significant advancement and the proportion of Island MPs with provincial experience has remained relatively high. In fact, this is even true of Island cabinet ministers (who do have full-time administrative responsibilities and who are, in fact, remunerated at a level commensurate with their counterparts in the rest of the country).

Even the position of premier has not customarily been regarded as a 'career' activity. While Nova Scotia experienced the leadership of George Murray for twenty-seven years, Newfoundland of Joey Smallwood for twenty-three years, and New Brunswick of Richard Hatfield for seventeen years, the norm in Prince Edward Island has been to serve as premier for one or two terms and then be 'elevated' to the bench or in the Senate.[23] The most recent ex-premier of the Island, Jim Lee, received a senior federal posting linked to the Department of Veterans' Affairs. Hence, while the Norwegian Storting has been characterized as 'a last stronghold of the political amateur,' it is clear that such a title applies equally well to the Prince Edward Island Legislative Assembly.

The traditionalist values in the Prince Edward Island political culture have found expression not only in the background of MLAs, but also in the non-professionalized nature of the Legislative Assembly. It seems clear that these values have also affected the timing, if not the content, of legislative reform. Most changes in the rules and structures of the legislature have followed those that have already occurred in other jurisdictions. What is significant in the present context is the extraordinarily cautious approach taken to legislative reform on the Island.

Admittedly, one cannot read too much into the fact that Prince Edward Island was, in 1851, the last colony in British North America to achieve responsible government. The British Colonial Office had made it eminently clear that what applied to other provinces did not necessarily apply to Prince Edward Island which, it felt, was too poor or too small to support the institutions of responsible government; and repeated entreaties to the contrary by the Island Assembly were suspiciously regarded in London.[24] Nor, given the intervening role played by the British government,[25] can much be gleaned from the timing of PEI's move to unicameralism.

Yet the fashion in which the province shed its second legislative chamber is certainly suggestive. In the years after Confederation, the Legislative Council (elected solely by property-owners) steadily lost influence to the more democratically representative Legislative Assembly. Characterized by one contemporary observer as 'the old ladies' end of the building,' it became, for example, increasingly impractical for premiers to lead their administrations from seats in the upper chamber.[26] Yet when unicameralism came in 1893, it arrived under a remarkably reactionary cloak. The Legislative Assembly was to have, as before, thirty seats, but fifteen of these would be elected entirely by property-owners. In other words, an undemocratically based chamber whose powers had been declining and whose members had constituted less than one-third of the legislative total was suddenly resuscitated and guaranteed half the seats in a reconstituted Assembly. It would be 1962 before this enclave of privilege would be eliminated; and while all meaningful distinctions between the two categories of MLAs have been eradicated, Islanders still continue to elect both an assemblyman and a councillor in each of sixteen dual-member ridings.

Other aspects of the electoral system have also been slow to change. Although the situation has improved since 1803, when Robert Hodgson was elected in three different constituencies on the same day (in one instance, unanimously), the pace of electoral reform has been lethargic. The secret ballot was not institutionalized until 1913, women and employees of the federal government were not enfranchised until 1922, and property-owners not only had an extra vote until 1962, but also had the right (if they were so inclined) to vote for both an assemblyman and a councillor in *every* riding in which they owned property.[27] While other provinces have periodically redistributed legislative seats in response to demographic changes, the last redistribution in Prince Edward Island occurred in 1963. Not surprisingly, this has gradually produced a severe case of malapportionment; in the 1986 provincial election there were almost five times as many valid ballots cast in the district of Queen's 5th as in the riding of King's 5th.

The Island has also been slow to respond to the realities of bureaucratic power. Admittedly, one former cabinet minister has recalled that 'the ministers, during most of the year, play a pretty large role in the administration of their departments. The systems are smaller, and you become familiar with most of the people in most program areas. It's a very "hands-on" kind of situation.'[28]

Parliament on a Human Scale

Yet despite the relatively small scale of the public service in PEI, and even assuming that a cabinet of competent administrators can be extracted from the relatively small pool that is the government party caucus, it would be a mistake to equate *political* control of the bureaucracy with *legislative* control. Even on Prince Edward Island, delegated legislation has become an increasingly prominent policy tool. Yet the provincial legislature has made no attempt to strengthen its supervisory powers. In Ottawa, observers wonder, 'can Parliament control the regulatory process?'[29] and suggest that when the federal government introduces new legislation to Parliament, it should also submit samples of the regulations that entailed by the legislation to the Joint Committee on Regulations and Other Statutory Instruments.[30] In Charlottetown such proposals are regarded with some bemusement. Concluded one former cabinet minister: 'If some other system has a committee in the legislature (to check bureaucratic regulation), I think that would be ridiculous. It's for the government to control the civil service, not the legislature.'[31]

Similar suspicions are voiced about another innovation designed to check bureaucratic power – the ombudsman. Nine Canadian provinces now have ombudsmen and, while the federal government does not have a multipurpose office, it does have a variety of special-purpose ombudsmen (an information commissioner, a commissioner of official languages, and so on). Prince Edward Island, however, has yet to initiate any moves in this direction, and interviews with one-quarter of the current group of MLAs elicited a distinct lack of enthusiasm for the office. One cabinet minister observed that he did not 'see any use in this province for an ombudsman. Everybody knows everybody in this province, and they will come on a one-to-one basis if there is a problem. They can usually work it out.'[32] Confirmed another former minister, 'I think our legislature is the ombudsman. We don't need one.' Echoed a third, 'No way.'[33]

The Island's committee structure has also retained a traditionalist flavour. If public input is deemed necessary, hearings on proposed legislation are held before a special committee. For most public bills and all of the government's spending estimates, however, detailed consideration is still provided by Committee of the Whole. Admittedly, the relatively small number of Island MLAs would militate against the erection of a sophisticated committee structure. Moreover, it is not clear that siphoning work off from entire legislatures to committees has had the desired streamlining effect in other jurisdictions. Comparisons may be misleading given the obvious differences in subject-matter; nevertheless, over a five-year period between 1980 and 1984 the Canadian House of Commons, working with the aid of an elaborate system of committees, managed to pass a total of 189 public bills (for an average of 38 per year). Over that same time, the Prince Edward Island Legislative Assembly enacted 213 public bills (for an average of 43 per year).[34]

In any case, Island MLAs are quite satisfied with their present committee structure and none of those interviewed envisaged PEI moving towards the Ottawa committee model. As one Conservative MLA asserted, 'I would never want to see the estimates, as we say go to the committee system. I am a firm believer that these should be done on the floor of the House. I just find that there is too much bureaucratic input in the committee system and sometimes they overshadow. After all, these are the experts and they sometimes overshadow the elected members. I am talking about Ottawa and also some of the other Houses that do have the committee system.'[35] Confirmed another, 'We have a much better system ... Every elected member goes through the Estimates of the government. It's not sloughed off to some committee.'[36]

Moreover, it is only very recently that an opposition member has been selected to chair the Public Accounts Committee.[37] That the government's accounts should not be reviewed by a body headed by a government supporter has long been an accepted principle at the federal level and in most of the provinces.[38] Yet before acting on this matter, Island politicians were either defensive ('Because it's standard practice somewhere else doesn't mean that it's the right thing to do. And I'm not sure it's the right thing to do') or somewhat sheepish ('I think it should be an opposition member who chairs the Public Accounts Committee, and I think maybe you will see that ... happen, but maybe not. We didn't change it when we were the government, and I suppose I would be a hypocrite if I started hollering for it').[39] Like both Senate reform and electoral reform, interest in an independent accounting of government finances has tended to be a function of distance from power; nevertheless, in the 1987 legislative session, the Liberal administration did appoint Conservative Albert Fogarty to chair the Public Accounts Committee.

Finally, the Island's traditionalism has been apparent in the absence of a written or visual record of legislative debates. Although a written record of the daily question period is publicly available, and although legislative proceedings are recorded on tape, Prince Edward Island remains the only Canadian province which does not produce a full *Hansard*. In fact, even the practice of reprinting the debates on the budget and the speech from the throne was terminated in 1973. Although cost was the major reason cited to explain the lack of a *Hansard*, one MLA expressed surprise that any jurisdiction would do otherwise. 'I mean,' he concluded, 'you wouldn't expect them to write all that down.'[40]

Nor has the Prince Edward Island Legislative Assembly reconciled itself to the age of television, although cameras were recently permitted on an ad hoc basis into some committee hearings. Yet the prospect of televising the proceedings profoundly disturbs most Island MLAs. There is a curious tinge to such suspicions; after all, as one analyst has observed, 'it seems paradoxical that citizens should be unable to see on their television screens the one institution which above all others is, or should be, public and accessible to everyone.'[41] Despite clear evidence to the contrary from other jurisdictions,[42] Island legislators remain convinced that permitting television cameras in the legislature would either trivialize or sensationalize the proceedings. Repeatedly, concerns were expressed that the legislature would be turned 'into a media event,' that 'the decorum of the institution' would be downgraded, that while some members would be inhibited by the television cameras, others would 'be playacting all the time.'[43] In this, as in other reforms to the procedures and structures of the legislature, Prince Edward Island politicians have been notably cautious; television is not likely to come to the Legislative Assembly for some time.

It would seem, therefore, that the traditionalist orientations of Islanders have found expression not only in the composition of the legislature and its non-professionalized nature, but also in the pace, if not necessarily the content, of past legislative changes. Contemporary legislators on PEI do not accord a high priority to legislative reform; apart from tinkering with the hours at which the Assembly meets, few MLAs could conceive of any constructive amendments to the existing set of institutional arrangements. Of course, one must be careful not to push this line of argument too far in the direction of cultural determinism. At times the size of the Assembly and that of the province have had a large impact on legislative rules and structures; on other occasions the need to husband scarce financial resources has played a critical role. Yet even if one must reject mono-causal explanations, it seems evident that the traditionalist orientations of Islanders have significantly shaped the evolution of the provincial legislature.

Yet any political culture contains a variety of political values; to characterize Prince Edward Islanders as traditionalist is not to capture the totality of the province's political culture. There also exists on PEI what one observer describes as 'a high degree of informality.' With respect to political party organization, for example, 'there has been a tendency to interpret the rules to conform to local practice and to the circumstances of the moment. If no one is interested in an annual meeting it can be permitted to lapse; an ineffective committee can be ignored; a rule can be interpreted with elasticity to permit or justify an action.'[44] Very similar observations can be made about the workings of the Legislative Assembly.

At first blush, there would appear to be some tension between the orientations of traditionalism and informality. In fact, the two values are complementary. Traditionalism has manifested itself in a reluctance to reform established rules and institutions. Accordingly, when the initial socio-political circumstances which generated such structures have altered, Islanders have responded not by reforming the rules and institutions, but by becoming more casual about their application. To Prince Edward Islanders, rules are made to be bent, not changed. At its best, this orientation generates a refreshing lack of pretentiousness; at its worst, it breeds an unhealthy cynicism.

How has the orientation of informality found expression in the norms of the Assembly? As might have been expected, its most visible manifestation has involved the role of the Speaker. After all, the Speaker in any parliamentary system is both the guardian and the interpreter of legislative rules, and without his or her tacit acquiescence, a casual approach to legislative niceties could not be sustained. In Prince Edward Island, the Speaker has generally governed less according to parliamentary texts such as Beauchesne, and more according to what the contemporary occupant has characterized as 'the feeling of the House.'[45] In particular, the daily question period in the Assembly tends to be very free-wheeling. As one former Speaker observed, 'if things are not bothering the members and it doesn't get vociferous or something like that, you tend to let it go along. Now if there were a genuine third or fourth supplementary and you can tell the difference where they're actually seeking information, well nobody minds if you allow an additional supplementary ... You try to allow as much latitude as possible to all debates.'[46]

Several members recalled their surprise when, upon visiting other provincial legislatures, they encountered Speakers who inflexibly applied the rules of procedure. In the Prince Edward Island Legislative Assembly, by contrast, the *de jure* rule of law has frequently become the *de facto* rule of men and women.

Caucus meetings have also apparently been infused with a spirit of informality. Even in the government party, where front-benchers have often outnumbered their back-bench counterparts, there have not generally been visible status differentials in caucus meetings. As one current Liberal back-bencher asserted: 'I would have to say that I have as much say in caucus as anybody else. I don't wait for senior members to necessarily express their opinions first.'[47] In fact, virtually all of those interviewed were able to recall numerous instances when caucus flexed its legislative muscles. In the words of one Conservative MLA, 'I think as a caucus we had to try to come to a consensus as best we could. But I can tell you that we had some very strong caucus members who were not cabinet ministers and many times ... when we as cabinet ministers would bring in a bill that we thought was the best possible bill, we often found that when we caucused our bill that we were changing some of our bill because we had strong caucus members who just were able to convince us that maybe our thinking wasn't the best.'[48] In Prince Edward Island caucus rooms, back-benchers are apparently heard as well as seen.

A relaxed attitude to the principle of cabinet solidarity has also been characteristic of PEI. While first ministers in most parliamentary systems have expected their governments to speak, at least in public, with a single voice, such has not always been the case on Prince Edward Island. At various times, ministers have publicly criticized their government's budget, complained that they have not been consulted on important measures of policy, and denied responsibility for their department's public accounts. In one particularly striking example, a minister without portfolio raged against his cabinet colleagues on the floor of the Assembly. 'When you fellows get an honest man,' declared John Archie Campbell, 'you chuck him out of office, and when you get a crook you hang on to him.' Yet in all of these cases, the dissenting minister was neither asked for, nor volunteered, his resignation from the cabinet. Even premiers have been guilty of publicly dissociating themselves from their own administration. As far back as 1880, Islanders witnessed the curious spectacle of a premier urging the lieutenant-governor to refuse royal assent to a bill that had just been passed in the Assembly. Premiers have also 'hinted' to ministers that something would have to be done 'to check the tendency of departments to run wild on their estimates,' and have attacked proposed government bills as 'exceedingly dangerous legislation.' Small wonder that one observer has concluded, 'there is often an extraordinary informality and elasticity in the (legislative) process ... Where Ministers have criticized the departmental estimates of their colleagues, condemned their own Government for extravagance, introduced Government bills and changed them entirely in one stage or other, and sponsored a number of other equally unusual practices, it is impossible to say that there is any definite, formal set of recognized rules, other than the ... skeleton procedure.'[49]

Finally, the informality of Island politics has been apparent in the immediacy of contacts between legislators and constituents. Admittedly, this is partially a function of size; whereas the average for the other nine provinces is one legislator for every thirty-six thousand constituents, in PEI the figure is one to four thousand. While the Island ratio seems extreme to most Canadian observers, it can be parenthetically noted that New Hampshire, with a state population of just under eight hundred thousand, has a *lower* house of four hundred members (for a ratio of one to two thousand). Yet even allowing for the relative ubiquity of legislators on PEI, two points stand out. First, Islanders expect to have direct personal access to their MLAs; despite their part-time status, legislators are always 'on call.' As one MLA ruefully observed, 'The people expect their elected representatives to be very accessible and available twenty-four hours a day, seven days a week, almost. And certainly with the Premier and Cabinet Ministers, Islanders just take for granted that if they walk into the office that you're there.'[50]

Secondly, Island MLAs perceive their role predominantly in terms of constituency service. In this respect, they are different from their counterparts in such major parliamentary democracies as Great Britain or West Germany, but similar to legislators in such societies as New Zealand and Ireland (of whom it is said that 95 per cent of deputies spend 95 per cent of their time working for their constituents). In fact, one study of provincial legislators recalled that Island MLAs were far more likely than their counterparts across Canada to suggest that they would subordinate their own views to those of their constituents.[51] Subsequent interviews by the author have confirmed the dominance of the delegate, rather than the trustee, role. One MLA recalled that when the provincial government was debating the merits of mandatory seat-belt legislation, she took the time to discover the views of her constituents. When it became clear that a significant majority in her district opposed the proposal, she felt bound, despite her personal convictions to the contrary, to act likewise.[52] And another long-time legislator observed that 'a good MLA's views should never [go against those of his constituents] because he's representing the constituents. I would have to go by the views of my constituents because they elected me to represent them in the legislature.'[53]

Party Discipline

It would appear, therefore, that a variety of legislative norms have developed which have been, at the very least, consistent with the orientation of informality in the Island political culture. Provincial MLAs (including the Speaker) have ignored rules of order, principles of solidarity, and differentials of status while remaining remarkably open and receptive to their constituents. All of this might lead one to believe that Island MLAs have been less constrained by what Richard Rose has dubbed 'the iron cage of party government,' and that party discipline has been only minimally apparent in the provincial legislature. Surprisingly, this has not been the case. Members of both parties unanimously agreed that intra-party splits have been confined to votes in the caucus rather than in the Assembly. Those who have, for whatever reason, felt unable to support the established party position have simply absented themselves from the legislature at the time of the vote. In fact, none of the newer legislators were able to recall a single instance in which an MLA had voted against his or her party, and while their more experienced cohorts were certain that such an event must have happened, they were unable to provide any details.

How is this strict party discipline to be explained? Some have attempted to root it in what appears to be a disproportionately large cabinet for the size of the legislature. Frank Mackinnon, for example, has suggested that because cabinet ministers comprise almost one-third of the Assembly, they occupy 'an unusually dominant position both in the Legislature and in the caucus, a fact which gives it a distinct advantage in controlling legislation and debate and in maintaining discipline in the party.'[54] Yet at least by Canadian standards, the political executive is not particularly big on PEI; in fact, six of the other nine provinces have cabinets which constitute a larger share of the legislature than exists on the Island. Others might look to the institutional imperatives of the parliamentary system. Where such structures exist, and especially in the parliaments at Westminster and Ottawa, the sources of many Island precedents, party discipline has generally maintained the necessary level of harmony between the executive and legislative arms of the state.

There are three problems, however, with the argument that the parliamentary system has constituted a necessary and sufficient condition to explain the consistent failure of Island MLAs to vote against their party in the Assembly. First, the separation of powers which characterizes the congressional model of representative democracy should render that system much less vulnerable to the excesses of party unity. Yet it is important to remember that voting along party lines was a much more frequent occurrence in the nineteenth-century American House of Representatives than it has become in the twentieth century.[55] Secondly, party discipline was once much weaker in the Island's Legislative Assembly; in the years immediately before and after the province joined the Canadian federation, religious splits frequently cut across party divisions.[56] Thirdly, the extent of party discipline has varied significantly not only across jurisdictions with the same institutional arrangements, but also over time within any given jurisdiction. Accordingly, the strong partisan discipline that now exists in the Prince Edward Island Legislative Assembly must be based on more than the mere existence of parliamentary institutions.

Does a scrutiny of the provincial political culture increase our understanding of this phenomenon? It would seem so. Numerous observers have commented on the intensity of political partisanship on PEI. Island voters have been less prone than their counterparts in the rest of Canada to change their partisan allegiances over time,[57] and one analyst of Island politics has concluded that, for some, 'being a Liberal or Conservative is of almost religious significance.'[58] Consistent voting along party lines in the Assembly, one is tempted to conclude, has just been the legislative manifestation of this broadly based political orientation.

Conclusion

This chapter has shown that the rules, roles, and norms of the Prince Edward Island legislature have been consistent with the dominant orientations of the provincial political culture, and, in this respect at least, the 'congruence' hypothesis would seem to have been sustained. Two caveats are necessary. First, it is appropriate again to stress the dangers of cultural determinism. A number of legislative rules and norms (such as the fact that the government sits on the left, rather than the right of the Speaker's chair) undoubtedly owe their existence to the vagaries of historical accident. Secondly, political culture is an abstract concept; the presence of any given political orientation must be entirely inferred from the presence of more visible political phenomena. Accordingly, the more sceptical reader of this paper might argue that political orientations are too amorphous to carry much explanatory weight. Given the heterogeneity that exists within virtually all political cultures, it might be suggested that one could always point to some value which might serve to support any particular institutional feature. Such reservations can never ultimately be uprooted. It is important to stress that, despite working from different data bases, most scholars of Island society and politics have stressed the pre-eminence of traditionalism, informality, and partisanship in the provincial political culture. That the Legislative Assembly has functioned in a fashion so congruent with these orientations can hardly have been entirely by chance.

GRAHAM WHITE

ONTARIO

A legislature in adolescence

We often think of political institutions in terms of human development. From this perspective, the Ontario Legislature might best be thought of as a teenager. With the growing pains of childhood behind it, it possesses the physical attributes of adulthood, but remains emotionally and psychologically immature. Though capable of sophisticated, responsible behaviour, and of powerfully influencing the world around it, its range of experience is limited and it often lacks confidence in its own abilities. Like the typical teenager, the Legislature is uncertain of its role and looks to others for guidance. Yet whatever ideas and advice others may offer, it will have to devote some serious thought to the way it is developing and to its inherent strengths and weaknesses; and ultimately some hard decisions will be required as to what it really wants to become.

Without over-extending the metaphor, the theme of this paper is that the Ontario Legislature has developed greatly in recent years yet it often fails to reflect seriously on its potential, so that many important possibilities – for reform, for contributing to the policy process, and for promoting governmental accountability – are not being realized.

Overview

In the course of the past two decades, the Ontario Legislature has travelled a long way down the road to becoming a mature, sophisticated parliament. The conventions and practices of Westminster-style parliaments are measured in centuries, but the Ontario Legislative Assembly as it existed prior to the mid 1960s is more of an historical curiosity than a guide to the present-day institution. To be sure, the traditional tenets of responsible government, as well as such formalities as the three readings of a bill, the passage of supply, and parliamentary privilege, remain fundamentally unchanged, but these are features common to all parliaments based on the British model.

The Legislature of the 1980s is marked by long sessions of six or seven months' duration with extensive committee activity for the balance of the year; an active, effective committee system; a broad range of services and facilities for individual MPPs, caucuses, and committees; considerable autonomy from the executive, symbolized by an independent speakership; highly institutionalized party organizations within the House, linked by sophisticated channels of inter-party consultation; occasionally significant impact on the policy process; powerful accountability mechanisms through question period and committees such as the Public Accounts Committee; a large, vigorous opposition; and repeated bouts of minority government. None of these features was present in the Legislature prior to the mid 1960s.[1]

That Ontario has been ruled by two coalition governments (Sandfield Macdonald's 'Patent Combination' immediately after Confederation and the Farmer-Labour government of the early 1920s) is of infinitely less moment than the fact that three of the last five governments have been minority governments. These minority situations not only greatly enhanced the power of the legislature with respect to the government and to the policy process, but also left a lasting legacy in terms of members' attitudes towards the House. These reforms withstood a return to majority government in 1981; moreover, a sense has developed that the Legislature has an important role to play in the governance of the province.[2] The principal advances date from the 1975-81 minority period, though the 1985-87 minority was responsible for some important improvements as well, most notably the introduction of comprehensive, high-quality television coverage of the House and its committees.

The second minority was marked by a NDP-Liberal accord, which featured pledges that for two years the premier would not seek a dissolution and the NDP would neither move nor vote non-confidence. The NDP was, however, free to defeat individual government measures, including budget bills, without the spectre of confidence being raised.[3] The accord eliminated the destructive brinkmanship of earlier minority times and demythologized the confidence convention; but its significance touches even more fundamental questions, most notably the extent to which the Ontario House is, in Nelson Polsby's terms, an 'arena' or 'transformative' legislature.

Transformative legislatures are true law-making (as opposed to law-passing) bodies; they have the capacity to transform ideas into law independent of other institutions, notably executives. An arena legislature, in contrast, primarily serves as the forum for the clash of ideas and policy proposals and for representation of the various interests and groups in society, but lacks an independent law-making ability.[4] Westminster-model parliaments are usually much closer to the arena end of the spectrum, but in limited though important ways the Ontario Legislature has moved towards becoming more transformative. Almost all this movement has been attributable to the influence of minority government.

Many of the most significant changes arising out of minority government, in the Legislature's corporate culture and institutional arrangements, can be interpreted as means of bringing order and stability to minority situations. The accord thus stands as the logical end result of the search for mechanisms to promote and ensure stability in what would otherwise be an innately unstable condition. Moreover, it was particularly in the interest of the NDP, traditionally the party most interested in making the Legislature more transformative, since it institutionalized the NDP's legitimacy in the policy-making process despite its third-party status.[5]

Every legislature reflects the politics of the wider society it represents. Without a long excursus into the nature of Ontario politics, a few points are particularly germane to an understanding of the Ontario Legislature. First, Ontario has a strong, diverse economy featuring extensive resource and extractive industries. It has the country's most concentrated secondary manufacturing sector as well as a highly developed service-based post-industrial economy. Thus while organized labour is a powerful force in Ontario and the province's politics continue to reflect the antagonisms of capital and labour typical of an urban, industrial society (principally through a strong NDP presence), Ontario's economy and society are too complex to permit polarization into two clearly defined political camps, as has happened in several western provinces. This has resulted in Canada's only stable three-party system (since 1943 the third party, usually the CCF-NDP, has never attracted less than one-sixth of the vote and normally garners between one-fifth and one-quarter of the ballots). In turn, this has made for the only provincial legislature marked by three strong parties; since 1967 the third party has always held at least sixteen seats.

Parliaments with three substantial parties are qualitatively different from those with only two parties. Aside from giving rise to the possibility of minority government, the presence of three parties complicates the political calculus in the House, mainly through the competition between the two opposition parties to prove which is 'the real opposition.' One of the keys to the long Conservative period in office (1943-85) was the government's success in ensuring that the Liberals and the New Democrats spent as much time and energy fighting one another as they did attacking the government. On an everyday level, in devising tactics for question period and for committee meetings, opposition strategists must worry not only about how the government will respond, but also about what the other opposition party may ask or what tactic it can employ.

The party enjoying the status of official opposition has an advantage over the third party in that it is recognized first in debate and in question period; but in other ways the third party is accorded better treatment than its numbers might warrant. The two opposition parties have equal status in question period, so that during the Thirty-Third Parliament (1985-87) the NDP, with twenty-three members, asked as many questions as the fifty-member Conservative party. Similarly, on a per member basis, the NDP received more funding than the Conservatives thanks to a policy (initiated by the Conservative-controlled Board of Internal Economy in 1981) that the third party should be funded as if it had thirty MPPs. The rationale behind these inequities is clear, and remains as persuasive for the current Liberal administration as it was for the previous Tory government: enhance the prospect of staying in power by equalizing the threat posed by the two opposition parties.

The party configuration is also significant. If the NDP is one of the opposition parties, as it is in Ontario, the question arises as to whether the basic division within the Legislature is a structural one – government versus opposition – or is based on ideology – the NDP versus the old-line parties.[6] (During the time of the accord right-wing lobby groups railed against the Liberal-Socialist alliance, but ideologically the Liberals have generally been closer to the Conservatives.)

The second point about the Ontario political culture is that it is essentially a melding of the more moderate elements of liberalism and conservatism, aptly described as 'progressive conservative.'[7] Moreover, though recent Ontario governments have been faced with unusually tough economic times and have consequently had to face uncommonly tough decisions, by comparison with the rest of the country the province remains prosperous and economically stable. These factors contribute to the generally moderate tone of Ontario political discourse and to the relative ideological moderation of all three major parties, which may be gauged by comparing their ideological stances with those of other provincial wings of the Liberal, Conservative, and New Democratic parties. This does not mean that disorder, unruliness, and bitter partisan squabbling are unknown in the Ontario House. It does mean that much of the barracking and verbal abuse is essentially theatrical, disguising extensive cross-party friendships and a generally high level of respect and understanding among MPPs for their opponents.

Finally, Ontario is unique among the provinces in that the political orientation of its populace is primarily national rather than provincial, so that Ontarians are more attentive to federal than to Ontario politics.[8] Ontario politicians must struggle to distinguish themselves and their concerns from goings-on in Ottawa. More generally, since provincial politics often rank below national and municipal politics in public interest, the Ontario Legislature probably has the lowest public salience of any Canadian legislature.

Structure

The Legislature is composed of 130 members, elected from single-member districts. It is the largest provincial House and, as discussed in the Introduction, size is a factor of some importance. The Ontario cabinet normally contains only about one-fifth of the membership of the House, and usually well less than half of the government caucus. Moreover, even without the Speaker, ministers, and party leaders (none of whom sit on committees), Ontario has more than ninety back-benchers available for committee duty.

Members of the Ontario Legislature bring a wide range of backgrounds and experiences to their tasks. In certain respects MPPs mirror the social composition of the province, while in other ways they are quite unrepresentative of the Ontario population.[9] Members are on balance much better educated and generally older than their electors. They are disproportionately drawn from small business and professional occupations (particularly teaching and law); relatively few Ontario MPPs have backgrounds in what might be termed working-class or lower middle-class (sales and clerical) jobs. In terms of their religious affiliation and their national origins, MPPs are remarkably representative of the provincial population, with one glaring exception: whereas 7 per cent of Ontario residents are of non-European origin – a great many in the so-called visible minority groups – in 1988 only three of 130 members of the Ontario Legislature did not trace their origins to Europe, and prior to the 1987 election only one did. At 16.1 per cent of the Legislature, women continue to be seriously underrepresented; but perhaps even more significant is the startling fact that the twenty-one women in the 1988 House constituted more than half the total number of women who ever served in the Ontario Legislature.

The Ontario Legislature combines substantial numbers of inexperienced members with a sizeable contingent of seasoned veterans. The Liberal landslide in the 1987 election brought in fifty-one first-time MPPs (39.2 per cent); one-third of the members in 1986 had less than two years' experience while another third had served in the House for more than a decade. A great many MPPs have previously held elected office at the municipal level. Virtually half the Ontario members are former municipal politicians, which is a far higher proportion than is found in any other Canadian legislature.[10] What effect this widespread background in local politics may have is unclear, but it does not, as might be expected from the general lack of organized parties at the municipal level in Ontario, incline MPPs away from strong adherence to party or from strict party discipline.

A strong independent speakership is essential to a mature, effective parliament. The prestige and power of the Ontario Speaker have increased markedly in recent years but in important respects the Speaker remains hamstrung by formal limits and by members' attitudes towards his office. Recent Speakers have worked diligently at presiding over the House in a neutral, non-partisan fashion, showing no favour to their own parties; MPPs have generally responded well to these efforts and certainly their respect for the institution of the Speaker has grown substantially. The Speaker has also assumed a host of administrative responsibilities unimaginable two decades ago and has played a leading role in promoting the Legislature's independence from the government in terms of crucial management and operational issues. Still, Ontario has some distance to go before its Speaker enjoys an equivalent position to that of the Speakers in Ottawa and Westminster. Only in late 1988 did the government turn over to the Speaker complete jurisdiction over the legislative building and nearby government buildings housing MPPs and Assembly staff offices. Procedurally, Ontario remains one of only a few Canadian provinces to permit challenges to Speakers' rulings. Most significantly, though, members still lack genuine respect for the office of the Speaker (as distinct from liking the Speaker personally) and readily dispute his authority in a fashion unthinkable elsewhere.

In addition to the party leader, each party in the Ontario Legislature has a house leader, a chief whip and deputy whips, and a chairman of caucus. Each party also has a dozen or more staff aside from individual MPPs' staff and leader's staff to look after caucus needs, communications, logistics, research, and the like. Save those in leadership roles, every opposition member has an assigned role as official party critic for a particular ministry or policy field; on the government side, a large proportion of back-benchers serve as parliamentary assistants to ministers. Parties in the Ontario Legislature, in other words, are large complex organizations. On both sides of the House individual MPPs and caucus staff can thus become minor cogs in the wheel, distant and alienated from the party leadership. Astute party leaders can and do take steps to counter this tendency but it is an inevitable fact of life in large caucuses. The role of caucus committees tends to be limited, though the opposition parties have in recent years expended considerable time and effort on mounting party task forces of MPPs to travel the province holding public hearings on policy issues such as occupational health and safety, youth unemployment, and the sale of beer and wine.

A measure of the institutional sophistication that the parties have achieved is the firmly established norm of consultation among parties on all matters of House and committee business. Short- and long-term House planning, setting of committee schedules, and many other matters are negotiated among the party house leaders and whips. While the government clearly maintains the upper hand, both Conservative and Liberal governments have proved quite accommodating to opposition requests and problems. By way of illustration, should a critic fall ill or be unavoidably absent, it is taken for granted that consideration of the estimates for the critic's ministry will be postponed until the member's return. Careful orchestration of House business, and the trust and co-operation it is built upon, finds its roots in both altruism and self-interest. It is in everyone's interest, especially the government's, that the business of the House be conducted as smoothly as possible.

Several hundred non-partisan staff, under the direction of the Speaker and the Board of Internal Economy, see to the needs of the members and their staffs. Both the size and level of competence of the Legislature's staff have been markedly enhanced in recent years. A key development was the establishment in 1974 of the Board of Internal Economy to assume financial and administrative control of the Legislature. Ontario's was the first such Canadian board to include opposition representation, and although the government maintains a numerical majority on the board, the opposition does exercise significant influence on the management and funding of the Assembly.

The Legislature at Work

Only a few highlights of the Ontario Legislature's operations can be touched upon here. The House sits for six or seven months a year (usually just over one hundred sitting days). Traditionally, sessions began in late March or early April, broke for a summer recess towards the end of June, returned shortly after Thanksgiving, and prorogued just before Christmas. In recent years, however, several weeks of sittings have been necessary in January and February to complete the legislative agenda. When in session, the House meets Monday to Thursday at 1:30 and adjourns at 6:00, with an extra sitting from 10:00 to 12:00 noon on Thursdays for private members' business. It is a telling fact that in 1986 the opening was moved ahead from 2:00 p.m. at the request of the press gallery.

The table on page 36 offers a breakdown of how the Legislature spent its time during the second session of the Thirty-Third Parliament (April 1986 to February 1987); in this period the House sat for 514 hours.[11]

In terms of time expended, the principal proceedings were question period, which took up just under one-fifth of all time, government legislation, accounting for roughly one-third of House time, and private members' business, which consumed 9 per cent of the time. Although they did not represent large proportions of House time, it is worth noticing that over ten hours were devoted to debating committee reports and nearly seventeen hours were given over to seven separate emergency debates. A measure of how the Legislature has changed in recent decades is the relatively small amount of time consumed by estimates and by the once-pervasive throne and budget debates: 13.6 per cent combined. In 1964, according to Schindeler, they took up 72.4 per cent of

House time.[12] The 3.1 per cent of legislative time spent on divisions may seem substantial at first blush, but appears quite reasonable by comparison with the nearly 10 per cent of time that they accounted for in 1973.[13] (The 'Ceremonial' category includes the throne and prorogation speeches, and an address to the House by Bishop Tutu of South Africa, but mainly reflects welcomes to distinguished visitors, tributes to deceased notables, recognition of various national days, and the like. Inevitably, unanimous consent is given for a representative of each party to speak on such occasions.)

**Time spent on various proceedings,
Second Session, Thirty-Third Parliament**

	%
Members' statements	3.4
Ministerial statements	6.3
Question period	19.8
Petitions	0.8
First reading	0.5
Second reading*	14.8
Committee of the Whole (legislation)	13.1
Third reading	4.7
Throne speech debate	4.0
Budget debate	4.1
Interim supply	1.8
Committee of Supply (estimates)	5.5
Emergency debates	3.2
Committee reports	1.9
Government motions	0.8
Private members' business	9.0
Ceremonial	1.3
Points of order/privilege	1.0
Divisions	3.1
Total	99.1

* Excludes private members' bills.
Total does not equal 100 because of rounding.

Except in certain limited circumstances, such as in emergency debates and for private members' business, time limits on speeches are unknown in the Ontario Legislature. Full-scale delaying tactics by the opposition are uncommon, but in recent years the government has occasionally found it necessary to resort to time allocation procedures in order to limit debate. Attempts at formalizing time allocation in the standing orders have come to naught, as have efforts at restricting the time that division bells may ring. If some debates drag on rather longer than the government might prefer, by and large obstructionism has not been a serious problem.

In terms of members' attendance, excitement, and media attention, the hour-long question period is clearly the highlight of the legislative day. To observers from other Canadian houses, two points about the Ontario question period are particularly striking. First, after the initial leaders' questions, the two opposition parties take turns putting their questions; this renders it difficult for a party to mount a concerted attack on a specific issue, and it greatly enhances the competition between the opposition parties.[14] Secondly, to a degree probably unique in Canada, question period in the Ontario Legislature is dominated by the party leaders. The opposition leaders are accorded special priority under the standing orders: their questions come first, and they are permitted two supplementaries to the one allowed other MPPs. Twenty-six per cent of all questions come from the opposition leaders.[15] Moreover, a high percentage of questions are directed to the premier rather than to ministers. One out of every five questions was directed to the premier, a much higher proportion than is generally found in Westminster systems.[16] Also significant is the extent to which the opposition leaders concentrate their attention on the premier: in 1986-87 one-third of both the Conservative and NDP leaders' questions were directed to Premier David Peterson. This concentration on the premier, which also characterized the Davis years, in large part stems from the opposition's belief that involving the premier brings extensive media coverage, whereas attacks on ministers (even if more successful) tend to go unreported. A number of rule changes over the past fifteen years have been directed at reducing the dominance of leaders; their universal failure attests to the inability of formal rules to overcome the realities of party life in the Ontario Legislature.

'Private Members' Business' provides a certain scope for members to pursue pet projects and to have a palpable, albeit minor, impact on the policy process. The significance of this period arises not from the slim prospects of private members' bills passing into law – since the procedure was established in 1976, only nine private members' bills have made their way onto the statute books and none have effected major policy changes – but rather in the sometimes substantial public interest private members' bills and resolutions can generate in public policy issues, their utility as trial balloons, and as levers for pressuring the government. The key procedural element which makes all this possible is the requirement that, after an hour's debate, items of private members' business must be put to a vote.[17] In other words, embarrassing bills and resolutions cannot simply be talked out; MPPs (most notably government members) must indicate publicly their support or rejection for the proposed measure.[18]

As elsewhere, private members in Ontario are constrained by the prohibition against their presenting money bills, though the rule tends to be interpreted in a much less restrictive fashion than in other jurisdictions. In the last year or two, there has been a tendency for MPPs to bring forward issues that are more in the nature of personal enthusiasms than clearly party-inspired measures. To be sure, the relatively enlightened approach to private members' business is not about to single-handedly transform back-bench MPPs into powerful policy-makers, but it does offer some possibility for them to influence public policy and to help set the province's political agenda.

Services to Members

No aspect of the Ontario Legislature has changed as radically over the past two or three decades as the services and facilities available to its members. Robert Nixon has recalled the response to his inquiry about amenities for members on first being elected in 1962: he was shown to his desk in the Chamber where he could do his correspondence and was told there was a pay phone in the hall.[19] Such primitive conditions are scarcely imaginable to present-day members, who take for granted their private, well-appointed Queen's Park offices, their publicly funded constituency offices, their personal staff, and a host of other services.

As of 1986-87, each MPP had a global staff allowance of $94,625 to allocate as he or she saw fit, subject to certain salary ceilings and anti-nepotism rules. This means that each member can hire some three or four staff. In addition, each caucus maintains a small research unit on which its members have call, and MPPs may avail themselves of the services of the economists, lawyers, political scientists, and other professionals in the research branch of the Legislative Library. Inevitably, some hyperactive MPPs are chronically understaffed even with these resources, but on balance members of the Ontario Legislature are well served with staff.

MPPs' personal staff spend most of their time on constituency business, as opposed to more broadly based policy concerns. Similarly, though resources certainly are available to assist members in their roles as legislators, far more services cater to the needs of the members as local representatives, as ombudsmen, as constituency case workers, and ultimately as incumbent politicians seeking re-election. The constituency offices, the thrice-yearly household newsletters, translation facilities, unlimited postage and long distance charges are but a few of publicly funded benefits which tend to give incumbent members such an important head start over their opponents. Yet the preoccupation of so many MPPs with the problems of individual constituents reflects more than a crass calculation of the most expeditious route to re-election. The so-called glorified social worker syndrome stems in part from the often underestimated degree of altruism which characterizes many members; it also is the natural extension of the essentially powerless position in which most non-cabinet members find themselves. Frustrated at being shut out of the principal decision-making structures, and at finding themselves able to influence policy only at the margins, many members – government as well as opposition – find great psychological satisfaction in the accomplishments they register on behalf of their constituents.

The Camp Commission, which carried out a wide-ranging independent review of legislative procedures and services during the early 1970s, insisted that only through improved services could MPPs move beyond constituency service to pay proper attention to their duties as legislators.[20] Though services have been vastly improved since then, members continue to devote great amounts of time to constituency casework at the expense of more policy-oriented pursuits. Casework is politically rewarding as well as psychologically fulfilling; it continues to grow in leaps and bounds as members exhort their electors, through householders, cable television shows, and other means, to bring all manner of problems to them. Casework, it might be added, need not always detract from policy or legislative concerns, for dealing with constituents' problems can give members useful insights into the operation and shortcomings of government policies. Similarly, the opposition can mount major campaigns to revamp policy on their casework experience; the NDP has been particularly effective in grounding policy critiques in specific cases of individuals.

Committees

The Ontario Legislature has for some years had a very active committee system. Members devote substantial time and energy to their committee work, recognizing that committees offer much greater scope than does the House for delving into, indeed influencing, policy. In turn, the work carried out by committees oftentimes carries considerable political and policy significance, though, to be sure, committees also engage in much futile busy work.

As is generally the case in Westminster parliaments, membership on committees reflects the party composition of the House. Since it has been tacitly agreed that each party should have no fewer than two members on each committee, the mathematics of proportionate party representation tend to make for committees that are larger than they otherwise would need to be. Thus in the 1985-87 minority Parliament, all committees had eleven members: four Liberals, four Conservatives, two NDP members, and a non-voting chairman; similarly, in the current majority setting, committees also have eleven MPPs (six Liberals, two NDPers, two Conservatives, and a chairman). A recent amendment to the standing orders formally divides chairmanships among parties (this had been done informally in minority times, but during majority governments only Public Accounts was chaired by an opposition MPP).

The important distinction lies not between standing and select committees but between the generalist, policy-field committees and the specialist committees. Select committees operate in precisely the same fashion as standing committees, differing only in their relatively narrow focus and in their disbanding upon completion of their assigned task; in 1988 three select committees (on constitutional reform, on energy and on education) were active. The four policy-field committees – social development, resources development, administration of justice, and general government – perform the lion's share of the routine work, principally the review of estimates and of legislation. These committees are also called upon to perform select committee-like special studies, which not only keeps them very busy but ensures that they deal with a tremendously wide range of subjects. Wholesale substitution of members (which is effected simply through presentation of a note from the party whip to the chairman) is thus a much-decried but generally accepted corollary of the committee system. Even with substitution, however, the parties, especially the government party, are sometimes hard pressed to find sufficient back-benchers to fill all their committee places.

The five specialist standing committees are active within more restricted realms. The Government Agencies Committee reviews the operations of the province's horde of semi-independent agencies, boards, and commissions. The Regulations and Private Bills Committee performs a cursory review of delegated legislation, but its prime function is as the private bills committee. The Finance and Economic Affairs Committee plays a role in the pre-budget consultation process, considers the tax bills arising out of the budget, and deals with related issues of macroeconomic policy. Up to the present, it has not, as was initially hoped, been assigned to deal with the entire package of government spending estimates.[21] The Legislative Assembly Committee advises on standing orders, procedure, and services to members, and it oversees the Legislature's television service. It also acts as the privileges committee; it has recently had before it recently several contentious privilege and conflict of interest cases. The Public Accounts Committee scrutinizes government spending for waste and mismanagement; it has consistently been the most partisan and politically significant of the specialist committees. The Standing Committee on the Ombudsman is unique in Canada in that it not only serves as liaison between the Legislature and the ombudsman, but also reviews in exhaustive detail and reports to the House on individual cases where the government has rejected the recommendations of the ombudsman.[22]

The specialist committees have unrestricted ability to pursue any matter coming within their broadly defined ambit. The policy-field committees can initiate studies or inquiries into a wide but not exhaustive range of matters; they do so through the polite fiction that they are reviewing issues raised in the annual reports of ministries and agencies which are referred to them (the limits on their scope arise in that only 'statutory' reports are within their mandates,[23] and several ministries and myriad agencies are not required by statute to table reports). Each committee has a clerk to see to its administrative and procedural needs and, except when they are engaged in estimates' review, committees typically have one or two researchers from the Legislative Library's research unit seconded to them, and may also hire their own consultants or counsel.

One of the more unusual features of the Ontario Legislature's committee system is that although most committees meet once or twice each week the House is sitting, they become even more active when the House is recessed or prorogued. During the summer recess, which usually lasts from late June until early October, and the interval between sessions (normally all or part of the first three months of the year), it is quite common for three or four committees to be meeting simultaneously. For weeks on end, committees may sit for fifteen to twenty hours a week. Such intense activity is usually given over to special policy studies or consideration of contentious bills requiring extensive public hearings, and may involve travel throughout the province and beyond.

Though technically a matter for decision by each individual committee, it is by now universally accepted that widely advertised public hearings should be held on all legislation sent to committee and on major policy studies. The influence exerted by public hearing process is open to debate and certainly varies greatly from case to case. Perhaps its greatest value lies in the dialogue it encourages between MPPs and interest groups (for almost all witnesses at public hearings are representatives of interest groups rather than private citizens), and in the legitimacy it fosters for the legislative process within the public.[24]

As with the House, the atmosphere in committees can swing between partisan pyrotechnics, mind-numbing tedium, boisterous frivolity, and constructive discussion of policy concerns. On balance, though, committees tend to be less partisan than the House, more conducive to compromise, and more likely to produce serious attempts at improving public policy. This stems not only from their smaller size and the less formal setting of the committee room, but also from the general lack of press attention and the common view among members that, whereas the House is mainly for political theatrics, committees can be important and useful forums for gaining valuable insights into political problems and for promoting policy ideas.

In addition to routine reports on legislation and on estimates, committees produce a good many substantive reports, often containing far-reaching recommendations on policy and administration. The fate of these reports is symbolic of the overall effectiveness of the committee system. Motions for adoption of (i.e., concurrence in) reports are routinely made by committee chairmen when their reports are tabled in the House. After some time, perhaps a year or more, most reports eventually come up for debate and disposition, though some are never debated. For the most part these debates are bloodless, pro forma exchanges largely confined to the MPPs who served on the committee. Yet the policy significance of committee work and committee reports may be much greater than this desultory ritual might suggest. Impact on policy, of course, depends on the extent to which the government is open to advice – which may be considerable, especially with inherently non-partisan issues such as family violence – and on the degree to which the committee members set aside partisan differences in favour of developing and improving policy rather than scoring political points. Even in areas characterized by strident partisanship and sharp political divisions, committees may have influence, although through rather different mechanisms. Committee attention to an issue often raises public awareness and concern, which may force the government to modify a policy or publicly justify its refusal to do so to hostile interest groups; it also offers the opposition good opportunities to put forward their alternatives.

Accountability Mechanisms

The success of the Ontario Legislature at holding the government – bureaucrats as well as ministers – responsible for its actions and policies is mixed. Question period is a powerful weapon, though it is often superficial and concerns of accountability tend to take a back seat to partisan attack and counter-attack. MPPs can and do utilize committee inquiries to review governmental activities in considerable detail, and to call upon senior civil servants to explain policies and their role in developing and administering them. In the Ontario Legislature, as elsewhere, the strength of both question period and committee review for fostering accountability may lie less in what actually transpires as in what ministers and bureaucrats fear might come out (whether specific facts or general images).

Two committees which contribute particularly to improved accountability are the Public Accounts Committee and the Government Agencies Committee. Working closely with the provincial auditor and his staff, the Public Accounts Committee regularly calls before it deputy ministers to account for errors and weaknesses in management, particularly those documented in the auditor's annual report. Although recent committees have frequently seemed more interested in scandalmongering than in more mundane attempts to improve management practices and government accountability, the PAC continues to have a salutary influence. The Government Agencies Committee, like its predecessor the Procedural Affairs Committee, focuses on semi-independent agencies, boards, and commissions. It examines in some detail perhaps a dozen a year, from major bodies such as the Ontario Municipal Board and the Ontario Lottery Corporation to such minor agencies as the Wolf Damage Assessment Board. Its review of agency operations is usually low key and non-partisan, but it does offer the Legislature and its members an institutionalized means of keeping tabs on the myriad agencies which would otherwise escape legislative scrutiny.

Through these means the Legislature registers important successes in the struggle to improve government accountability. Other methods by which accountability might be enhanced, most notably review of estimates and of delegated legislation, are abject failures. Each year the House and its committees spend hundreds of hours reviewing ministry estimates, to almost no purpose. On occasion, valuable policy debates arise between the minister and the opposition critics; in addition, members sometimes find estimates useful as a means of raising constituency concerns – a modern-day 'grievance before supply.' For the most part, though, debates on estimates are little more than tedious, pointless rituals which have no connection with their ostensible purpose of scrutinizing and approving future government spending; their contribution to accountability is limited indeed.

Delegated legislation is not even subject to any formal legislative review, save in a highly legalistic way by the Committee on Regulations and Private Bills. This committee, or rather the committee counsel, examines the hundreds of regulations passed annually to ensure that they do not exceed the scope of the enabling legislation, that they have no retroactive provisions, that they do not impose fines or imprisonment, and so on. To be sure, this review is a useful check, but it is rare that regulations breach such principles; moreover, the far more significant question of the regulations' policy content lies outside the committee's jurisdiction. Thus, review of the merits of regulations is not possible, nor is there any mechanism, as has recently been instituted in Ottawa, for the House to overturn delegated legislation. Accordingly, the vast range of governmental activities carried out through regulations constitutes a black hole for accountability.

Reform

Evaluation of the progress of reform in the Ontario Legislature depends on whether one is considering services and resources or procedure. Signal improvement in resources, begun in the early 1970s, has continued through the

1980s. As indicated earlier, the level of services is sufficiently high that, aside from a thorough and long overdue renovation of the legislative building,[25] few major reforms are needed. On the procedural front, progress has been more sporadic. The 1970s were marked by thoroughgoing, imaginative changes which clearly put the Ontario Legislature at the forefront of parliamentary reform in Canada.[26] The record in the 1980s has been much less impressive: changes have been relatively minor and reform proposals have been mainly revivals of ideas put forward in the 1970s or derivative of those emanating from the House of Commons.

The impetus towards procedural reform in the 1970s stemmed from an unusual confluence of circumstances: a six-year period of minority government came just as a major independent study – the Camp Commission – recommended a wide range of far-reaching yet practical reforms. The opposition, after years of pent-up frustration at executive dominance and bulldozer tactics by the government, was keen to press its advantage. The government, if not always enthusiastic, also recognized the need for and the legitimacy of reform. Among the more significant advances were an innovative and effective procedure for private members' business, heightened powers for committees, formal and informal restraints on government control over House business, and mechanisms for the opposition to force legislation and policy issues before standing committees.

Following the return of majority government in 1981, the reform process came to a screeching halt. Predictable as this may have been, it was less significant than the fact that the government saw no need to reverse any of the changes made during the minority years. The Procedural Affairs Committee, which had taken over from the Camp Commission as the chief promoter of reform, continued to issue reports recommending changes but was unsuccessful in persuading the government to implement any of them.

Parliamentary reform ranked as a high priority in the Liberal-NDP accord, but few significant procedural reforms were registered during the 1985-87 minority. Within a few months of the 1985 election, the Procedural Affairs Committee tabled a report proposing a wide range of reforms, mostly recycled from its earlier reports and from Ottawa's Lefebvre and McGrath committees. The provisional standing orders adopted in April 1986 implemented only some of the committee's proposals; generally these were among the less significant ones. To be sure, some of the new rules embody welcome and desirable changes: civilized meeting hours, which have made evening sessions a thing of the past; a ten-minute period at the beginning of the day's proceedings for MPPs' statements; opposition right of reply to ministerial statements; a McGrath-style ten-minute question and comment period following members' speeches. Many of the more important reforms suggested by the committee, such as enhancing the power and independence of the Speaker, major restructuring of the committee system, and a sensible solution to the hollow charade of estimates, did not survive the inter-party negotiations on the new rules. Similarly, the proposal in another committee report of legislative committees' reviewing order-in-council appointments, as may now be done in the House of Commons, was effectively rejected by the government on the grounds that it would entail 'a significant departure from parliamentary tradition.'[27] The appointment of senior House officers, including the clerk, the ombudsman, and the provincial auditor, may now only be made with concurrence from various committees, and in certain cases the committees are the ones which effectively make the appointments. On balance, despite some undoubted improvements, the scope and impact of the 1986 rule changes pale by comparison with the reforms of the 1970s. Their overall effect in enhancing the influence of individual MPPs and in strengthening the Legislature's position with respect to the government has been slight.[28]

Attitudinal change on the part of members is widely and accurately believed to be an essential prerequisite to significant parliamentary reform. This is nowhere truer than in Ontario. Several key areas may be identified where attitudes require change if fundamental reform is to come about. First is the pervasive view that procedure is essentially technical and boring. This results in a widespread lack of interest in the possibilities of reform; beyond the Speaker, the members of the Legislative Assembly Committee and the whips and house leaders, precious few MPPs are in the least concerned about reform. Secondly, altogether too many members, even those who are interested in change, fail to reflect seriously on the purpose of a legislature and are thus content to tinker with the rules rather than pursue more far-reaching changes. A perfect illustration here is the opening ten minutes given over to ninety-second statements by private members. It is very popular among MPPs and is widely regarded as a tremendous success, but it has enhanced the effectiveness and influence of the House and its members not a whit. Finally, party leaders and private members must come to realize that the sky will not collapse, or wholesale Americanization ensue, should party discipline be loosened. Hopes that party leadership on either side of the House will willingly renounce this key source of power are quite misguided. The force of party discipline lies far less in the threats and sanctions imposed by party managers than in the limits which members impose upon themselves. These limits reflect in part a commendable desire to be supportive of one's party, but they also arise from a deep-rooted belief that they are necessary evils required by 'the system.' Suffice it to say here that less Pavlovian adherence to the party line not only is justifiable but has been demonstrated not to cause the demise of the parliamentary form of government.[29]

Conclusion

Repeatedly throughout this paper facets of the Ontario Legislature have been described as having changed dramatically in the past fifteen or twenty years, mostly for the better, yet as still falling short of what might reasonably be expected. To return to the metaphor which began the paper, it is as if a person, physically but not emotionally ready for adulthood, lacked the self-awareness and self-confidence to step out into independent life and depend on his own abilities to reach his full potential.

The achievements of the Ontario Legislature over the past two decades have indeed been noteworthy in services, in institutional sophistication, in attaining independence from government, in streamlining procedure, in developing means for private members to influence the policy process, and in other ways as well. These formidable advances have had impressive results in enhancing the effectiveness of the Ontario Legislature; however, they signal a tremendous potential for further improvements which remains essentially unfulfilled.

Ontario MPPs are exceedingly busy men and women, preoccupied with the political battles of the day and with legions of constituency concerns. Perhaps it is not surprising that they have generally not asked themselves what their institution is all about and what features of it should be altered or jettisoned. To what extent, to take one key example, can and should the Ontario Legislature combine elements of the arena and transformative legislative models? A clear indication of its sometimes significant transformative capacity is the increasing attention paid to MPPs and to legislative committees by sophisticated, professional lobbyists. And yet there has been a singular lack of serious discussion by the members themselves as to the proper balance between arena and transformative elements, as to how that balance might be achieved now that the accord has lapsed, or as to what roles might be appropriate or practical for the Legislature and for MPPs in the policy-making process.

The Legislature's collective failure to reflect on its reason for being and on its potential is well indicated in the narrow range of sources it turns to for inspiration as to future directions. First and foremost, Ontario MPPs look to the House of Commons in Ottawa and have followed Ottawa's lead to a sometimes embarrassing extent. They also seek ideas in Westminster and in American legislatures. They have shown no interest in reviewing the practices of European parliaments, many of which retain some or all elements of responsible cabinet government and would thus seem far more suitable models for emulation than the US congressional system.

Still and all, Ontario does possess a sophisticated, active, oftentimes effective legislature. Its accomplishments and its strengths should not be belittled; yet it is neither unfair nor unrealistic to expect further growth and maturity.

DAVID E. SMITH

SASKATCHEWAN

Approximating the ideal

Perhaps parliamentary tradition is too inflated an appellation for what has gone on in the Legislative Assembly in Regina. Now that there is an opportunity to see complete television coverage of proceedings in the Chamber, the comic and sometimes mordant picture transmitted often seems to belie so grand a description.

And yet, if within their sphere of jurisdiction the legislatures of the provinces are sovereign, why should the description of a parliamentary tradition fit uneasily with the Saskatchewan legislature? Is it because the members appear uninterested in playing the roles that political theory assigns them? More generally, is it the failure of the Saskatchewan legislature to conform to the academic stereotype of how a parliament is supposed to act? Indeed, both the electorate and the elected display a disconcerting lack of attention to the legislature as an institution. The Saskatchewan Archives Board, which houses one of the country's most complete collections of provincial public documents, holds no papers of the Legislative Assembly's eighteen former Speakers and none of its five former clerks. In the only taped interview with a provincial Speaker (a man who occupied the Chair for twelve years, longer than anyone else in the legislature's history), only ten minutes of four hours of conversation deal with his speakership.[1] By comparison, ministerial papers, departmental records, and political party literature seem to abound.

The answer to the conundrum posed by the legislature – occupant of the province's most magnificent building but perennially eclipsed in the public mind by the executive and its administration – is to be found in a long-standing misconception of its function. This misconception arises from the application of a standard of parliamentary practice which, whatever else it implies, suggests a measure of balance between executive and legislative institutions that has never been realized at any time in Canada. To the extent that practice falls short of the standard and the executive dominates the legislature, so too has interest in the legislature flagged. Moreover, love of legislative fiction in preference to fact explains the failure to notice that the Saskatchewan legislature's role has evolved through the decades. In the last half of its life it has begun to move in the direction of the ideal; though the gains appear minute and the speed of change glacial, the balance has altered so that the legislature has acquired greater powers of scrutiny over the executive than it once had. This change is due to a variety of factors, of which, paradoxically, a more active executive is one of the most important. None the less, even in the early decades when the legislature was less active as a scrutinizing body, it still had an important role to play in the political system. The Saskatchewan Legislative Assembly has worked in practice if not always according to parliamentary theory.

Brief History and Current Political Context

By any measure Saskatchewan is one of Canada's most politically competitive provinces. In the last half-century voter turnout at fourteen elections has dropped below 80 per cent only twice and then only by one or two percentage points.[2] Again, in thirteen of twenty-one elections since 1905, the vote cast for the two major parties has stayed above 80 per cent, while in ten of the twenty-one elections the spread between the popular vote for each of the two major parties has stood at less than eleven percentage points. In 1986 the spread between the Progressive Conservative (PC) and New Democratic Party (NDP) vote was less than 1 per cent, and in favour of the NDP, who lost. No stronger evidence than this could be cited to illustrate the continuation of the long history of party competition in the province.

Intense party competition is a fact of Saskatchewan life, but so too are long periods of one-party rule. There have been six changes in government (1929, 1934, 1944, 1964, 1971, and 1982), and except for the Co-operative government between 1929 and 1934 (composed of Conservatives, Progressives, and Independents) and the current PC government, elected in 1982, the alternation has been between Liberal and CCF or NDP parties.[3] Longevity is confined to governments, however: on thirteen of nineteen occasions between 1908 and 1982 the turnover of MLAs has exceeded 40 per cent (and in seven of these instances 50 per cent) of the legislature's total membership. Gross percentages disguise significant differences among parties; Liberal and Conservative (as well as PC) MLAs generally exceed the average turnover figure in each legislature, while CCF or NDP members generally fall short of the average.

These characteristics – competitive elections, stable one-party government, and higher mobility among representatives of the old parties than among the CCF or NDP – have had immense importance for the operation of the legislature. First, the strength of electoral competition has extended into the Chamber making it a partisan body, though more so, it will be argued, after the CCF came to power in 1944 than in earlier decades. Secondly, notwithstanding the coalition of 1929-34, the Co-operative government proved the rule that Saskatchewan politicians prefer one-party government. This premise guided Liberals such as J.G. Gardiner – who as a result of the 1929 election (twenty-eight Liberals, twenty-four Conservatives, six Independents, and five Progressives) had the singular opportunity to contemplate coalition but then rejected it, saying: 'The only type that would usually join a coalition [was someone] that does not have any strong convictions on anything' – and was a view later shared by CCF and NDP politicians.[4] Thirdly, since 1948 the contrasting rates of turnover among MLAs of the different parties have given the edge in legislative experience to the CCF or NDP. Only once, in the seventeenth legislature (1971-75), did the NDP caucus have a smaller proportion of members with greater legislative experience (that is, eleven to fifteen years) than some other party, and even then in absolute members there were thirteen NDP members to the Liberals' nine.

Another distinguishing feature of Saskatchewan rests in the manner of its creation. Like its sister prairie provinces, Saskatchewan is a creation of the Parliament of Canada. For years, certain of the terms of autonomy – the separate school provision, the federal government's retention of natural resources, and the exemption of the CPR from local taxation – were the subject of much debate and numerous resolutions in the Legislative Assembly. They also laid the ground for antipathy toward the central government which has waxed and waned ever since. But the creation of the province *de novo*, within invisible, geometrically determined boundaries and at a time of exceptional economic and demographic growth (a sixfold increase in population between 1905 and 1916), created exceptional demands on government and on the legislature. More public bills were passed at the first session of the first legislature than at any other session but one before 1917. In the *Canadian Annual Review of Public Affairs for 1907*, J. Castell Hopkins wrote that 'the previous year had seen the making of a Province in the way of much foundation and creative work of an administrative character; this year saw the passing of various laws dealing with fundamental institutions.'[5] More than any other institution, it was the legislature which defined Saskatchewan, which provided the frame that in time was filled in by private activity. State preceded society in Saskatchewan, and pre-eminent in defining important aspects of the state – courts, municipal government, education, and highway systems – was the legislature. Of no Canadian province could it be said with greater accuracy than of Saskatchewan that its early history was recorded in its legislation.

Settlers who flooded into the province after 1905 looked to the legislature for solutions to their problems. How those demands for solutions were translated into legislation is worth a brief comment, for if the parliamentary tradition in Saskatchewan has changed over the decades since the province's birth, then this early period affords an illustration of the original understanding of the place of the legislature in the political system. Commentators on the early Saskatchewan scene never failed to remark on the dominance of what some called the Farmers' Parliament, by which they meant not the legislature but the annual meetings of the Saskatchewan Grain Growers' Association (SGGA). The *Canadian Annual Review for 1911* said of the SGGA that it 'rivalled the legislature in serious debate.'[6] No one, least of all the province's Liberal governments, denied the assertion. Indeed, they fostered the belief that through overlapping Liberal and SGGA membership and officers, the Liberal government acted as servant to the organized farmers. But the relationship was never so personal nor the government so suppliant as this interpretation suggests. Instead, through the use of royal commissions appointed to investigate farmers' complaints and their proposed solutions to perceived problems, the government successfully held the organized farmers in check as an electoral challenge.[7]

In a situation where the government stood yearly in danger of losing control of a single pressure group on whose support its life depended, the Legislative Assembly offered the government a unique forum in which to expound and defend its views on proposed policy. It was in the legislature where the converts were made to Liberal policy, who, once educated, would return to their constituencies to spread the word. Policy decision did not come through the party – there was only one Liberal convention between 1905 and 1946 – nor in any regular manner through senior advisers who stood at the head of a small, patronage-based bureaucracy; it evolved as a result of contact between party and interest group leaders, sometimes supplemented by the opinion of experts temporarily hired to work on royal commissions. The legislature's job was to ratify government's decisions and by its assent to lay the foundation on which an electoral majority might be sustained. Occasionally, legislative debate might help inform the public, although even here the organized farmers performed a superior educational role. Whatever description might be applied to the work of the legislature, no serious claim could be made that it scrutinized the government's actions or held it accountable.

Two decades later the government's extraordinary relationship to a single farm organization had become a memory. The rise of the Saskatchewan Wheat Pool, which eventually became Canada's largest grain-handling company, and the disappearance of the SGGA into the United Farmers of Canada (Saskatchewan Section) in the 1920s were only a prelude to more drastic changes brought about by depression, drought, and war in the next decade. When the CCF came to power in 1944, there was no counterpart to the SGGA on whom the new government depended, had that been its wish. The CCF was unlike the Liberal party in several respects, each of which contributed to the new party's having a different perspective on the place of the legislature in the political system. First, it was a programmatic party, whose policies deliberately appealed to the urban working class as well as to the farmers. Secondly, it was a party that placed great emphasis on accountability to its rank and file members rather than to an extra-parliamentary organization. Finally, it was a party that sought to reform the province's bureaucracy by introducing not only the merit principle and competitive examination but the first central policy agencies to implement its program. As a consequence of these innovations in government, the legislature found its place in the scheme of politics necessarily changed.

Had Castell Hopkins still been producing his annual review after 1944, he could not have written of CCF legislation as he had of a hail insurance bill in 1912: 'Its main principles were submitted to and approved by the Grain Growers' Association and various details afterwards [were] threshed out in the Legislature.'[8] The Liberals said responsible government had ended after 1944 and a regime of rule by experts had taken its place. That was inflammatory language, but it signalled the changes in legislative atmosphere and activity that became evident in the post-1944 period. Among the few comments on the House during his time as Speaker from 1944 to 1956, Tom Johnston refers most directly to the rise in partisan temperature: for example, he claimed to be the first Speaker to 'name' a member. More concrete evidence of the evolution under way can be seen in the expansion of the Assembly's committee structure, most particularly in the creation of the Standing Committee on Crown Corporations. The rise to power of the CCF marked not only the introduction of activist government in the province but also the end of a quiescent legislature whose task, according to the long-dominant Liberals, had been to sustain and approve the process of political accommodation at which past governments had proved themselves masters.

Political Culture and the Legislature

If there is one characteristic of Saskatchewan that has received more comment than any other, it would have to be the co-operative tradition reflected in the associational structure of the province. In *Agrarian Socialism*, Seymour Martin Lipset explored the co-operative principle at work in the Pool and credit unions and concluded that it made a fundamental contribution to the rise of the CCF.[9]

The CCF had no monopoly on the co-operative tradition, however. The Liberals claimed, with justice, that they had introduced it through legislation into such diverse concerns as local elevators, creameries, telephones, and hail insurance, and had done so over Conservative opposition which favoured government ownership and operation of basic services. In time the Liberals were to charge the CCF with introducing partisan politics into the co-operative tradition, so that Pool elections, for example, became a kind of primary contest in the province's politics. It is an indication of the strength of Saskatchewan's party spirit that the contenders for power should eventually compete over the question of who was the more faithful exponent of co-operation.

Certainly, the legislature never offered sanctuary to the co-operative spirit. Here, instead, was a partisan coliseum whose very structure, one foreign observer noted, accentuated the combative spirit that characterized elections:

The existence for twenty years in Saskatchewan of the only Socialist government ever known to the North American continent on the one hand and strongly characterised version of Liberal policies on the other may account for the bitterness with which politics are fought in Saskatchewan. Few of the influences which tend to bring members of different parties together at Westminster are effective out there. There are few parliamentary delegations on which they can get to know each other personally; select committees on the Westminster pattern, which tend to develop the 'consensus' view, are in their infancy; 'pairing' is rare; Members sit by party in the cafeteria (there is no bar in the Legislative Building: politics in Saskatchewan are officially 'dry'); and outside the building there appeared to be little fraternisation. In an Assembly with as few as sixty Members, moreover, the tendency to concentrate beneath the party banner is marked: the public expression of dissenting views within a party appears to be a luxury that an Assembly with a small membership cannot afford, at least when the majority between the two largest parties is so narrow.[10]

The subject of the size of legislatures and its influence on their operation needs closer attention than it has so far received. Since colonial days, membership in Canada's legislatures has tended to be small in number with the effect, as Lord Elgin remarked, of accentuating division.[11] One of the few modern commentators on the subject has argued that in addition to partisan rigidity, small numbers suppress the representation of minority interests.[12]

The representational defect of small chambers has not been perceived as a problem in Saskatchewan. This is explained by the strong sense of provincial community fostered in large part by an overriding interest in rural and agrarian matters. The one segment of Saskatchewan society excluded from the community has been the native people, who until the early 1960s were concentrated in the northern, or Shield, section of the province. To the degree that provincial politics responded to native questions, it was as a matter for administration, not representation. Until 1973, when the first independent commission drew constituency boundaries, electoral maps were prepared by the government and considered in Committee of the Whole. Although the charge of gerrymandering was common, and the electoral impact of the enterprise disputed, its effect on the legislative expression of interest was minimal because agriculture's interests were so uniformly spread across the southern, settled grain belt.

The 1971 census revealed for the first time that the rural-urban balance had shifted in favour of the cities (53 to 47 per cent), a development the 1981 census indicated had accelerated (58 to 42 per cent). The electoral implications of this change became starkly evident in the 1986 elections, which saw the PCs win only four of the twenty seats in the two major cities and only three of the other eight urban seats. Conversely, the NDP was excluded from all but four of the thirty-six rural seats. Ruling parties in Saskatchewan have always sought, with varying degrees of success, to embrace both urban and rural voters. While each party still retains considerable voter support in city and country, the most recent shift in voter preferences, coupled with the presence of an electoral map unrevised for six years, has transmitted the rural-urban cleavage into the legislature's institutionalized dichotomy of government and opposition.

The near coincidence of urban-rural and partisan divisions is unprecedented, as would be a coincidence between party and any other socio-economic or demographic division. Saskatchewan is not a fragmented society. Once, in the period up to 1929, racial and religious divisions may have been reflected to a degree in the pattern of party support but that disappeared half a century ago. In fact, the province which Statistics Canada regularly shows to be among the most ethnically heterogeneous in Canada is one where ethnicity is least significant in politics. The Ku Klux Klan, with its anti-Catholic and anti-foreign appeals, disappeared in the searing experience of the great depression, and J.G. Gardiner's later dictum that no Roman Catholic could become leader of the Liberal party or premier has been proved false by two of the last three of that party's provincial leaders, and by the present premier.

Normally, the legislature is divided by partisan feelings, although; on occasion those sentiments may be submerged to a higher cause; the provincial interest can be regularly invoked against a common enemy, the federal government. Part of the parliamentary tradition in Saskatchewan is the use of the provincial legislature to petition or attack the federal government. This strategy is more complicated and devious than a simple all-party assault on some perceived federal inequity or transgression. Depending on which party is in power and which in opposition at each level of government, a resolution attacking Ottawa may have several objectives. It could be a straightforward, even annual, request that Ottawa carry out some public work of benefit to the prairie provinces (for example, in the era of the First World War, the Hudson's Bay Railway or, in the era of the Second World War, the South Saskatchewan River Dam).[13] As such, the resolution would receive unanimous support and be directed at whatever party was in power federally. Indeed, in J.G. Gardiner's protracted but ultimately unsuccessful campaign to convince his Liberal cabinet colleagues to support the dam, the Saskatchewan legislature's unanimous resolutions in the early 1950s urging construction of the project were welcome ammunition even when they included favourable reference to the CCF government's own actions on behalf of the dam.[14] Again, resolutions might be introduced by the provincial CCF government to embarrass the provincial and federal Liberals (for example, regretting that sections to the Criminal Code failed to give adequate recognition to labour's right to strike and picket). Or they might be intended by the provincial Liberals to embarrass the provincial CCF government (for example, calling upon the CCF to live up to its promise of a complete system of socialized health services) and then be amended by the ruling CCF majority so as to demand that the federal Liberals take action on health insurance.[15]

The rare appearance of a party in power in Ottawa without a counterpart in the Saskatchewan Assembly had an immediate and adverse impact on the resolution industry of the legislature, as it did on the frequency of recorded divisions in the House. The return of the Liberals federally in 1963 and provincially in 1964 might have been expected to prompt the NDP to indulge in a new round of resolutions calculated to disconcert Liberals or cause friction between federal and provincial Liberal camps. The *Journals of the Legislative Assembly* for the 1960s do not bear out this supposition. Part of the explanation lay in the bellicose spirit of the provincial Liberals under Ross Thatcher who, preoccupied with discrediting CCF and NDP policies, were not easily embarrassed. And part of it lay in the emerging split between federal and provincial Liberals which often revealed that the provincial NDP had more in common with the governing Ottawa Liberals than did the Saskatchewan Liberals.

It would take more research than has been possible here to unravel the skein of partisan calculations that linked legislative procedure to electoral campaigns; and yet that was the principal motivation behind the tapestry of resolutions the *Journals* reveal. Those that dealt with federal matters had an additional purpose: they allowed provincial proponents to state their position on federal issues and, even better, they forced their opponents to do the same. In 1909 the Saskatchewan Liberals argued, 'elaborately' says Castell Hopkins, for a Canadian navy. They did the same in defence of Laurier's Reciprocity Bill, going so far as to propose a vote of censure on those Conservatives who had voted for the reciprocity resolution and then campaigned against the policy in the 1911 federal election.[16] The reason for the Liberals' action Walter Scott, the premier, made clear to a party worker in a provincial by-election in 1913: 'Reciprocity and naval policy you may very well say are not matters of Provincial concern but in reply I would venture to say that in the event of the Conservative candidate winning the Hanley Division we would not be long in hearing that the result meant that the Saskatchewan farmers have lost their interest in Reciprocity and that they also are quite willing to approve the $35,000,000 naval contribution.'[17]

Although the activities of the Assembly as a provincial political forum changed with the arrival of activist government, the provincial legislature has consistently provided a ready stage on which local politicians might declaim their federal political loyalties. As with almost every other aspect of government, cabinets receive the lion's share of attention in studies of federal-provincial relations, while the legislatures are ignored or dismissed as subservient to the executives. Investigation of the Saskatchewan parliamentary tradition suggests, however, that this is too one-dimensional an interpretation and that in practice an element of intra-state federalism occurs in the battle over federal issues in provincial legislatures.

Structure of the Legislative Assembly

As already indicated, archival material on the Speakers of the Saskatchewan legislature is scarce. In an interview taped in 1963, Speaker Tom Johnston singled out the partisanship of the House as the greatest problem he and his predecessors had had to face. It was, he said, 'hard to be unbiased when the Speaker has been a devoted party worker, when the appointment is made for services to the party and when his future political career might depend upon his actions in the Chair.'[18] He favoured the appointment of a permanent or continuing Speaker, whose constituency would be the Assembly itself and who once selected would hold office through several legislatures regardless of changes in the governing party. James Snedker, a Liberal and Speaker from 1965 to 1971, expressed similar sentiments in an interview with this author in 1969. These reforms would encourage the growth of independence and dignity in the office by removing the Speaker from the heat of the partisan contest.

In fact, there have been no specific reforms to neutralize the Speaker and it seems unlikely in the Saskatchewan context of intense partisanism that there will be any, unless they should enter the political system through contagion from the federal level. It is not unreasonable to expect that provincial opposition parties will express support for the introduction of an innovation similar to that in the House of Commons where members recently elected a Speaker by secret ballot. Legislative reforms have a way of permeating the jurisdictional walls of federalism by force of imitation. At the same time, developments within Saskatchewan are conducive to freeing the Speaker from his partisan ties. For example, the Speaker is chairman of the Board of Internal Economy, created in 1981, which is composed of two cabinet ministers, two opposition private members, and two government private members. The board is responsible for the day-to-day operations of the Assembly and it is to the board that such legislative officers as the clerk of the Legislative Assembly and the legislative librarian report. According to Gordon Barnhart, the clerk of the Legislative Assembly: 'The control of the purse strings for the operation of the Legislature has [now] been placed in the hands of Members representing the Legislative Assembly as a whole rather than in the hands of the Executive only, as was the case previously.'[19] From this perspective the board is an important step in helping to strengthen the legislature vis-à-vis the executive and can be seen as contributing to greater balance between the two branches of government. The Speaker and the members generally are clear beneficiaries of this change.

Furthermore, the legislative fortunes of Saskatchewan's parties have fluctuated widely in the last decade. The decline of the Liberals, the rise of the PCs, defections within the Chamber, and the establishment of new legislative parties – the Unionest with two members in 1980 and the Western Canada Concept also with two in 1986 – have presented the Speaker with a series of difficult challenges. Never before in Saskatchewan have events conspired to underline the central place of the Speaker in the orderly operation of the Assembly. Party government and parties in the legislature are so fundamental a part of the modern constitutional process that the mechanisms of the system occasion little comment or investigation. Yet recent Saskatchewan experience illustrates that the Speaker plays a crucial role in determining the players and the rules of the game. It seems fair to say that recognition of his importance has made legislators and members of the interested public more sensitive to the conditions of his office and more willing to contemplate reforms that would strengthen his independence from partisan influence.

A second office of major importance to the development of the Saskatchewan legislature is that of the clerk. Among the smaller provinces of Canada, Saskatchewan is unusual in having so well-established an office: as late as 1966 the only other provinces with a separate establishment for the clerk were Ontario and Quebec. Unlike the Speaker, more is known about this office, as a result of the research and writing of its current occupant, Gordon Barnhart. In a history of 'The Saskatchewan Table,' he has traced the parallel development of the office of clerk and the evolution of responsible government in the North-West Territories and Saskatchewan.[20] The first clerk, A.E. Forget, named in 1876, later became the province's first lieutenant-governor. Not only has Saskatchewan been fortunate in the continuity of this office but it has benefited as well from the experience which clerks of long tenure have acquired: between 1917 and 1960, there were only three clerks.

The numerous contributions of the Saskatchewan clerks to the province's parliamentary tradition will become evident later in this paper. At this point it is their general influence which should be stressed. The clerks have been responsible for keeping alive a view of the legislature independent from that held by government or by political parties. The nature of the accomplishment is suggested in the following comment by a previous clerk, C.B. Koester, later clerk of the House of Commons:

All Clerks are aware by instinct of the subtle differences in mentality between themselves and civil servants. Only those who have served a small legislature can know the solitude of the parliamentary officers surrounded by even the most genial government employees. It is one thing to adapt Westminster procedures to local conditions; it is quite another to avoid, in the process of simplification and adaptation, doing violence to the principles embodied in those procedures. To defend the parliamentary faith alone in a world which ranks parliament a poor third after government and politics is a task which can be unduly fraught with doubt and sorrow.[21]

In a House whose turnover generally is high – for example, in situations like that following the 1975 election, when none of the seven-man PC caucus had any legislative experience, or following the 1982 election, when thirty-nine of the fifty-five PC members were new – the independence of the clerk's office and the value of its collective memory is unquestioned. In such circumstances (and even, in other instances, for members with legislative experience) there is profit to be gained from attending the orientation and information seminars the clerk and his staff organize. As the current clerk has said: 'The seminars ... offer the Members an opportunity to evaluate the Legislature as an institution and their role within it. Too often, Members become involved in representing their constituencies and running the government (as Cabinet Ministers) and forget their role as parliamentarians.'[22] The constructive influence of the clerk's office goes beyond orientation seminars for individual MLAs and extends to sessions organized to help individual committees of the legislature: in 1982, for instance, the Saskatchewan Public Accounts Committee was composed entirely of members without experience on that committee.

Speakers and clerks help to define the corporate identity of the legislature. The legislative organization of a political party, the caucus in particular, can have an analogous impact in the sense of promoting back-bench influence over front-bench leaders. To the extent that today's individual member enjoys a greater opportunity than in the past to participate in his legislative party's deliberations and discussions, the legislature's hand will have been strengthened in its resistance to executive domination. The impact of this development is more immediate in the case of the governing party, but similar adjustments within the opposition party might be expected to carry over to government after the next election if that party is successful at the polls. If the foregoing sounds tentative, it is because of two Saskatchewan political realities: first, moves to increase back-bench participation are so recent that no party has had the chance to hone them in opposition before coming to power (the PC rise was too tumultuous and rapid to allow any structured back-bench/front-bench relationship to develop); and secondly, a veil of mystery and uncertainty hangs over the subject.

What happened to the current governing party after 1982 is an illustration of the confusion that can occur. With their huge majority, the PCs set about finding tasks for their caucus. The limit on the number of legislative secretaries was removed so that, in addition to a cabinet of twenty-five, another eighteen MLAs were named as assistants to ministers. The result of this change as to increase the percentage of members receiving more than the basic indemnity, from 52 per cent in early 1982 to 75 per cent a year later. For the remaining members of caucus, the promise was held out of ad hoc committees, in agriculture for example. The fate of this last experiment is difficult to trace.

A more certain guide of a modern Saskatchewan party in power is the NDP before 1982. In this era a set of caucus committees with interests in departmental matters such as agriculture and resources was established. They were expected to examine draft legislation or more general policy questions following cabinet discussion of these matters. In the normal course of events, Saskatchewan's governing parties number between forty and fifty members of whom nearly half are ministers. The assignment of personnel and the allocation of committee duties are largely dictated by the premier's prior selection of his cabinet. As well, major issues (for example, in the 1970s, the constitutional negotiations, the potash takeover, and the land bank) are not seen as appropriate subjects for committee study but for full caucus debate. For the ministers, caucus discussion provides the opportunity to secure more allies for controversial policies than does committee examination, while for the private members, the Saskatchewan political arena is deemed too small to carve up the government's program for small group discussion. If functional committees of the legislature have been slow to develop, it is hardly surprising that the appearance of comparable committees in caucus should be equally hesitant in emerging.

The formula for caucus research, which depends on party standings and is based on statute, is described in the current issue of *Canadian Legislatures*. A Special Committee on the Library, which reported in 1981, rejected a proposal that a research unit be established in the legislative library; it reasoned that such a unit would detract from caucus research. Thus committees must function without research assistance, a condition the Public Accounts Committee in 1982 noted with regret.[23] Saskatchewan has no legislative internship program, though in the absence of committee research facilities PAC members suggested that were one established, interns might provide this service.

A substantive contribution by caucus toward establishing a distinctive legislative mentality depends on a level of familiarity with government operations. Because the NDP has monopolized legislative experience in Saskatchewan, it is that party's caucus which appears to have put in place the more independent structure. It is worth recalling, however, that NDP leaders, as inheritors of the CCF tradition, have had more experience than any of their counterparts of the need for rank and file accountability. It has been an article of faith with them 'to safeguard the party organization from domination by ... members of the legislature.'[24] Current observation of this tenet is to be seen in a caucus Outreach Committee intended to keep elected members in touch with those groups historically seen as key units of their ideological constituency.

Legislative officers and party organization are the principal structuring agents in the Saskatchewan legislature. Because Saskatchewan society is unfragmented, representational concerns, such as the proportion of Roman Catholics or Protestants, or of native or non-native English speakers who are elected to the House, have not entered political discussion for years. None the less, in the eight decades since autonomy, the proportion of Anglo-Saxon Protestants elected to the legislature has consistently declined. As to sex, in 1986 the five woman MLAs comprised less than 8 per cent of the membership of the Assembly. Noting that the first women to be elected to Canada's provincial legislatures were concentrated in the West, a recent writer has hypothesized that the explanation lies in the less formalized political system in this region.[25] This may be true, although there is equal merit in observing that by their participation in the many activities of farm organizations in the early years of this century the majority of western women were afforded an opportunity for political training denied to their sisters elsewhere in Canada. The results of the most recent provincial election (1986), in which twenty-eight women competed for election in twenty-two constituencies but only five were elected, two of them incumbent ministers, are not inspiring.

Routine Operations and Services to Members

The Saskatchewan Legislative Assembly has a reputation for innovation. Radio broadcasts of selected proceedings began in 1946, while soon afterward it became the first Canadian legislature to go on the air regularly. As early as 1939, the legislature seriously considered using dictaphone technology to transcribe debates. The war intervened, but in 1947 an experiment began which matured into what George Stephen, then clerk of the Legislative Assembly, called 'machine-made *Hansard*.'[26] Thirty some years later, in accordance with a 1981 recommendation of the Rules Committee, TV coverage of proceedings was introduced, using automated television equipment. Similar influences were in operation in each instance: short sessions, a small chamber, and a province large in area but sparse in population.[27] These imperatives dictated that if the legislature was to experiment, it could not just copy the more expensive and sophisticated precedents established in larger jurisdictions. It is in the procedures whereby innovation was accomplished as much as in its substance that Saskatchewan broke new ground.

While the presence of suitable technology explains the concentration of these experiments in the second half of the legislature's history, the early Liberal view of politics saw no need for experimentation which had as its goal the strengthening of the bond between the elected and the electorate. In the Liberal idea of government, the forum for debate was the floor of the Assembly. It was here where the case for government policy was to be made and where converts were to be won. The *Journals of the Legislative Assembly* reveal that the *average* number of returns (requests by MLAs for information from government) ordered when the Liberals were in opposition between 1929 and 1934 totalled fifty-three, a figure surpassed during their long period in government in only four sessions (1916, 1939, 1940, and 1944). Again, the annual number of questions they asked while in opposition averaged 247, surpassed when in power on only three occasions: 1937, 1938, and 1939. Despite their reputed electoral prowess, the Liberals were essentially a legislative party. In contrast, and in part because it was an ideological party, the CCF looked outside the legislature and spoke directly to the voters. For the Liberals control of the legislature was the apogee of their political orbit; for the CCF it was but a point (albeit an important one) en route to a more distant objective.

The effect of televising the legislature on the political attitudes of Saskatchewan residents is open to question. As opposed to impressionistic and anecdotal evidence, no studies have been published to indicate either a positive or negative influence of these innovations on voter preferences or on perceptions of the political system. But commentators suggest that the presence of the media has had a determinative effect on the Assembly. One of the major reasons for a revision of the rules in 1950 (only the second time since 1905) was to accommodate to the demands of radio broadcasting.

Broadcasting of part of the daily proceedings has had other than procedural effects. It tended to make each Session follow a fairly well-defined pattern, which the new

Standing Orders tend to make more rigid. Heretofore, the terminal day of the Budget debate was a variable, a fact which had to be considered in making arrangements with the broadcasting companies. Now, however, the terminal day may be calculated fairly accurately in advance of the Session, and thus firm contracts for radio time may be made. These contracts more or less dictate the pattern of the Session ...

Whether or not it will be possible to maintain the rigidity of pattern imposed by this *quasi* guillotine, particularly with respect to the Budget, already is a moot question. A future Provincial Treasurer might find the commitment irksome that he deliver his Budget Address on the Friday of the fourth week of each Session. It has become evident, too, that an astute Opposition can so take advantage of the fixed hour of the fixed day for termination of the Budget debate, as to deprive the Provincial Treasurer of any opportunity to exercise his right to reply to criticism of his Budget.[28]

While the introduction of television is not responsible for the flourishing health of the oral question period (rule changes in 1975 provided for a 25-minute period each day), the pressure of the electronic media to encapsulate news has helped to 'downgrade the importance of the debates which follow later in the day.' Of equal importance, and perhaps of greater concern for researchers, 'the procedure of written questions with notice (a useful mechanism for searching for factual information) has nearly been abandoned.'[29] In 1975 fifty-three such questions were asked, but in 1980 only sixteen and in 1981 and 1982 none. For the private member, however, the gain of a sharper prod with which to irritate the executive may be considered benefit enough to counter the scholar's lament. Other advantages accrued to back-benchers as a result of the 1981 change in the rules. Among these was greater emphasis given to private members' day; a special 75-minute debate now takes place at the commencement of every second private members' day on a topic chosen alternately by government and opposition members. Also, the new rules provide for the establishment of special legislative inquiries, without government necessarily initiating them, on topics of interest to the members. The first such committee (on fire prevention-protection) reported in 1984.

Excluding six sessions of eight or fewer days, between 1905 and 1983 there were eighty-five sessions of the Saskatchewan legislature. If 1944 is used as the mid-point, forty of these were held before that date and forty-five after. Of the first group, six lasted less than thirty days, eleven lasted more than forty days, while the majority (twenty-two) extended between thirty-one and thirty-nine days. Of the second group, only three lasted less than thirty days, while twenty-six extended beyond forty days; only sixteen sessions fell in the intermediate range (thirty-one to thirty-nine days). The lengthening of the sessions is a response to the growing complexity of government, but the statistics do not convey the impact of this larger work-load on the members. Nor for that matter would an accounting of the number of public bills passed or sessional papers tabled. In any case, these statistics, easily available in the index to the *Journals,* do not depict long-run change so much as they record the rhythm of legislative activities: the numbers of public bills peak in the sessions that follow a change in government, and the numbers of sessional papers rise when a new government begins to explore the political ground vacated by its vanquished opponents. A more telling commentary on the change in condition experienced by Saskatchewan legislators and those who serve them is the following comment by the current clerk:

Within the last decade, the budget for Members' services has increased by approximately 628 percent, the parliamentary staff has grown from eighteen persons to nearly one hundred persons, yet the size of the Legislative Assembly has increased by only two Members and the Sessions have increased in length by a further forty sitting days per year. The difference is in the public expectations of the elected Member and in his view of his own role.[30]

Committees and Accountability

As with other aspects of Saskatchewan politics, the year 1944 marked a break in the practices and traditions surrounding the mechanisms to enhance accountability in the legislature. The Liberals – non-programmatic in policy, dependent upon a patronage-based civil service, and holding a restricted view of the functions of the Assembly – perpetuated a climate in which executive accountability could not mature. C.E.S. Franks has described this earlier period as one in which 'the Legislature was a debating platform for the parties, but not an autonomous institution holding the Government to account.'[31] He also notes that it was reform of the executive branch, particularly the desire of the CCF to implement its program and introduce administrative experiments, that provided the stimulus for legislative change. The implication which different styles of governing have for the operation of the legislature is a subject in need of exploration, for the Saskatchewan experience suggests that changes in government have been of signal importance in the evolution of the Legislative Assembly.

The advent of the CCF is a clear example of this fact. Writing in 1950, George Stephen, the clerk of the Legislative Assembly, said of the Saskatchewan Crown Corporations Committee that it was 'the most fecund source of extra-cameral news';[32] an opinion which most observers still share. The CCF inherited two public corporations (Telephones and the Saskatchewan Power Commission) and within five years had established eleven more. In 1946 a new Committee on Crown Corporations was created to scrutinize their operations. While it was originally expected that the new committee would act like the Public Accounts Committee and conduct a post-mortem examination of crown corporation activities, from the outset its members brought to their task a much wider perspective. Partly because the committee's creation preceded receipt of the first annual reports of the crown corporations, the scope of investigation immediately assumed that of a more general inquiry; and this approach was never revised. In fact, characteristics of the Saskatchewan legislature already noted discouraged limited perspective: 'The Provincial General Election of 1948 brought many new members into the Assembly; and the new Committee included many wholly unfamiliar with past proceedings and lacking knowledge of the details of the capital structures of the various corporations.'[33] In time, the practice grew of referring all questions about crown corporations on the order paper to the committee; the questions posed and answers received are then included in the committee's final report to the Assembly, which is treated as a sessional paper. As a result of this custom, the House itself was denied information on this perennial topic of provincial political debate and the spotlight turned completely onto the committee. It became a para-legislature, subject to the constraints which six-week sessions and high turnover in personnel impose. It was perhaps to be expected given the subject and the circumstance that the Crown Corporations Committee should become one of the principal forums for opposition and media attention.

The lineage of the Public Accounts Committee extends back to the first decade of the province but its potential as an effective instrument of accountability remained minimal until the mid-1960s. The first extensive study of legislative control of public accounts occurred in 1963 with the appointment of a Special Committee on Public Accounts Procedure. In essence, that committee recommended that the separate functions of approving government's disbursements and auditing its accounts should be performed by different officials and that the latter job should belong to the provincial auditor who should report to the legislature. That recommendation, among others, was adopted in 1965 and with it, Professor Franks says, Saskatchewan became 'the first Canadian province to begin the process of reform to its system of legislative control of finance.'[34] The operative word in that statement must be 'begin,' for changes in budgetary practices and a continuation in electoral practices have undermined the practical implementation of reform.

A recent observer of the new and complex budgetary processes, introduced in the 1970s and 1980s, has suggested that in the western provinces they have posed substantial problems for enforcing accountability. On the one hand governments 'seem reluctant to provide more information to legislatures [and on the other hand] legislatures seem uninterested in demanding more information.' He goes further and, in the context of Saskatchewan's practice of transferring sums from one subvote in the same vote to another subvote, cautions that 'it is difficult to be optimistic about the expanded use of government instruments to emphasize responsible government when governments are playing fast and loose with the existing safeguards.'[35]

Part of the problem, again, is the high turnover of legislative members. At no time has this been more evident than in the plight of the Public Accounts Committee after the 1982 election. For the two opposition members on a committee of nine, the problem was a combination of lack of numbers and experience. The opposition chairman, Ned Shillington, a former minister in the last NDP government, had never sat on the committee and confessed that 'it was not initially contemplated that I would be chairman ... then they shuffled the roles around and I came forward in this.' But that was only the beginning of the opposition's problems. Adhering to a tradition no longer common in the Assembly, Mr Shillington carried on another occupation during the session (in this case a legal practice). During the committee's early days he tried to reschedule meetings so they would not conflict with his court appearances. It was eventually decided to convene at 7:30 a.m. after the other committee members had rejected his suggestion to meet in his absence. The senior PC member (who had been substituted for a freshman member), referring to his own experience in 1975-78 as the sole representative of his party, advised that 'the custom has always been to wait for one opposition member.' Nor was the argument accepted that an NDP member was less needed in 1982-83 because the committee would be examining NDP expenditures. One new PC member pointed out: 'This is a brand new experience to me and since you were part of that previous administration, you may be able to shed light on some of the things that are very hazy and foggy to me at the moment.'[36]

The opposition's problem did not end here, however. Another NDP member of the committee (absent at the beginning and later replaced) sat for one of the northern constituencies and could not be expected to attend inter-sessional meetings unless they were of sufficient duration 'to make it worthwhile for [him] to come.' Thus, the expanse of Saskatchewan (eight hundred miles north to south) is one more problem to be added to those of personnel, scheduling, and a recurrent imbalance in size between government and opposition caucuses which affect all aspects of a small legislature's operations. It is no exaggeration to say that geography is one factor in explaining the problem the Saskatchewan legislature encounters in enforcing accountability.

By tradition there have been ten or twelve standing committees in the legislature but except for the two mentioned, the subjects they discuss are so procedural as to cause little comment (for example, radio broadcasting or the legislative library) or so fundamental as to warrant full House debate (for example, agriculture or education). Since 1971 there has been a

Non-Controversial Bills Committee which has an opposition majority and which is basically intended to streamline the Chamber's work by removing routine matters from its consideration. Most of the estimates are considered in a Committee of the Whole (it is now called Finance but it has passed under different names) where there are no time limits on speeches and no guillotine on supply procedures. Finally, there is a Special Committee on Regulations, with an opposition chairman, which reviews the regulations of the executive and its agents and the by-laws of professional associations to determine if they are made within the authority of the delegating act. More exhaustive scrutiny of delegated legislation was attempted in 1972, with the setting up of a Special Committee on Statutory Instruments. That experiment was later abandoned, an action which, in light of recent developments in the Saskatchewan legislature, is cause for regret among opposition members.

In December 1986 the government introduced Bill 5, An Act Respecting the Organization of the Executive Government of Saskatchewan. Clause 5 of that bill allows the Lieutenant-Governor-in-Council

to assign to any minister any power, duty or function conferred or imposed by law on a minister, to transfer any power ... to any other minister, to transfer any power ... conferred on any department, to any ... other department; either absolutely or limited for any period and in respect of any purpose or area of Saskatchewan. [Moreover] the Lieutenant Governor in Council may assign to any minister or transfer from one minister to another the administration of (a) any Act or portion of an Act; (b) any part of the public service ... [and] may also transfer ... the whole or any part of the moneys appropriated in respect of that Act or part of the public service.

In the debate on second reading, during which the speeches of government members filled only three of ninety pages of *Hansard*, the opposition argued strongly against the proposal on the grounds that it would delegate the power to make rules which would effectively amend, repeal, and replace existing legislation; it would reduce the function and the power of the Assembly, leaving scrutiny only to the regulations committee with its narrow terms of reference; it would seek to change the party which makes the law and thus would be *ultra vires;* and, in short, it would deprive the opposition of 'its window on the operation of government.'[37]

The pragmatic argument was also invoked that Saskatchewan was not 'a large and complex jurisdiction [where] government can no longer function effectively if we involve the Assembly.' In this regard the province was unlike 'Great Britain with a population approaching 48 million, and with a House that has 650 members, and where it might make some sense to restrict the involvement of the House in the detailed affairs of government.'[38] As spokesmen on the government side intervened just twice during the debate – the most substantive comment coming from Bob Andrew, the justice minister, who labelled the opposition and, in particular, the NDP house leader, Roy Romanow, 'hypocritical [for saying] some small Bill is now destroying parliament and destroying democracy [when he] championed the charter of rights that took the power away from parliament'[39] – the government's reason for seeking change remained as originally expressed at the opening of second reading: to improve efficiency by saving time. It is not appropriate here to evaluate the purpose of Bill 5 or the arguments presented by the opposition against it. In the context of a discussion of accountability and the Legislative Assembly, however, it is appropriate to say that legislation such as Bill 5 will detrimentally affect the opposition's opportunity to debate and scrutinize government actions. In a political system where the balance between executive and legislature has traditionally leaned toward the executive and where an adjustment in favour of the legislature has only slowly become evident, Bill 5 must be interpreted as a move in the old and not the new direction.

Reform Processes

Gordon Barnhart has argued that the watchword of legislative reform in Saskatchewan is 'efficiency, not speed.' In a lucid and succinct article with that motto as its title, he notes there have been three major rules changes in the Legislative Assembly since 1970 and that each set has embraced a general theme: procedure (1970), communication (1975), and administration (1981). These reforms have had a substantial effect on making the operation of the legislature more streamlined, in bringing its deliberations closer to the interested public, and in improving the orderly conduct of its business. 'Throughout these reforms,' he asserts, 'one major trend has been developing. The role, rights, and responsibilities of the Private Member have been slowly improving and increasing not because they were given but because the Private Members began to work as a group to improve their lot.'[40]

In the context of Saskatchewan's slowly evolving parliamentary tradition, these innovations must be seen as major advances toward approximating the ideal of greater executive-legislative balance, which this paper argues has been hesitantly realized in the province's past. The prospect of further reform is inevitable, if only because the provincial legislature does not exist in a vacuum and the example of change elsewhere is ultimately too strong to resist for a province with Saskatchewan's record of experimentation. Over a decade ago a political scientist argued that 'a diffusion of legislation [takes place] among the Canadian provinces,' which is explained by factors other than physical proximity or socio-economic similarity.[41] Arguably, if emulation in policy is in order then emulation in procedure can be expected.

Within Saskatchewan the most pressing factor for change emanates from what might be called 'the legislator's world.' The introduction of television into the legislature's proceedings and the establishment of a Board of Internal Economy are two recent and important products of private member pressure. In the immediate future Saskatchewan may expect a period of strong opposition, provided by the provincial party possessing record legislative experience and the lone Liberal leader who made 'responsible opposition' his party's principal platform in 1986. Not for the first time the province's governing party appears less at ease in the world of the legislature than do the opposition parties.

For those who want further reform aimed at creating a still more independent and critical legislature, the task is to convince the electorate of the merits of their case. In Saskatchewan, at least, the public either equates the government with the executive or, to the extent that the legislature impinges on this limited view of the political system, identifies it with one or other of the principal political parties. There is no doubt that the partisanship of the Saskatchewan electorate strengthens popular democracy in the province, but the supplementary question remains whether high participation and the passion it engenders are not bought at a price to parliamentary democracy. Respect for independence in the Saskatchewan legislature is less notable than fervent support for partisan sides. In the provincial political system, where the crown is even less visible than it is at the national level, the concept of the legislature as a constitutional entity of primary importance in assuring good government is an idea seldom expressed. It is, however, an ideal worth seeking through a parliamentary tradition that is still evolving.

LOUIS MASSICOTTE

QUEBEC

The successful combination of French culture and British institutions

Those who believe that the obvious distinctiveness of Quebec society, officially acknowledged by Canada's first ministers in 1987, must unavoidably result
in distinct parliamentary institutions will be disappointed by the results of an in-
depth exploration of the historical evolution, structures, and working of the Assembly. The National Assembly does not differ markedly from other Canadian
elected assemblies. What some persist in denouncing as an unmistakable sign of
collective alienation, others perceive as a shrewd borrowing that successive
generations have adapted to the needs of their society and which, so adapted,
today represents the least questionable part of its colonial heritage.

Peculiar Features of the Quebec Parliament

The first characteristic of Quebec's parliamentary institutions is their longevity:
indeed, they will soon be two hundred years old, since the Constitutional Act
was adopted in 1791, belatedly honouring a promise made twenty-eight years
earlier to create in Lower Canada the first elected legislative assembly that the
descendants of the country's French settlers had ever known. If this date appears
respectably old when compared with the dates of the establishment of elective
chambers in many states of continental Europe, it is none the less much later
than the creation of the legislative assembly of the colony of Virginia (1619),
the oldest of the American legislative bodies. Parliamentary government arrived
in Quebec at the same time as in Ontario, but representative institutions had
been granted as early as 1758 in Nova Scotia, 1773 in Prince Edward Island, and
1785 in New Brunswick.

A second feature of parliamentary government in Quebec is its discontinuity, resulting from the vicissitudes of the constitutional evolution of French Canada. From 1791 to 1838, under the Constitutional Act, Lower Canada had a distinct legislature which, after an eventful existence, was abolished as a result of the troubles of 1837-38. From 1841 to 1867, the elected members of Lower Canada sat in the legislature of the United Province of Canada, whose jurisdiction covered the present provinces of Ontario and Quebec, and in which Lower Canada held, first to its disadvantage, later to its benefit, exactly half the seats. Confederation in 1867 brought with it the rebirth of a separate legislature, but one whose powers were limited to the areas defined by the Canadian constitution. The first interruption was the result of a popular rebellion followed by the abolition of the Assembly and an authoritarian reorganization of constitutional frameworks by the colonial power. The second stemmed essentially from the choice of representatives elected by the population.

Bicameralism is another characteristic of traditional parliamentary government in Quebec, since each of the regimes mentioned above included, alongside a legislative assembly elected by the population, an upper chamber called the Legislative Council. Members of this were appointed by the crown, with the exception of a brief period under the Union (1856-67) during which they were elected by the same voters who elected the Assembly.[1] For forty years Quebec was the only Canadian province to maintain a legislative body of this kind; its abolition in 1968 coincided with a new and ambitious name for the elected, and henceforth the only, chamber: the 'Assemblée nationale.'

The two-party system is a fourth long-standing characteristic of parliamentary government in Quebec. Despite occasional breakthrough by third parties in 1935, 1944, 1970, and 1976, the political configuration in Quebec has been clearly bipartisan, although the identity of one of the partners varied. The first-past-the-post electoral system played a major role in the advent, and more particularly in the maintenance, of this two-party system. There are, however, many examples, some quite close geographically, to show that multipartism can continue for a long time despite the presence of such an electoral system. Since 1981 the Liberal party and the Parti Québécois have held between them all of the seats in the Assembly, have received approximately 95 per cent of the votes, and have collected or accounted for an even higher proportion of the contributions and electoral expenses reported in the province.[2]

The tendency for one party to remain in office for long periods of time has long been considered a basic trait of political life in Quebec. Indeed, after Confederation the Conservatives held power for thirty years with two interruptions, the first rather brief, under Joly de Lotbinière (1878-79), and the second more significant under Honoré Mercier (1887-91). The first of these governments was brought to office following an authoritarian intervention by the lieutenant-governor, and was defeated by a vote in the Assembly. The second was born and died in identical circumstances, but in the reverse order: brought to power by a vote in the Assembly, it perished at the hand of a lieutenant-governor! This very lively period in Quebec's parliamentary history was followed by two long terms of office: the uninterrupted reign of the Liberals (1897-1936), and that of the Union Nationale (1936-39 and 1944-60), interrupted only by the second Liberal government of Godbout. During these two reigns, the opposition was numerically quite weak. Only two of the sixteen elections held between 1900 and 1956 left it with more than one-quarter of the seats in the Assembly, with predictable consequences on the effectiveness of parliamentary control. Malapportionment of legislative districts significantly contributed to this.[3] The election of 1960 began a new period, in which the fate of governments appears less assured and the possibility of alternation more likely. Since that date, no government has succeeded in being re-elected more than once.

Quebec not only has no real experience of minority government, but the majority of the ruling party in the Assembly has tended to be enormous throughout the history of the province, even when compared with assemblies elected under the same electoral system. Indeed, since 1867 the governing party held more than two out of three seats for no less than eighty-seven years. The comparable figure is fifty-four years in Ontario, twenty-nine in Ottawa, nineteen in the United Kingdom, and sixteen in the U.S. House of Representatives. Many other provinces are closer to the Quebec pattern.

An Assembly Embedded in Quebec History

All the characteristics just described have their importance, but there is one that might be said to transcend them all and make the Parliament of Quebec an institution unique of its kind. Modelled for a long time on the British Parliament, to the point of being described as a replica in miniature, and still strongly marked by that model in its essential features, this Parliament remains none the less the representative organ of a province which is overwhelmingly French in terms of its language and culture, and which is firmly resolved to remain so. This duality has been and continues to be perceived in various ways.

To some Québécois intelligentsia, the marriage of British institutions and a French Catholic population could not last. A product of circumstances, it could culminate at best in the imposition of a thin and fragile liberal, democratic, and parliamentary surface on a social body imbued with quite different cultural traditions.

This pessimistic assessment found much of its source in the special circumstances of the 1950s and 1960s. Unanimous in their condemnation of

Duplessisism, both Cité Libristes and neo-nationalists condemned outright the type of democracy operating in Quebec at the time they were developing their respective systems of thought, towards the end of the 1950s. They objected to the open buying of votes, undue ecclesiastical pressures, and authoritarianism of the premier in the chamber. But their prescriptions differed. For the Cité Libristes, French-Canadian society of the time was not worthy of the model: imbued with clericalism, corporatism, and anti-democratic principles, its official ideology was not conducive to the normal functioning of parliamentary institutions. Only with a radical transformation of outlook in French Canada could such a system find fertile ground for its harmonious operation.[4]

The neo-nationalists of the 1960s laid the blame elsewhere. Equally unedified by our political and parliamentary life, they blamed its vices not on the society but on the institutional apparatus that had been 'imposed' on it. The system, whatever value could kindly be conceded to it for other parts of the world, suffered here from one original and indelible flaw. A product of the Conquest and of the British approach to politics, it could only constitute in Quebec an odious colonial veneer which the nation, when it finally reached maturity, would replace with original institutions of its own.

These two schools of thought, so different in their ultimate explanations, so unanimous and categorical in their condemnation, were based on a common and pessimistic view of Quebec parliamentary history. According to this, in 1791 the parliamentary institutions had been 'imposed' on Canadiens who then used them for essentially national purposes, which in the eyes of the Cité Libristes amounted to perverting their spirit.

Is that interpretation universally accepted? In fact, democratic and parliamentary values were not a part of the intellectual inheritance that France handed down to the sixty thousand settlers whom it abandoned in 1763. The French empire in America had been founded by a country which was overcoming at the same time the final obstacles to the emergence of absolute royal power. What Richelieu and Louis XIV dreamed of building in America was based on the principles by which they were governing France. The political institutions of New France were based on centralization and the authority of the governors and intendants. They made no concessions to any popular expression by the people.[5] From that standpoint, the Conquest merely replaced the absolute authority of the crown of France with that of the crown of England, although it is true that the latter was less sensitive, particularly in the beginning, to the religious and linguistic aspirations of its new subjects. At the same time, the Catholic Church deeply distrusted liberalism, democracy, and parliamentary government, at least until the end of the nineteenth century.

Parliamentary institutions were established in Lower Canada not at the request of French Canadians, but rather at the initiative of the anglophone merchants, often newly arrived from the former American colonies, and accustomed to a representative system. Many francophone leaders strongly opposed this innovation, not, it seems, because they were fanatically anti-democratic but because they feared new taxes. If taxation implied representation, they believed, did not representation imply taxation?

Strenuous insistence has been placed on this 'foreign' origin of parliamentary government in Quebec. It has been claimed that this is the definitive proof that the parliamentary system has no authentic roots, as if the story ended there. But the story had only begun.

What was granted in 1791 was a very incomplete parliamentary system.[6] The elected Assembly was in fact framed by two non-democratic institutions, the governor and the Legislative Council, representing respectively the home country and the anglophone merchant oligarchy. Far from being merely checks on the Assembly, they constituted the driving elements of the system, and it was the Assembly that was looked on as a mere counterweight. Apart from its linguistics aspects, this constitutional arrangement closely resembled the one from which the American colonies had just emerged in revolutionary circumstances. Fifteen years after a spectacular failure on the banks of the Hudson, the system was given a 'second chance' on those of the St Lawrence. Seen from this perspective, it is scarcely surprising that the enterprise turned out badly.

Too many criticisms directed at the lack of 'roots' of parliamentary government in Quebec overlook an essential fact. The institutional framework introduced by the Constitutional Act and reaffirmed by the Union Act was profoundly transformed in 1848 by the advent of responsible government. This made the elected Assembly the source of governmental power and over the long term reduced to very minor importance the old royal prerogatives and the powers of the upper chamber. Responsible government was not imposed by the mother country, but was won after a hard-fought struggle by the elected representatives of the population. In the long process that led to this essential change, England played an ambiguous role. Because of the resistance with which its proconsuls greeted the demands of the parliamentarians, it was generally thought of as an *obstacle*. But it also constituted the *example* to be followed, insofar as Patriotes, then Reformists, could base their claims on the rich British parliamentary tradition. In this way the governors were on the horns of the following dilemma: either they accepted claims that in the long run diminished their own status, or they had to assert that what was good for the British (and generally admired abroad) suddenly stopped being valid as soon as one proposed to apply it to Her Majesty's North American subjects.

It is true that the British inspiration was very strong in the development of the nuts and bolts of the Quebec Assembly. Until only twenty years ago, procedure, terminology, ceremonial, and customs readily betrayed their origins. Paradoxically, a desire to reinforce the value of the government of Quebec was often the direct cause of this borrowing. The transposition of solemn ceremonies underlined the importance of the provincial government, and its desire to be more than a big municipal council. Many of the rites that were ridiculed in the 1960s had stemmed from the desire to affirm the status of the provincial government.

A few initiatives reveal, none the less, the eagerness of the parliamentarians of the past to adapt the institution in which they were evolving to the cultural values of Quebec society. One need not be a purist to acknowledge the deficiencies of the parliamentary terminology of 1867; the official French terms and expressions of those times were a cascade of slavish imitations of the English, and reading them aloud today would drive any audience in Quebec to thunderous laughter. In 1885 more correct French expressions began to replace some of the literal translations that had been satisfactory up to then, and the description of the customs that constituted such an important part of parliamentary procedure was translated into the language spoken by the majority of members. The standing orders adopted that year provided for the primacy of the French version over the English in cases of conflict. In 1914 all the constitutional rules, standing orders, and customs were integrated into one code of more than six hundred sections. Though the final product became the lengthiest rule book in the British empire, thus discouraging more than one novice MLA, it satisfied the predilection of jurists of the French tradition for codification. This enterprise was completed between 1969 and 1972, when there was a terminological revision and a welcome simplification.

The need to adapt the Westminster parliamentary model to the requirements and values of a society with a French majority also made itself felt with regard to the symbols of monarchy. The history of popular French-Canadian feeling about the British monarchy has yet to be written,[7] but it seems fair to say that the monarchy maintained at least the implicit support of the majority until the early 1960s. The traditional ideology conveyed by the church taught respect for the established order, and maintained for a long time a bias in favour of hereditary royalty. The official speeches of Quebec political leaders of the time brimmed over with loyalty to the crown, all the more readily because the crown had ceased to involve itself in partisan debates.

The signs of a change of attitude in this regard emerged at the beginning of the 1960s. The more ardent Quebec nationalism found an easy target in an institution recalling, if only in a symbolic way, a foreign subjection identified as the source of all evils. As early as 1962 a poll revealed the disaffection of Quebec opinion toward the monarchy, while the demonstrations that marked the visit of Queen Elizabeth to Quebec City in 1964, and then the 1970 refusal – at least to begin with – of the newly elected Parti Québécois MNAs to swear the oath of allegiance to the queen stipulated in the constitution, revealed the depth of this hostility, at least among separatists.[8] The same period saw a growing number of plans for reforming political institutions and providing for not only the disappearance of the crown but the establishment of presidential systems on the French or American model.

So far the only result of this widespread opposition has been a reduction in the visibility of the monarchy in Quebec institutions. In point of fact, the office of lieutenant-governor is beyond the legislative power of the Quebec Assembly, and no government, including that of René Lévesque, has seen fit to launch an in-depth debate on that question. Successive governments have preferred to reduce the expense allowance of the lieutenant-governor and systematically eliminate references to the crown scattered throughout the standing orders of the Assembly. Since 1969 the throne speech read by the lieutenant-governor has been replaced by an inaugural message or opening speech delivered by the premier. Bagehot described the British political system as a 'republic in disguise.' As to more fundamental reforms, they appear for the moment to be supported by only a minority, although the polls hint at a degree of public sympathy at least for certain aspects of such systems.

The Quebec approach to this matter is reminiscent of the Irish experience. The historical disputes between England and Ireland at the turn of the century were far deeper than those between Quebec and the colonizing country. Achieving power in 1921, the Irish nationalists adopted a parliamentary form of government, even though it strongly resembled the institutions of the detested colonizer. The constitution of 1937 replaced the governor general by an elected president with reduced powers, and the head of government and his deputy received the very Irish titles of *Taoiseach* and *Tanaiste*; but behind this façade is played a parliamentary game closely inspired by the Westminster model.

Any attempt to replace this model with a replica of the American constitution or the French semi-presidential regime might well encounter serious obstacles. A thorough public debate would make clear the limitations of a purely 'cultural' approach to political institutions, which dictates that a community should sweep away a proven and well-established system solely to distinguish itself from certain of its neighbours (even though this means substituting institutions modelled on those of another neighbour). Various indications give us reason to doubt the purely electoral profitability of such proposals, even among those whom they obviously seek to win over.

Legal and Political Leadership in the Assembly

The Speaker of the Assembly is elected for the duration of a legislature, by a motion proposed by the premier after consultation with the opposition. As everywhere else in Canada, the Speaker plays both a procedural and an administrative role. The first is the more visible, although the Speaker now tends to occupy the Chair only during the oral question period and other important periods.

Except between 1878 and 1881, the Speaker and the Deputy Speakers have always been members of the party in power. Nineteen Speakers were subsequently appointed to the cabinet, while only three followed the reverse course. The premier's choice was ratified by the Assembly in all cases except in January 1887, when the election of the Speaker, following the ambiguous result of the general election of the previous fall, gave the National opposition party an opportunity to prove that it well and truly held the majority in the Chamber, by rejecting the candidate proposed by Premier Taillon and electing instead Félix-Gabriel Marchand.

The method of choosing the Speaker appeared at first glance to guarantee the presence in the Chair of an active partisan of the government. Thus, the relative impartiality of Speakers between 1867 and 1936 is all the more surprising. Many times their casting vote settled a question in a way contrary to the preferences of the government. If the rarity of appeals from Speakers' rulings constitutes a convincing indicator of their authority, one can consider that the Speakers prior to 1936 generally enjoyed the respect of both sides of the Chamber, since in that period of nearly seventy years there were only sixty-one appeals, related to 11 per cent of the decisions rendered by the Chair. The previous parliamentary experience of the Speakers of that era, generally longer than that of their successors, may explain this high regard. Certain Speakers, like LeBlanc (1892-97), raised the ire of the opposition, and others sometimes gave rulings favourable to the government on quite questionable grounds. Nevertheless, a procedural expert like Maurice Duplessis, then in opposition, could obtain favourable decisions from a Liberal Speaker.

The situation changed utterly beginning with the session of 1937, when appeals became epidemic. Between 1937 and 1959, 256 Speakers' rulings (91 per cent of the total) were appealed. From 1959 to 1968, there were 206, covering almost all decisions of the Speaker, Deputy Speaker, or acting chairman. Few practices have contributed so much to tarnishing the image of Parliament as this multiplication of appeals according to an almost unvarying scenario which may be summarized as follows. The premier interrupted an opposition member, alleging a violation of the standing orders, or perhaps the opposition accused him of the same thing. The Speaker invariably ruled in favour of the government, basing his decision on grounds sometimes as subtle and sophisticated in their content as they were transparent in their origin. In a Pavlovian response, the opposition immediately appealed the decision to the Assembly. As the standing orders did not permit a debate on this point, raised hands immediately showed a majority in favour of the ruling. The opposition then demanded a recorded vote. The bell was set ringing and the contentious decision was confirmed by a vote along strict party lines.

The Speaker's position in such a system was untenable. If by any chance he ruled in favour of the opposition, his decision could be reversed by the government majority. Most successive Speakers chose rather to sanction the government position in cases of dispute, even if it meant being looked on as a hostage of the majority. As Daniel Johnson, then Deputy Speaker, acknowledged humorously one day, the Speaker, like any motorist, should 'keep to the right.' Moreover, there is reason to believe that the opposition appealed even well-founded decisions, in order to delay the progress of business in the Assembly by requiring recorded votes.

One can discern an outside inspiration in the decision taken in 1969 to abolish appeals of the Speaker's decisions. Taken four years after a similar move in Ottawa, this innovation had in the long term the same positive effects. Despite the minor skirmishes that have occasionally marked their terms of office, the Speakers of the Assembly have, since that date, enjoyed general confidence in their impartiality, and this has been confirmed by their habit of no longer attending their respective party caucuses. A few Deputy Speakers, however, have seen their prestige diminished as a result of opposition motions of censure against them, although such criticisms do not appear to have been justified.

The party leadership structures in the Assembly, originally rather slight, have become more complex since the 1960s. Traditionally, the leader of the government party in the House was the premier himself, or one of his colleagues if the head of government sat in the Legislative Council. It was only from 1965 that a minister assumed, along with the title of government house leader, the organization of business in the Assembly, a practice which has continued ever since. One or more ministers can be appointed deputies to him in this responsibility.

The fluidity of partisan allegiances at the beginning of Confederation quite probably explains why the office of leader of the opposition did not appear until March 1869. Its first incumbents, Joly de Lotbinière, then Chapleau and then Mercier, quickly asserted their rights, including that of being asked to form a government in case of a change of majority. A 1918 statute enshrined this function in law, and provided its incumbent with a salary equivalent to that of a minister. On several occasions the leader of the opposition party, defeated in his own riding or not yet elected to the Assembly, had to be represented in the House by one of his colleagues. The most recent cases are that of Robert Bourassa between 1983 and 1985 and Jacques Parizeau since 1988. Like the government, the opposition has had a house leader paid out of public funds since 1971.

Though the status of the main opposition party was quickly established, the same was not true for third parties, whose members for a long time were treated as independents under parliamentary law. The breakthrough by third parties in the general election of 1970 – which elected twelve Créditistes and seven Péquistes – immediately brought about a change in official thinking on this point. Any parliamentary group with at least twelve MNAs, or which represented a party whose candidates had received at least 20 per cent of the votes cast in the most recent general election, was recognized as a party. These purely arbitrary criteria were made to measure for the two third parties of that time, and the split in the Créditiste group in 1972, like the election of eleven Union Nationale MNAs in 1976 and the break-up of this group a few years later, necessitated laborious adjustments. The head of such a party receives a supplementary allowance and privileges with regard to the right to speak.

The actual planning of Assembly business gradually slipped from the hands of the party leaders to those of the house leaders. Under the standing orders, the house leaders must meet even before the government may resort to closure.

A complete list of party whips is not available, but the fragmentary data suggest that this function was performed without remuneration by private members prior to 1967, when a law recognized these duties by providing for the payment of a supplementary allowance to their incumbents. For a long time, in addition to maintaining party discipline, the whips chaired the party caucuses, but a recent development separated these two duties. Little is known of how caucuses functioned in the past. In 1959, 1960, and 1968, the caucus of MLAs and legislative councillors of the Union Nationale formally ratified the choice of the new party leader and petitioned the lieutenant-governor to send for the elected leader as premier. Until party leadership conventions became common (the Conservatives began this practice in 1929, and the Liberals followed in 1950), the caucus had the right to elect the leader of the party when in opposition. There is no indication that the government caucus exercised much control over government actions prior to 1976, although a caucus revolt in 1905 forced Premier Parent to resign. Jérôme Proulx reports that in 1969 a piece of legislation as important as Bill 63 was discussed in caucus before being introduced in the Chamber: it was the first time such a precaution was taken in over three years.[9] The scarce data available suggest that caucuses play a more active role today. In November 1987 a caucus revolt forced the resignation of Pierre Marc Johnson as leader of the Parti Québécois.

Sociological Profile of the Assembly

Like most parliamentary assemblies, the Quebec Parliament is more representative in the political sense than in the sociological sense. The most obvious imbalance between the composition of the Assembly and that of the population relates to sex. There were no women in the Assembly prior to 1961, when Claire Kirkland-Casgrain was elected. There was only one woman until 1976. Since then, progress has been rapid, although many consider it quite inadequate. At least the election in 1985 of eighteen women (then the highest proportion in the country as well as in the French-speaking world) exploded the myth that the first-past-the-post electoral system blocked the entry of women into the Assembly.

The socio-professional composition of the Assembly has been studied by Robert Boily, Marc-André Bédard, Réjean Pelletier, and Gaston Deschênes.[10] It is characterized by the overwhelming and continual preponderance of three major strata: professionals such as lawyers and doctors; owners of small and medium-sized businesses; and administrators, business people, and industrialists.[11] These three groups alone have traditionally accounted for more than three-quarters of the members. In contrast, the proportion of farmers has never exceeded 10 per cent, and has been steadily eroded over the years, while workers have always made up a negligible portion of Parliament. Rather than profession, today it is the previous work environment of their members that distinguishes the two parties: 35 per cent of the present Parti Québécois MNAs worked prior to their election in the private sector, compared with 70 per cent of the Liberals.

MLAs have traditionally distinguished themselves from the mass of electors by their advanced level of education.[12] In 1867 one-quarter of the members possessed a university education. From 1886 this proportion exceeded 40 per cent (and often 50 per cent). After the elections of 1976 and 1981 nearly three-quarters of the members possessed such a degree, and the percentage was 68 per cent in 1985.

The average age of members has fluctuated between 42 and 52 since 1867. This apparent stability masks the fact that members are becoming relatively younger since, as Gaston Deschênes observes, 'a forty-year-old of today is younger than his counterpart a hundred years ago.'[13] This infusion of young blood has been evident not only relatively but in absolute terms since 1956. From 52 in that year, the average age of members has gradually declined to 43.6 in 1985. The election to the Assembly of Claude Charron at 23 years of age, and Michel Pagé at 24, symbolizes this breakthrough by the younger generation.

Linguistically, the striking feature is the steady erosion of anglophone representation. From 30 per cent in 1867 it dwindled to 20 per cent in 1900, 10 per cent in 1940, and 6 per cent in 1976. The English language, used frequently in the Assembly in the past – from 1867 to 1878 the budget speech was *always* delivered in English[14] – is now heard more rarely. Section 80 of the BNA Act protected the boundaries of twelve ridings, mostly anglophone, against any gerrymander designed to reduce that group's representation, but this privilege seems to have done nothing to check the decline in the relative influence of the anglophone group. Such an evolution may stem from the traditional ethnic sharing of responsibilities, with francophone preponderance in provincial politics coexisting until a few years ago with the massive presence of anglophones in business. A slight recovery in the numerical strength of anglophones occurred in the elections of 1981 and 1985, probably linked to the Quebec government's interventions in the area of language. For the last ten years or so, the Assembly has also included representatives of some of the various cultural communities, including Quebeckers of Italian, Greek, or Haitian origin.

The end of the era of long terms of office for one party and the more frequent changes of government since 1960 have resulted in a decline in the number of members with long parliamentary experience. In 1956, the last time Duplessis was re-elected, the percentage of members who had sat in the Assembly for at least six years was 57 per cent. It fell successively to 40 per cent in 1962, 29 per cent in 1966, 26 per cent in 1970, and 18 per cent in 1985. This evolution has increased the relative strength of newcomers, to the point that the total absence of parliamentary experience is no longer a decisive obstacle to entering cabinet, a fact which to some confirms the decline of Parliament. Moreover, it has probably facilitated the adoption since the end of the 1960s of numerous parliamentary reforms which a 'coalition of elders' could have delayed. Parliamentarians who can boast over thirty years' experience in the Assembly, like Gérard D. Levesque today, remain exceptions. Alexandre Taschereau holds the absolute record with an uninterrupted career of thirty-six years.

The Parliamentary Calendar

The marked lengthening of sessions is one of the major differences between parliamentary government in Quebec in the past and today. From 1867 to 1960 the average number of sitting days per year was forty-five, and a typical session lasted approximately three months. There were few deviations from this average, and the short sessions of 1949 and 1950 (twenty-six and twenty-eight days respectively), like the longer sessions of 1959-60 and 1944 (sixty-five and sixty-seven days respectively), were exceptions.

This relative brevity of the sessions appears to stem from the conception of the role of government that prevailed at the time. Non-interventionist governments would naturally result in parliamentary assemblies that sat only a few months a year. At that time a member received only a modest sessional allowance rather than an annual salary, which meant that he had to return to the exercise of his profession once the session was prorogued. Perhaps this helps to explain the consistent preponderance of business people and members of the liberal professions. The working conditions of the time made it difficult for employees to enter politics. Was the position of members vis-à-vis ministers strengthened by it? The answer is not obvious. Perhaps members could view exclusion from the caucus for the 'crime' of independence of mind with a more philosophical eye because for them such a sanction merely meant returning to a profession they had never really left. However, ministers were exempt from normal parliamentary controls for nine months out of twelve, and could pose more easily than mere MLAs as real professional politicians.

In that regard, the Quiet Revolution signalled a complete change. The advent of a more activist concept of the role of the state was reflected in a marked lengthening of sessions. Since then, the Assembly has been sitting an average of eighty-seven days per year, close to double the average of previous decades. This upward trend would undoubtedly be even more noticeable if the working methods of the Assembly had not been reformed and simplified from 1964 onwards. By delegating to its committees tasks formerly reserved for the Committee of the Whole, the Assembly succeeded in dealing with a much larger quantity of work than was indicated by the number of sitting days alone. The average length of sessions remains well below that recorded today in Ottawa, approximately 175 days.

The Quebec Assembly was in the vanguard in Canada with regard to the establishment of a proper parliamentary calendar. For a long time the convening and proroguing of sessions remained entirely at the discretion of the government, subject to the constitutional rule calling for the holding of one session per year. From 1978 onwards it was ordered that the Assembly must be adjourned on set dates a little before St. Jean Baptiste Day (24 June) and Christmas, a rule supplemented in 1984 by the establishment of set dates in March and October for the resumption of business. More intensive periods of work marked the three weeks preceding each adjournment. These new rules made official the practice of having two parliamentary semesters, one in the spring and one in the fall, which dates back to 1968.

Role of the Private Member

In this framework, the balance of power between the government and private members is clearly to the former's advantage. Almost all public legislation originates with the government, and in votes taken in the Chamber, the government can normally count on the total support of its caucus. This state of affairs, despite its obvious drawbacks, is so deeply entrenched that it has almost been forgotten, even in official circles, that in its early days the Assembly functioned quite differently. Accustomed to a Chamber that acts merely as a rubber stamp, a student who is willing to carry out patient investigations of earlier periods often feels he has landed on another planet, so striking is the contrast between yesterday's Assembly and that of today.[15]

The table below could be entitled 'the harnessing of the private member.' It shows the evolution over a long period of three key indicators: the percentage of divisions in the Assembly in which some government members broke with the party line, the percentage of public legislation that originated with private members, and the number of government defeats in the Chamber. Each of these indicators would require many explanations and qualifications, but it is the overall evolution that is of interest here. That evolution is quite clear.

Indicators of members' independence, 1867-1985

	Percentage of divisions in which government members dissented	Number of government defeats	Private members' public bills as a percentage of public bills passed
1867-1897	50.8	105*	42.0
1897-1936	33.0	67	28.4
1936-1960	1.8	0	6.9
1960-1985	4.0	0	2.0

*Three governments were forced by the Assembly to resign or dissolve the legislature (1878, 1879 and 1887)

In the nineteenth century more than two-fifths of the *public* bills passed by the Assembly had been introduced by private government or opposition members. More than half of the votes revealed open disagreements within the government caucus, and the premier found himself in the minority nearly four times per session. A closer analysis reveals at least two clearly distinct spheres in Assembly business. Government legislation received the support of the Assembly, occasioned a lower rate of dissent, and very rarely resulted in the defeat of the government. However, at that time it was accepted that private members would introduce legislative measures which, although they did not have financial implications, were none the less of obvious public interest: amendments to the Civil Code, the Code of Civil Procedure, the Municipal Code, and electoral law were the major spheres of action of the private member as legislator. In those areas, party discipline was clearly less strict, and the cabinet often lost the divisions.[16] If there was a 'golden age' of the Quebec Parliament, it is here that we should be looking for it. A parliament in which private members would become true legislators is the dream of many observers and of some private members (and the nightmare of ministers and their advisers). Such a model may be part of the future of the Assembly, but is undoubtedly part of its past.

Should one therefore advocate a 'return to basics'? It has been amply demonstrated that the flexibility of the constitutional rules governing our parliamentary system allows it. The survival of the government is at stake only on motions of censure, its annual spending estimates (but not an individual item of spending), and motions the government has explicitly and in advance designated as tests of confidence. The room to manoeuvre is therefore quite large, constitutionally speaking, for private members who would decide to use it fully.

Nevertheless, such a development appears quite improbable if one reflects on the causes of the end of the golden age just described. That age coincided with an era of limited suffrage in which private members were wealthy, influential persons capable of paying the costs of their own electoral campaigns. Universal suffrage increased not only the number of electors but the cost of election campaigns. Gradually, private members came to depend for their re-election on the financial, symbolic, and intellectual resources provided by their parties. In return, the parties demanded unfailing support in the Chamber and greater conformity among members. Moreover, the growing complexity of public affairs necessitated the systematic use of legislation whose preparation required means that only the government had at its disposal. As early as 1881, Justice Loranger criticized the inconsistencies introduced into Quebec law by the 'mania' of private members 'for legislating.'[17] In short, it was the change in the role of government and, to a lesser extent, the advent of universal suffrage, much more than the emergence of more authoritarian leaders, that overcame the independence of private members. A similar evolution was observed in Great Britain, Ottawa, and the other provinces. It is difficult to reverse such a fundamental movement.

Does this condemn private members to choke in an iron collar? Most seem to accept the limitations of their current status with good grace. Absorbed in constituency work, they find in it an awareness of their own importance and the justifiable impression that they are being useful to their fellow citizens. A good number are aware that they owe their election (and will owe their defeat) more to the popularity of their party, the sociological characteristics of the riding they represent, and the performance of their leader than to their legislative performance. Private members are engaged in a career whose ideal culmination is entry to the cabinet or, failing that, positions of lesser responsibility (which have tended to multiply in the last thirty years). There is much truth in Mr Denis Vaugeois's witty comment that, for most members, 'The Chamber is really the antichamber of the cabinet.' In this race, the value and dynamism of individuals count for a lot, but so does the confidence they inspire to the party leader. Such confidence is rarely earned through repeated disagreements, dramatic declarations, or harassment of ministers. Moreover, is it not the job of the opposition to exercise – in a disciplined and systematic way – the critical function in the Assembly? Whether one calls it loyalty or conformity, party discipline has a rosy future.[18]

Government and Opposition

The government is in a position to control the progress of business in the Assembly. For a long time this predominance seems to have been taken for granted, even in a much earlier era when parliamentary rules placed no restrictions on the right of private members to speak. During its first century of existence the Assembly saw only two examples of systematic obstruction. The success of the second, in 1936, when Duplessis succeeded in preventing the adoption of the annual supply bill authorizing government spending, thereby forcing the government to hold an early general election at the worst possible moment for itself, showed to what extent a determined and able opposition could take advantage of a favourable opportunity. Three years later a limit of one hour was placed on the length of most speeches, and in 1941 a very strict procedure for adopting interim supply prevented a repeat of the feat of 1936. The maximum length for speeches was reduced to thirty minutes in 1969, then to twenty three years later. In 1972 the Assembly adopted a closure mechanism enabling it to put an end to the study of a bill in committee, as well as a procedural guillotine for the adoption of budgetary estimates. Despite this procedure (or because of it?) filibusters have multiplied over the last fifteen years. In cases of emergency, the Assembly suspends its own rules on the initiative of the government and establishes an ad hoc procedure guaranteeing the passage of a controversial bill – often a bill putting an end to a labour dispute – in a short period. The enumeration of the various provisions in the standing orders that limit the right to speak or the total duration of debates would quickly prove tedious. These different means are in no way exceptional in the Canadian context and, here as elsewhere, are designed to ensure the majority will prevail in cases of systematic obstruction by the minority.

If the opposition is assured of losing any confrontation in which neither its arguments nor public reaction have succeeded in shaking the government's resolution, at least it now has a better chance of seeing its arguments reach a wider public. In 1964 the Assembly resumed the practice, which it had encouraged between 1879 and 1893, of publishing a verbatim account of its debates. Unlike the old *Hansard*, this account is exhaustive. It constitutes the transcription of tape recordings rather than stenographic notes, and is prepared by the services of the Assembly. Greater still seems to have been the impact of the televising of debates, introduced in 1978 and limited for the moment to sittings of the Assembly and only a few committee meetings. Through this medium, the debates are broadcast throughout Quebec and reach a much wider public.

If private members have given up trying to impose their own legislative priorities, at least they have tried in recent years to exercise more control over the administration of the Assembly. For a long time this was the responsibility, under a system established in 1875, of a Board of Internal Economy composed of the Speaker and three ministers. The executive thus had complete control in the area. Since 1982 the administration of the Assembly has been entrusted to a board including not only the Speaker but also four government and three opposition members.

Scrutiny of the Government by the Assembly

Stripped de facto of its initiative in the area of policy, has the Assembly developed mechanisms for effectively controlling the executive? The majority of observers hesitate to say it has.

Written questions were authorized as soon as 1867 by the standing orders, and the text of questions and answers has been printed in the *Journals* since 1879. In the beginning, government members did not hesitate to use this device; 28 per cent of the questions asked between 1879 and 1916 originated with them. Since that date, opposition members have held a virtual monopoly in this area. There is no evidence that this has been particularly troublesome for the government. At times the opposition freely asked questions on the most diverse subjects, the answers to which could be found in public documents accessible to everyone. Thus, the government was asked in 1913 for the number of species of wild birds in the province! Sometimes government members diverted the procedure. On the eve of the prorogation of the first session of 1912, during the last sitting before the general election, the Gouin government was pleased to table together the answers to forty or so questions asked by its own members. These questions were designed to elicit favourable comparisons with past governments, to detail government expenditures in various sectors, and to illustrate the progress it had achieved in recent years. The minutes of proceedings of the day were then ready for use as a manual for Liberal candidates in the coming election. Under the pretext of complying with the requirements of parliamentary representation, the government had its election propaganda prepared and published at taxpayers' expense!

It was only in the early 1960s that oral questions became a common procedure in the Assembly. From the outset they came almost exclusively from the opposition ranks and quickly became the most popular time in the sittings of the Chamber. As everywhere else, they are designed to embarrass ministers rather than obtain answers. Preambles, questions, and answers tend to be long and elaborate, and the whole process often looks like a debate rather than an information session. Since 1972 members dissatisfied with answers provided can raise the issue at the end of the sitting, a procedure equivalent to the Ottawa 'late show.'

Though the development of delegated legislation has raised fears in many quarters, the Assembly has not developed effective controls in this regard.[19] There has never been a special committee for this purpose, although it has been proposed that one be created. Controlling the regulations pertaining to each sector is in principle the responsibility of the competent parliamentary committee. In practice, each committee feels that it has more crucial matters to deal with. Though some committees examined draft regulations in the past, none has done so during the first two years after the parliamentary reform of 1984. The recent adoption of a long-awaited law in this area (Quebec was the last province to do so) opens interesting prospects, since this law establishes a procedure whereby the Assembly could disallow a regulation. The insertion into this law at the very last minute of a provision exempting draft regulations which the government can determine by order-in-council has confirmed the scepticism of many observers as to the political will that exists in this regard.

In the financial area, parliamentary controls have been notably weak until recently. So-called statutory expenditures, which are not subject to the scrutiny normally given to budgetary estimates, until 1960 made up an enormous proportion (between 31 and 87 per cent) of total expenditures. Estimates were traditionally examined in Committee of the Whole.[20] Starting in the mid-1960s, certain estimates were examined in smaller committees, and this procedure became standard practice in 1972. It was the desire to free the floor of the Chamber for other purposes, rather than to strengthen parliamentary control in this area, that appears to have motivated this innovation. To our knowledge, not a single estimate has ever been reduced or cancelled as a result of this review by committee, whose principal interest has more to do with the in-depth discussions facilitated between private members, ministers and their senior aides or bureaucrats.

A study on the scrutiny of the estimates by a particular committee between 1969 and 1980 led an author to conclude: 'The influence of parliamentary control over decisions on government spending is limited ... Debates in the House or committee scrutiny do not modify in any way the estimates tabled by the Minister of Finance ... Nothing in this study backs the idea that through parliamentary control, elected representatives influence political decision-making.'[21]

The Assembly has not tried to control the activities of departments and crown corporations very strictly. No committee is exclusively responsible for scrutinizing the activities of the latter. The occasional appearance of their executives illustrates the discrepancy between the resources available on each side: the executives of Hydro-Québec customarily inundated parliamentarians with complex documents that only the initiated could truly master. Nevertheless, the televised parliamentary inquiry into the out-of-court settlement of lawsuits with respect to the havoc on construction site LG 2 in 1984 provided the opposition with an opportunity to cast doubts on the credibility of the premier and his advisers. From 1984 the standing orders provided for the appearance at regular intervals before committees of senior officials directly responsible to the Assembly. Two years later, one of these senior officials in his annual report lamented the fact that he had never been invited![22]

In 1978 the Assembly adopted an original control procedure first called 'question avec débat,' and renamed 'interpellation' in 1984. The opposition may, on a subject which it designates, cause the holding of an in-depth debate in committee on Friday mornings.

On the whole, parliamentary controls are not considered as effective as they should be. It is not so much the structures and procedures that are in question. Used fully, they could produce satisfactory results. The problem is more in the attitude of parliamentarians themselves. They have rarely displayed the 'corporate' attitude that would have helped them to overcome partisan divisions. When it is attacking an administration, the opposition aims less to correct its abuses than to discredit the ministers responsible. Government members, whatever their deepest feelings may be on the merits of an issue, are reluctant to embarrass the government they support. The presence of ministers on committees has undoubtedly contributed to dampening the ardour of private members in the area of control. In these circumstances, it is scarcely surprising that party discipline has become the prime target of those who wish to strengthen Parliament.

Committees

During its first century of existence, the Quebec Assembly only rarely used the standing committees formed at the beginning of each session, except in the area of private legislation. In that respect, the Quebec practice is similar to that of many other legislatures. In public matters, the details of bills and budgetary estimates were scrutinized in Committee of the Whole. More often than not, the standing committees met only once at the beginning of the session, to elect a chairman, after which they were never heard from, although committees sometimes initiated studies on specific subjects.

The Legislation Committee, which in 1914 became the Committee on Miscellaneous Public Bills, was an original institution. Created in 1882 following a recommendation by the commissioner responsible for the revision of provincial statutes, this committee had referred to it in a fairly systematic way the numerous bills initiated by private members, and was asked to sort through them and ensure that the proposed innovations were consistent with the existing statutes of Quebec. Under Taschereau, this committee was even referred a substantial number of government bills. Duplessis ended this experiment, and the committee, despite its designation, became a second committee responsible for reviewing private bills.

The reactivation of committees dates from the end of the 1960s, when the principle of using standing committees for the review of budgetary estimates and of bills after their second reading was established. Contrary to the impression that prevailed in certain quarters, this reform was designed less to restore the influence of private members than to free the floor of the Chamber, which had been visibly overburdened since the early 1960s. In that respect, the objective was achieved, and the trend to longer sessions, so evident in 1960-65, was checked. By distributing responsibilities among several 'sub-assemblies' sitting at the same time as itself, the Chamber succeeded in saving one of the most precious parliamentary commodities: time.

Since 1969 the committee system has been the object of frequent reorganizations which do not seem to fit into a long-term plan. In 1969 there were twenty-seven specialized standing committees. This number was reduced to sixteen three years later, increased to twenty-seven in 1978, and was reduced again to nine in 1984. Such fluctuations betray a degree of uncertainty as to the optimal formula. The present standing committees deal with broad sectors of policy in a multi-functional perspective.

It is sometimes said that the effectiveness of a committee is in inverse proportion to the number of members above fifteen. If that is the case the standing committees in the past must have been extremely ineffective, since their average size during the century before the reorganization of 1969 varied between 12.9 and 46.7 members. Some standing committees had become so swollen that the Assembly had to be adjourned in order to allow them to sit! The committees were trimmed to a more realistic size later, that is, between ten and fifteen members on average. At the time of writing, the average size of committees was 15.8 members.

Until 1972 each committee elected its own chairman, invariably from the government ranks. In that year, the so-called banque des présidents was established: a panel of six to ten members (most from the government side), designated by the standing committee of the National Assembly, chaired in turn one of the standing committees and received remuneration for this. Since 1984 each committee elects a chairman and a vice-chairman representing both sides of the Chamber, and the chairmanships are divided in a proportion of five to three between the government party and the opposition, while the Speaker chairs exofficio the ninth committee. A chairman is now expected to act as the driving force behind the work of the committee.

The reform of 1984 included a very interesting innovation: mandats d'initiative. Briefly the formula allows a committee, with the consent of the majority of members of the two parliamentary parties, to examine a particular issue on its own initiative. Such a mandate may focus on a draft regulation, a public agency, financial commitments, or 'any other matter of public interest.' The last category, called mandat d'initiative pure, recently resulted in a report on demographic trends that attracted considerable attention.

Wide and frequent consultation of the public has been done by advisory committees within the government structure rather than by parliamentary committees. The Assembly, however, started an original practice under which a bill may be referred to a committee after first reading for hearing witnesses. This has allowed the public to express its opinion on the most important public policies before the Assembly adopts their principles of second reading.

Although the standing orders authorize committees to sit outside the Parliament Building, few of them availed themselves of this right, since only 3 per cent of the sitting hours in 1984-85 took place outside. However, committees frequently meet between sessions, 25 per cent of meetings being held during such periods.

Committees do not have permanent research staff, and since 1984 have used the research division of the Assembly library to summarize documentation and prepare background reports. The standing orders do not require the government to respond in detail to committee reports, although certain reports have clearly influenced subsequent legislation. The committee system of the Assembly is viewed in general rather favourably. The use of committees has enabled the Assembly to carry out its legislative and financial work more effectively. The predominance of party divisions prevents them from becoming centres of power in the same way as the committees of the U.S. Congress.

Parliamentary Reform: Perspective and the Future

For almost a century the procedure of the Assembly remained basically unchanged despite occasional rewritings of the rule book. The Quiet Revolution necessitated in-depth reforms which took place in the peak periods of 1969, 1972, and 1984. The predominant concern of this period was to enable the government to secure the adoption of the complex laws and increased finances required by a government in full expansion. Consequently, the rights of parliamentarians were limited and procedures simplified. Moreover, the emergence of a more intransigent nationalism necessitated a symbolic adjustment which was seen in the introduction of a more accurate French terminology and a reduction in the visibility of the monarchy.[23]

This reform perspective ignored the frustrations of private members, whom a century of evolution had gradually reduced to a support role. The reforms of recent years were designed to reduce their increasingly open dissatisfaction: increasing members' salaries and paid responsibilities, providing support staff and better working conditions, and guaranteeing their presence on the Board of the National Assembly (the Committee on Internal Economy). Certain control mechanisms, such as oral questions, developed rapidly. Such trends could be carried much further if private members had the collective desire and will, but there is no evidence at the moment that this is the case.

The planning of work at the end of sessions is always a target of critics. Despite the improvements of recent years, the Assembly persists in its century-old habit of functioning at a slow pace for two months, only to expedite a considerable amount of work in three weeks of intensive sittings. Night sittings are one of the traditional scourges of the Quebec Parliament. They increase the risks of error while exhausting the principal actors.

For some, as always, the only admissible solutions are global. Though intellectually appealing, proportional representation and the presidential system raise, in terms of their possible consequences, nagging questions that are asked far beyond parliamentary and ministerial circles. By constantly harping on the flaws in the present system, one may well lose sight of the real benefits that many consider it provides: elections that decide who is to rule, rather than the dealing out of cards among a select club of kingmakers; clear identification of responsibility for public policy; and a firmly entrenched system whose operation and rules are grasped and understood by the political élites and the population as a whole. The odds are that Quebeckers will continue to choose, not major upheavals, but the route that they have always preferred: that of constantly adapting existing institutions to meet new needs.

ANDY ANSTETT and PAUL G. THOMAS

MANITOBA

The role of the legislature in a polarized political system

For three decades the Manitoba Legislative Assembly has been undergoing a process of institutional adaptation in response to changes in the political system, particularly the increased demands being placed upon it. Legislatures are always subject to outside influences, but they vary in the extent to which they are open to change. The pace of change within Manitoba has quickened in recent years as the institution has begun a process of modernization. However, adaptation to changing conditions within the political system has been made more difficult by the polarized nature of the province's party system since 1969 and by the highly adversarial nature of the province's legislative politics.

While partisanship will always provide most of the energy needed to drive a cabinet-parliamentary system, deep divisions between the parties can pose barriers to organizational change. In such a political setting, parties will be reluctant to accept organizational and procedural changes that might disrupt the political equilibrium to their disadvantage. Where there is not a tradition of executive-legislative balance, but instead a history of executive predominance, as is the case in Manitoba, it becomes even harder to enhance the power of the legislature so that it can contribute more meaningfully to the formulation of public policy and to the accountability of the cabinet and of the bureaucracy.

Over the past two decades there have been gradual, but significant, improvements to the Manitoba Legislature. Previously neglected functions have been developed. The job of the member of the Legislative Assembly has become more full-time; and legislators have been given more of the tools necessary to carry out their responsibilities. As a group, MLAs have gained more control over their own working conditions rather than having the political executive decide these matters unilaterally. As an institution, the legislature has grown in organizational complexity in terms of the number of internal offices and structures and the variety of tasks performed by them. Committees have played a more significant role over time. Caucus involvement in the formulation of party policy development and in the determination of tactical approaches has increased. Problems remain, of course, and some of them are severe. Without flattering the institution unduly, it can be said to be moving in the right direction in terms of bringing the legislative process in line with the requirements of more active and complex government activity.

The Historical Background and Current Political Context

A cynic might suggest that attempting to strengthen the Manitoba Legislative Assembly is a bit like trying to revive a corpse that never lived. This is too strong a condemnation, but there is no denying the fact that the legislature has never been a potent force within the political system. All the talk of parliamentary decline during the twentieth century presumes there was a previous period when the Assembly was relatively influential with respect to legislation, spending, and the enforcement of accountability. In Manitoba's case no such period is easily identified. A limited role for the legislature, and domination by the cabinet, has been the prevailing historical pattern from the outset.

Manitoba was rushed into provincehood in 1870 and while it immediately acquired many of the formal trappings of British parliamentary government, there was a definite rustic quality about the early legislatures. The first session was held in a log cabin, the mace was made from an ox-cart wheel, and the members wore open-necked flannel shirts.[1]

The Manitoba Act of 1870 provided for a bicameral structure, consisting of a legislative council of seven members appointed for life and an elected Assembly of twenty-four. The upper house represented the economic elite of the fledgling provincial community and provided a safeguard against rash actions by the popularly elected lower house. Six years later the legislative council was disbanded, largely for reasons of costs.

Early sessions of the Manitoba Assembly were short and dominated by local and patronage concerns. Firm party alignments did not begin to appear until the 1880s, after the influx of settlers from Ontario who brought with them attachments to Liberal and Conservative labels. During the initial years from 1870 to 1877, the province's first two lieutenant-governors took responsibility for nearly all legislative initiatives and MLAs divided into 'government' and 'oppositionist' factions.[2] Legislative attention to the principles of sound public finance was undermined by the local expenditure concerns of most MLAs and by the fact that Ottawa was supplying most of the provincial revenue through transfer payments. While debates in the early legislative sessions could hardly be described as refined, they were usually not lacking in vigour, especially when topics such as boundary disputes with Ontario and federal disallowance of provincial railway legislation were under discussion.

The portrait of legislative life down to the early twentieth century which emerges from the available, albeit sketchy, accounts is hardly flattering by today's standards: raucous debates reported by a press gallery manned by strong partisans, regular adjournments for lack of a quorum, frequent challenges to the Speaker's rulings (even one attempt to tar and feather the presiding officer), and a kind of rambunctious camaraderie amid heavy drinking and smoke-filled rooms. When the legislature convened for its short sessions, it seems to have resembled more an army barracks than a serious deliberative assembly.

Reconstructing the history of the legislature is made more difficult by the absence of a full *Hansard* service until 1958. From 1949 to 1958, tape recordings of debates were kept, which were made available to MLAs on request. Committee hearings have been recorded and transcribed since 1974. Televising of the proceedings has been allowed since 1979 but is usually limited, by media choice, to the question period, the speech from the throne, and the budget address.

The Manitoba Legislative Assembly began its existence as a truly bilingual institution reflecting the relative equality of the two linguistic groups within the province during the 1870s. The twenty-four seats in the original legislature were split equally between English- and French-speaking representatives.[3] Use of the French language in the legislature was guaranteed in the Manitoba Act and during the first several sessions francophone MLAs regularly availed themselves of this right. As demographic changes rendered francophones a permanent minority, two developments ensued. First, French-speaking MLAs adopted English in the legislature in order to be understood by their anglophone colleagues and dropped their insistence upon bilingualism in certain proceedings and documents. Secondly, in 1890 an act was passed to abolish French as an official language of the legislature, civil service, and the courts.

An effective judicial ruling on the constitutional validity of the 1890 language act did not take place until 1979, when the original guarantees for the use of the French language were upheld. In response to a Supreme Court ruling in June 1985, the Assembly has required all legislation to be prepared in both official languages, all legislative documents are required to be produced in a bilingual format, and since 1982 a simultaneous translation facility has been installed in the Chamber and, upon reasonable notice to the Speaker, francophone MLAs can have their speeches interpreted into English. Use of French in the legislature is infrequent, however.

While government activity grew in scope and complexity, during the twentieth century the pace was moderate because of the prevailing public philosophy in favour of limited state intervention. Governing parties viewed provincial government as something like a glorified municipality with a limited range of responsibilities, an overriding need to balance revenues and expenditures, and a desire to keep partisan warfare from getting in the way of sound administration.[4] As an economy measure, the cabinet was deliberately kept small at six or seven members. A managerial approach to governing prevailed through successive administrations from the early 1920s onwards.

The United Farmers' organization (UFM) came to power in 1922 on a platform which rejected party politics.[5] Known as the Progressives in office, the UFM group was led by John Bracken, who believed in co-operative group government as a way to ensure honesty and economy. A non-partisan approach would also end cabinet domination of the Assembly. Except for financial measures which would involve the life of the government, all legislative votes would be free votes. Technically, of course, all votes were already free and the Bracken government which held power until 1942 never took steps to formalize an actual system of free votes.

Anti-party sentiment actually contributed to a downgrading of the legislature because it led to non-partisan and coalition governments. During the early 1930s, the Liberals became reliable allies of the Progressives and the label of Liberal-Progressive became attached to the Bracken government. At various times, the Conservatives, CCF, and the Social Credit were part of coalition or non-partisan governments. Agreements were reached among the parties to share cabinet posts and to forgo electoral competition in certain ridings. In elections held throughout the 1940s, nearly half the seats were filled by acclamation. According to Professor Murray Donnelly, the long period of coalition government did grave damage to political institutions in Manitoba: '... debate in the legislature almost ceased and the cabinet became a kind of regulatory board, a shadow of what such a body should be. The theory, held so strongly by Bracken, Garson, Campbell, and Willis (successive Premiers from 1922 to 1958), that political parties were unnecessary shows how little they understood the parliamentary system which, of course, is based on party government. Indeed, they very nearly succeeded in destroying it.'[6]

Premier Bracken's biographer described the legislature during the 1930s as 'a dull and dreary place, lacking in ideas, humour, vigour and incisiveness.'[7]

While profound changes were taking place in its external environment, the legislature seemed to be caught in a time warp of an earlier, simpler age. Despite the prevalent philosophy in favour of small government, new departments and programs were being created, non-departmental entities like regulatory boards and crown corporations sprang into existence, and the overall complexity of government increased markedly. Nevertheless the legislature underwent little by way of modernization and professionalization. A committee system from an earlier age remained unchanged, committees met infrequently, and ministers dominated their proceedings, often serving as chairmen. During the 1940s only three of the fifty-seven MLAs were officially in opposition. Within the governing coalition apparently little caucus democracy was practised. Much of the legislation passed during the 1940s consisted of 'housekeeping' amendments to existing statutes. Not until the breakup of the governing coalition and the re-establishment of party competition after the 1958 provincial election did the process of revitalization of the legislature begin.

After having broken away from the coalition in 1954, Duff Roblin subsequently led his Progressive Conservative party to minority government status in the 1958 election and to a majority government position the following year. Part of Roblin's success was due to his recruitment of younger, often professional, individuals to stand as candidates for the party. It was at this point that the social composition of the legislature began to change. From 1958 to 1973 Manitoba had a three-party system in action, although by the 1966 election the Liberal party had begun a cycle of decline which would see it hit rock bottom with no seats and only 7 per cent of the popular vote after the 1981 election.[8] The New Democratic party's first electoral victory came in 1969 when it elected twenty-eight MLAs to face a combined opposition of twenty-nine members. The NDP has three subsequent victories to its credit, the latest in March 1986 when the government of Premier Howard Pawley was returned for a second term. When the Pawley government unexpectedly came to the end of its second term, the party had been in power for fifteen of the last nineteen years. Prior to the achievement of minority government status in the snap provincial election of April 1988, the Progressive Conservative party had won only once since 1969, that being in 1977 when it was led by Sterling Lyon, a strong proponent of a neo-conservative philosophy. The ideological rift between the parties, when combined with highly divisive issues, such as French-language services and public auto insurance, has led to intense conflicts in the Assembly. At times this has resulted in bitter personal attacks across the floor, a trend which might be moderated by the emergence after 1988 of a three-party line-up in the legislature and the Liberal party as the official opposition.

The Present Legislative Assembly

Since 1949 the Assembly has consisted of fifty-seven MLAs elected on the basis of a first-past-the-post system. From 1924 to 1949 Manitoba had operated a proportional representation system within Greater Winnipeg where ten members were returned from a single constituency using a preferential ballot. After 1949 Winnipeg was split into three four-member constituencies still using a preferential ballot and in 1958 the city was finally divided into single-member seats. Outside of Winnipeg, single-member constituencies elected on the basis of a preferential ballot was the pattern from 1927 until 1958 when an ordinary ballot was adopted.[9] Prior to 1957, redistribution of constituency boundaries was done on the basis of a government bill and gerrymandering was clearly evident on some occasions. For the first time in Canadian history, the redistribution of 1957 was carried out by an independent commission under terms of reference set by the legislature. Those terms of reference explicitly provided for overrepresentation of rural areas, a pattern which had existed for many years. Seven urban residents were deemed to be equal to four rural residents. The last boundaries commission to report in 1978 added two seats in the City of Winnipeg, giving it twenty-nine of the fifty-seven provincial seats. The commission observed that an enlargement of the legislature to sixty members before the next redistribution in 1988 should be considered.[10] No change was made by the legislature and the 1988 commission created fifty-seven seats, with thirty ridings in the City of Winnipeg.

The Personnel and Working Conditions

In terms of their social and economic backgrounds, Manitoba MLAs are not representative of the population they serve. Unless one subscribes completely to a theory of social determination, which maintains that only people of similar backgrounds can represent effectively individuals and groups, this finding is not particularly disturbing.

The average age of MLAs has not changed significantly since 1958. It was 47 years in 1958 and 46.7 years in the mid 1980s. Since 1969 the NDP caucus has usually been slightly younger than that of the Progressive Conservatives. There were no women in the legislature in 1958, whereas in the second Pawley government term there were eight female MLAs, including four cabinet ministers, the Speaker, and the leader of the Liberal party. Today there are nine women in the House, two of whom are in the Filmon cabinet. The average years of service for MLAs during the period 1958 to 1986 was 5.5 years. In 1986, eighteen MLAs were elected for their first term; in 1988, twenty-five new MLAs were elected.[11]

In terms of their educational backgrounds, MLAs as a group are somewhat better educated today than in the recent past. In 1958 the fifty-seven MLAs possessed twenty-two university degrees compared to twenty-nine in 1986. Professionals (including teachers) were 28 per cent of the MLA population in 1958 compared to 32 per cent in 1986. There was a significant decline in the number of MLAs with a business background from 1958 (45 per cent) to 1981 (13 per cent), but a slight increase (to 18 per cent) occurred after the 1986 election. Up to the late 1950s MLAs with a farming background were more than 40 per cent of the Assembly's population, whereas after the 1986 election they were 21 per cent of the membership.

MLAs have recently gained greater control over their working conditions. The management of the Legislative Assembly underwent a dramatic change in 1983 with the establishment of the Legislative Assembly Management Commission (LAMC) in place of the Board of Internal Economy. The old board consisted of only the Speaker and two government ministers, whereas the new commission includes opposition representation and government back-benchers and is chaired by the Speaker. The new commission has complete jurisdiction over the affairs of the legislature and its agencies: the ombudsman, the provincial auditor, and the chief electoral officer. This change reflected a gradual evolution in the perception of the assembly and its members over the previous fifteen years, from part-time sessional legislators to full-time constituency servants as well as lawmakers.

The LAMC prepares the estimates for the legislature and approves services for members, albeit only changes favoured by the government caucus tend to be positively received by the commission. The LAMC's independence is compromised only to the extent that its estimates must be approved by the minister of finance before inclusion in the estimates. The original proposal for the LAMC in 1982 provided for complete financial independence from the government, but the opposition balked at the loss of ministerial responsibility for all spending. The commission also has responsibility for the provision of facilities and services to members, caucuses, and opposition leaders, the formulation of administrative policies respecting the operation of the Assembly, its officers and staff, and the provision of a proper system of security for the Chamber and the Assembly offices. Some of these responsibilities are carried out by departments of the executive branch of government under the direction of and in co-operation with the commission.

With the advent of the commission, members services have been improved. Members are allowed three 'franks' (constituency-wide household mailings), including printing costs, each year. Members receive an accountable constituency allowance of $9,500 per year for constituency service expenses such as an office and the associated costs. The commission has established guidelines for allowable expenditures. All members from constituencies outside of Winnipeg are allowed reimbursement for the cost of fifty-two return trips to their constituency each year and a living allowance of $65 per day for the cost of maintaining a separate Winnipeg residence during legislative sessions. All of these services have been improved since the establishment of the commission.

In some cases, such as the constituency allowance, the commission initiated the new service capability, while other changes have been improvements on existing services which were deemed inadequate. Manitoba has a history of providing less than adequate resources to MLAs and ministers, and the new commission is making some strides to correct this situation for MLAs. Ministerial service improvements are a government prerogative.

As recently as 1969, Manitoba MLAs did not even have access to a caucus room or government telephone lines when the House was not in session. The caucus rooms were closed as soon as the session ended, and the part-time secretary was returned to a government department or laid off. Opposition leaders did not have offices or staff. Only ministers had any of the resources we associate with members of legislatures today, and they derived those resources from their departments. MLAs were clearly part-time and those who wanted to be full-time did so from their homes. In less than twenty years this has changed dramatically. Most MLAs elected in 1986 are full-time and use the services provided to them by the Legislative Assembly Management Commission. The changes have been gradual and the Schreyer, Lyon, and Pawley governments have contributed to varying degrees to the enhancement of the ability of members to meet the growing demands of their position. Manitoba salaries for legislators are at or near the national average; however cabinet salaries, including that of the first minister, are among the lowest in the country.

The LAMC and the Standing Committee on the Rules of the House have some overlapping responsibilities and some potential areas of conflict; this has been avoided because the membership of the two bodies has coincided substantially. Such areas as television coverage and Chamber security are within the mandates of both bodies, but neither question has been an issue in the last six years. The sergeant-at-arms performs a ceremonial and administrative function, with security handled by the regular legislative building protective staff in the employ of the Department of Government Services subject to direction from the LAMC with respect to the Chamber and offices.

Party Structures

Party caucuses meet daily when the House is in session. Since the governing party has the initiative, the opposition caucus focuses mainly on such tactical issues as how it will use question period or react to the legislative and spending proposals of the government. On the government side, available accounts for the 1950s and 1960s suggest a limited, largely passive, role for government caucuses, which consisted mainly of listening to the plans of the cabinet. Caucus involvement gained some ground during the Schreyer administration, although there were still complaints that cabinet took caucus for granted. Perhaps this is not surprising since the cabinet members usually represent at least half of the total caucus membership. With the last Pawley government there were twenty-one MLAs in cabinet and only eight back-benchers. The current Progressive Conservative minority government has a cabinet of sixteen and seven back-benchers. An innovation of the Pawley administration was to have the chairman of caucus sit on the Legislation Review Committee of cabinet, and back-bench MLAs participated as ex-officio members of other cabinet committees.

There are designated house leaders for both parties, although exactly when these offices came into existence is lost in the mists of history. Down to the late 1950s, the main line of communication among the parties for the purpose of arranging House business was the party whips. The whips have lost some of their role to the house leaders and are now mainly responsible for ensuring attendance, a task which can be delicate in a closely divided legislature like the last Pawley majority (thirty NDP, twenty-six Progressive Conservatives, and one Liberal) or the present minority (twenty-four Progressive Conservatives, twenty-one Liberals, and twelve NDP). Whips receive an extra stipend, but lack some of the prerogatives available to their counterparts in larger jurisdictions. They do not assign seating, offices, or MLAs to parliamentary delegations. Up to six government MLAs are also appointed as legislative assistants to ministers, for which they receive an additional stipend, and a number have always served on the boards of major crown corporations.

The Office of the Speaker

As in all cabinet-parliamentary systems, Manitoba's Speaker must strive to balance the right of the government to have its business dealt with reasonably expeditiously and the rights of the minority to highlight, for the benefit of the public, the problems or dangers of what the government is proposing. Impartiality in the office of the Speaker is usually seen to be essential to the successful performance of this balancing act. In Manitoba not many steps have been taken to protect the speakership despite the more intense partisanship featured in the legislature since 1969.

In formal terms, the Speaker is elected by the Assembly, although in practical terms the choice is the premier's. In recent years there has been advance consultation with the leader of the opposition. Of the thirty-six elections held to choose a Speaker, twenty-six were based on a motion by the premier.[12] In only six instances (including four of the six most recent elections), did the leader of the opposition second the premier's choice. During the second term of the Pawley government, the official opposition refused to support the premier's nomination because his choice was regarded as too partisan an individual. In the past, cabinet ministers and government MLAs have also seconded the premier's nomination. There is no case in Manitoba history of an opposition MLA serving as Speaker, although Premier Schreyer did offer the job to a Conservative in 1969 when the NDP had twenty-eight seats and the combined opposition had twenty-nine. The offer was refused.

The Speaker's job is widely, but perhaps inaccurately, interpreted in the media as a consolation prize for government members who do not make it into the cabinet. Excluding the present Speaker, only five of the past twenty-four Speakers went on to serve in cabinet. Conversely, four former cabinet ministers have been elected Speaker since 1871.

The Speaker must interpret and apply the rules. Appeals against rulings by the Speaker are still allowed in Manitoba. While the right to challenge rulings leaves ultimate control in the hands of MLAs, if appeals are frequent they can bring the office of Speaker into disrepute. Both the opposition and the government have come into conflict with Speakers in recent years. In 1982 James Walding became the first Speaker to be subjected to a non-confidence motion by the opposition. It was alleged that the government influenced the Speaker to change a decision. The motion of censure was defeated. In the latter stages of the French language controversy, at the height of a prolonged bell-ringing crisis, the premier wrote to the Speaker insisting that votes should be held even if the opposition chose to absent itself. The Speaker refused, arguing that this was not provided for under the rules, would be unprecedented, and would compromise the integrity of his office.[13]

The most visible role of the Speaker involves presiding over question period. This is a delicate task, especially during recent sessions when ideological divisions have been wide and emotions have run high. Upon assuming office, the present Speaker indicated her intention to try to bring greater order and decorum to the question period. Also in relation to his or her procedural role, the Speaker chairs the legislature's Standing Committee on the Rules.

Permanence in the position of Speaker was broached in the late 1950s and again in the early 1980s. In the first instance, the Liberal government of Premier Douglas Campbell raised the idea, partly for short-term political ends. The most recent advancement of the concept came from Speaker Walding (1982-86). He raised two points in support of greater permanence in the chair: as a solution to the impossibility of being at once a party member and being seen to be impartial, and the fact that the riding from which a Speaker was chosen was denied full representation in the legislative process. At the time of his statement in favour of a permanent Speaker, Mr Walding was facing a fight to retain the NDP nomination in his constituency and there was speculation in the media that the premier's office was working behind the scenes to replace him. In neither case did the idea of a permanent Speaker advance very far. There seems to be no political will to explore this issue in depth.

The Legislative Process

The legislative process in Manitoba follows the British parliamentary model, with several significant departures that reflect local circumstances. These include the use of public hearings on legislation at the committee stage, the 'speedup' resolution, and the split committee of supply system used for estimates review.

Many jurisdictions in Canada provide for committees to hold public hearings on specific legislative proposals. However, in Manitoba all legislation, except bills referred to the Committee of the Whole House, is potentially exposed to public delegations at the commencement of committee stage. This has been a long-standing practice of the Manitoba legislative process. While other provincial assemblies and the federal House have often divided over the question of holding public hearings on specific bills and have debated expansion of the practice, Manitobans view committee stage as their point of access to the law-making process. There is never a question of whether there should be public input, just a question of when. This question is of some relevance because of the absence of a sessional timetable.

Typically a Manitoba session begins in late winter and runs for about eighteen weeks or until late June or early July. The session is usually characterized as the 'Spring' session, although no other sessions are regularly held. During the last three decades the practice of governments has been to print and distribute most legislation in the latter half of the session, with a concomitant pressure on members to deal with bills in a constricted time frame. A date for prorogation or adjournment is not set on a calendar, but it is understood that the government's legislative program will be debated and decided before a session ends. Unlike in some jurisdictions, unfinished legislation is not carried forward on the order paper through a summer recess to a fall session. This timetable means that the government must be ready to move its legislation through the House at the one annual session and interested groups and individuals must be ready to make their submissions during the hectic final weeks.

Public participation in the legislative process is further complicated by the fact that committee hearings are scheduled on the basis of forty-eight hours or less notice. Interest groups and the general public must be well prepared in advance of second reading if they wish to make representations on a specific bill. All public delegations are heard and questioned by the members of the committees before clause by clause consideration of bills; however, ministers occasionally give notice of amendments when they close debate on second reading or at the beginning of committee hearings. While this practice can frustrate the public hearing process by changing the bill in midstream, it is often used to respond in advance to public or opposition criticism at the committee stage.

The government is often in receipt of semi-confidential (i.e., everyone concerned has a copy except the media) submissions on legislative proposals from special interest groups during second reading debate. Sometimes it chooses to respond positively to these submissions, both because they have merit and also to avoid the publicity which would surround a similar or identical public submission at the committee hearing. This latter practice is not substantially different from that in other jurisdictions where public hearings are not regularly held; however, the leverage available to the public and special interest groups is greater in Manitoba, if for no other reason than the government's desire to avoid embarrassment.

Perhaps the greatest advantage of the more open and accessible committee hearing system in Manitoba is that it forces special interest groups to make their pitches to government publicly and encourages other groups who might not normally participate to get involved in preparing briefs and making representations. The number of individuals who appear at committee solely on their own behalf has always been a small percentage. Participation by individual citizens is greater when committees advertise hearings throughout the province, usually on an intersessional basis. Such hearings usually involve a topical issue or a subject on which the government is seeking advice in advance of legislation. In 1983, for example, the Standing Committee on Agriculture held hearings throughout rural Manitoba on the issue of the Western Grain Transportation Initiative proposed by the federal government.

The second procedural variant is popularly described as 'Speedup.' It involves a procedural resolution which, when passed, allows the House to sit three times a day, in three separate sittings, for six days a week, with no adjournment time prescribed for the evening sitting. Under this system, the House can sit virtually around the clock, and on some occasions has done so. During this period near the end of a session, private members' hour is set aside. Bills move through readings at an accelerated pace and committee hearings are held in the evenings and on Saturdays, with two committees often meeting simultaneously to deal with legislation. As in the House, there is no set adjournment time for these committees, and public representations are heard until the list of delegations is exhausted. Not all prospective witnesses have the patience or the stamina for such late-night marathons, and many go home only to learn that their names were called during the early morning hours.

'Speedup' has its origins in earlier Manitoba sessions when rural MLAs who dominated the legislature numerically wanted to get away quickly when spring seeding weather arrived. More recently the practice has been used by governments, with the concurrence of opposition members, in order to complete the sessions by the end of June. The reference earlier to cleaning the order paper rather than adjourning to the fall has been a major impetus to the use of 'Speedup,' despite all of its negative implications and regular criticism by the public through the media.

A 'Speedup' motion was last used in the 1983 session. Resistance had gradually built up among members to the negative aspects of accelerated debate, particularly the criticism that it represented 'legislation by exhaustion' rather than serious deliberation. Since 'Speedup' was almost always introduced immediately after the estimates debate was concluded in the Committee of Supply, the finance and taxation bills were debated and considered in the Committee of the Whole House under this accelerated procedure. This practice was not viewed as the best method of affording critical scrutiny of the government's fiscal measures, and a further pressure for change resulted.

Despite this criticism, Manitoba had developed a unique process for estimates review. Up until the mid seventies, the Committee of Supply considered departmental estimates for a specific time period – eighty hours during the fifties and sixties and ninety hours during the early seventies. At the conclusion of the allotted time the committee was required to vote on all outstanding appropriation motions and report to the House. Debate continued in the House on concurrence motions and on the supply bills. However, this debate usually occurred during 'Speedup' because the government would hold the motions and bills until near the end of the session to deliberately limit the debate at a time when members were unwilling to prolong the session. The effect of this practice was to shift queries and comments about the estimates into other forums such as the daily question period, which then operated with no time limit. Members recognized this inappropriate use of question period and all parties agreed to a fundamental procedural change in 1975.

At that point the time limit for estimates was removed and the Committee of Supply was divided into two sections, but remained as a Committee of the Whole (all MLAs are still members of the committee). Estimates for two departments can be considered simultaneously, with one section of the committee sitting in the House and the other in a committee room. In exchange for this procedural innovation, question period was limited to forty minutes and concurrence motions were abolished.

The effect of this change has been to allow the House to examine the estimates in greater detail, while avoiding an expansion in the total length of the session. Total hours spent on estimates review by the two sections of the committee expanded immediately to an average of 290 hours over the last decade. The rules also allowed either section of the committee to sit beyond the normal 10:00 p.m. adjournment time. In practice, the committee seldom goes past 11:00 p.m.

The changes to the supply process necessitated other rule changes respecting the adjournment of the House, the taking of votes in committee, and the right of the official opposition to be consulted on the order in which departments appear before the committee. There is general acceptance of the new procedure, which represents an improvement because more actual examination of departmental spending takes place and, particularly in the committee room section of supply, there is less formality and fewer purely political speeches.

The session of 1987 witnessed further changes to the supply process, which to some observers represented a turning back of the clock. Limits were again placed on the debate: 240 hours for all estimates including interim, capital, and supplementary as well as the main supply motions. In exchange, an all-inclusive concurrence motion was reintroduced, not to take place in the House, but in Committee of Supply. To prevent undue delay on the concurrence motion, the government was given the authority to invoke the 'Speedup' rule, but only with respect to debate on the concurrence motion.

New rules are also in place respecting bell-ringing. The Manitoba Legislative Assembly experienced a series of bell-ringing delays during the debate on the Pawley government's French language proposals of 1983-84. As a result, in June 1984 limits were placed on the length of time that the bells could ring to call members to a vote. These rules required the bells to cease and the division to be recorded after fifteen minutes, with a provision for an extension by the Speaker of up to twenty-four hours after consultation with the whips. Late in 1986 the division bell limits were changed from fifteen minutes to one hour and the twenty-four hour maximum extension was changed to a vote deferral of up to seventy-two hours. Both changes will accommodate members, particularly ministers, who may be away from the legislative building on government or constituency business. The experience of members during the 1984 through 1986 sessions clearly indicated that the initial rule was too restrictive. However, it was a liability more for government members because of the narrowness of the government's majority. In Manitoba narrow majorities are the rule rather than the exception; as a result Manitoba's rules contain more provisions to protect the government's majority in voting situations than do those of other legislatures.

A new rule respecting constitutional amendments also flows from the Assembly's experience with the French language services debate. It provides that a specific period of ten sitting days be set aside for debate on the constitutional amending resolution and that public hearings on the resolution be held prior to the sixth day of debate. The exclusive debate provision makes this debate akin to the throne speech or budget debates in most legislatures, except that the resolution does not necessarily come to a vote at the end of the ten days. Instead, if debate remains unfinished, it becomes a regular government motion on the order paper. The new rule is silent on whether the government can hold the committee stage prior to the commencement of the debate. The novelty of a committee stage requirement, replete with public hearings, for a matter which requires only one reading by the House should be noted. This is an innovation which applies the Manitoba practice on bills to a particular type of resolution. Since Canadian experience with legislative procedures flowing from the new amending formula under Part V of the Constitution Act of Canada is very limited, the Manitoba rule bears watching in practice.

Finally, it should be noted that Manitoba's experience with rules changes has almost invariably been a consensual exercise. The last set of changes, of which only the major items have been noted above, were passed unanimously by the Standing Committee on the Rules of the House. The only time the House divided over a rules change in recent memory was in 1984 when the first bell-ringing limits were introduced. That lack of consensus was clearly attributable to the lingering ill-will associated with the French language debate that precipitated the new rule.

A minor, but significant, modification in procedure occurred in 1983 when the estimates were tabled at the conclusion of the budget speech. In prior years, the estimates were tabled weeks before the budget and a complete picture of revenues and expenditures was not immediately available. The simultaneous tabling is politically advantageous to the government during periods of fiscal restraint, but there is no guarantee the practice will continue if financial flexibility returns.

Accountability Mechanisms

Ensuring the political accountability of the cabinet directly, and of the bureaucracy indirectly, is largely the responsibility of the opposition parties, since government MLAs will not normally wish to highlight the problems or mistakes of their cabinet colleagues. While question period provides a useful spot check on executive performance, systematic inquiry is more likely to take place through the committee system. While strong committees are not the only gauge of the independence of the legislature, the absence of effective committees will mean inadequate scrutiny of government activity. The tradition in Manitoba has been to view committees mainly as devices to expedite the completion of the government's business. Continuous scrutiny of the executive has not been central to the role of committees. Only in the case of intersessional committees have the government and the Assembly sought to use committees for inquiry purposes.

In recent sessions, the Manitoba legislature has created eleven standing committees.[14] Most committees have eleven members. The law amendments committee is deliberately kept much larger (thirty members) because it considers about half of the bills which receive second reading. The remaining bills go to the other standing committees whose jurisdiction applies. Membership on all committees is proportionate to party standings in the House and ministers serve on all committees. Prior to 1969 they chaired the majority of committees. During the first session of the Thirty-Third Legislature (1986) there were six ministers on the agriculture committee, six on economic development, and five on public accounts. While the small size of the legislature and the growth of the cabinet's size make the presence of ministers on committees inevitable, when they constitute the majority it becomes questionable whether an objective review of government performance is possible. With the exception of public accounts, standing committees are now chaired by back-bench government MLAs. In one instance during the first session of the Thirty-Third Legislature a cabinet minister briefly chaired a committee and presented its report to the House.

Activity by individual standing committees fluctuates from one session to the next. In the 1986 session there were thirty-three committee meetings and eighteen reports were filed with the legislature. In 1985, there were twenty-seven meetings, eighteen reports were presented, and only one committee failed to meet. Standing committees are used to consider legislation and to review the annual reports of non-departmental agencies. As mentioned earlier, annual spending estimates are considered in the two-part Committee of Supply, not in the standing committees. Amendments to legislation are seldom proposed by committees, and those which are often originate with the government. Apart from a clerk, the committees do not have staff resources. Reports for committees holding a series of public hearings (i.e., on an inquiry basis) are usually drafted by departmental staff. Three of the standing committees are particularly important to the attainment of accountability.

Manitoba was the first jurisdiction in Canada to provide for some legislative scrutiny of regulations through a Standing Committee on Statutory Regulations and Orders created in 1960. Regulations are supposed to be reviewed in terms of eight principles, which were adapted from the British report on ministers' powers.[15] The committee can comment on the technical propriety of regulations but not on their merits as a form of public policy. It can recommend the revocation or amendment of regulations. Administrative manuals fall outside the scope of committee review because they are not regulations of a legislative nature as defined in the Regulations Act. In practice, all these points are rather moot because the standing committee has not met for the purpose of reviewing regulations since 1970, when the Manitoba regulations were last consolidated. From being a leader in this field, the Manitoba Legislative Assembly has allowed its procedure for the scrutiny of regulations to fall into disuse. The Standing Committee on Statutory Regulations and Orders is appointed for each legislature, but is now used to review bills. For example, during the fourth session of the Thirty-Second Legislature, it held six meetings on Bill C-5, the government's freedom of information bill, which passed but was not proclaimed until 30 September 1988.

The Manitoba legislature does not operate a standing committee on crown corporations, but two other committees regularly review the annual reports of a select number of the province's nineteen crown corporations.[16] During recent sessions the Standing Committee on Economic Development has usually spent two hours on each of six small crown corporations. The Public Utilities and Natural Resources Committee has reviewed the annual reports of the province's two large public utilities, the Manitoba Hydro and the Manitoba Telephone System (MTS). Usually three or four meetings are held on the Hydro's report. While there is an opportunity to examine the performance of certain crown corporations, in-depth reviews are not possible in the time available. Committee proceedings are often partisan in nature so that an objective inquiry is really not possible. Government control is evident. The designated minister for each corporation serves on the committee and at times the government MLA who chairs the committee also serves as a director on the board of the crown corporation under examination. The larger crown corporations represent enormous repositories of expertise but no staff, beyond the clerk, is available to the committees. This apparent handicap has not completely blocked the opposition from uncovering problems in the crown corporation sector. For example, during the 1986 session the Public Utilities and Natural Resources Committee spent ten meetings investigating the misdeeds of an MTS subsidiary, including the potential loss of up to $30 million. Chairs of the boards and chief executive officers are available for questioning, but legislators have found it difficult to identify the respective contributions of corporation officials and government ministers to particular actions by crown corporations. Substantive reports from committees reviewing crown corporations are rare. The standard committee report lists who has appeared and always ends by affirming that 'the fullest opportunity was accorded to all members of the committee to seek the information desired.'[17]

The Standing Committee on Public Accounts considers the public accounts and the annual report of the provincial auditor. By precedent both documents are automatically referred to the committee, but during earlier sessions the committee often failed to meet. It usually takes its cue in terms of lines of inquiry from the provincial auditor's report. In 1979, the committee considered and declined to grant the auditor authority to practise comprehensive auditing. Still, the auditor does conduct broad-scope auditing, which goes beyond the financial attest function to examine the adequacy of financial and management information systems.

The committee is now chaired by an opposition MLA. Until the election of the Schreyer government in 1969, it was chaired by a cabinet minister. Four ministers serve on the committee, ministers are usually the primary witnesses, and public servants seldom appear alone to account for their management of public funds. Reports from the committee consist of a paragraph or two and are never debated in the House.

It would be wrong to leave the impression that government control is the only, or even the primary, reason for the limited scrutiny achieved by legislative committees. While no government will welcome the revelation of information that might prove politically embarrassing, it is also the case that opposition parties can usually be counted on to focus on the sensational disclosures and bypass the more routine aspects of government performance. In the highly charged partisan atmosphere of recent Manitoba legislatures, the idea of an impartial search for economy, efficiency, and effectiveness in government operations is not widely practised because of the adversarial approach adopted by all parties.

Media Coverage of the Legislature

Television coverage of the Assembly in session and its committees is potentially unlimited, but at the expense of the broadcast stations. The Chamber's sound system required restoration in the late seventies. A broadcast quality sound system was installed then and the lighting in the Chamber was revamped to a suitable candle-power for television. Question period is covered live on a local cable channel and taped for use by news outlets under a pool arrangement established and maintained by the receiving media outlets. Broadcast quality sound feeds were part of the sound system replacement in 1979-80 and no additional expenses are incurred by the government by giving access to these facilities to the media. This approach has provided the public with reasonably thorough television and radio coverage of the Assembly at no ongoing public cost. Major events such as the throne speech or budget speech are covered live by some outlets, while others use the capability solely for newscasts. The cost of providing television coverage and the complexity of the administrative rules and political sensitivities associated with control of an 'in-House' operation in other jurisdictions were primary reasons for the external service option chosen by the Rules Committee in the mid seventies. That decision has created few, if any, problems for members or the Assembly staff.

In terms of regular print and electronic media coverage, the focus is almost entirely on the daily question period. Debates on legislation are rarely reported extensively. Most of the committee work is done during the evenings and most of the media representatives have left the building for the day by this time. Only the prospect of a controversial hearing will draw the media representatives back at night. The result is to create some almost perverse incentives for MLAs, especially on the opposition side. During the last session, the Progressive Conservative opposition was determined to examine estimates systematically, but they found there was little publicity value in their efforts since the dual committee of supply was meeting at night and all the media attention focused on the MTS-MTX scandal. By emphasizing the sensational aspects of legislative performance, the present media coverage gives the public a misleading impression of how the legislature spends its time.

Reform

Prior to the late 1960s changes to the organization and the rules of the Legislative Assembly were infrequent. Since then the rules have been under almost continuous examination, first by special committees up to 1977, and since then by a Standing Committee on Rules. Several major packages of reforms have been presented. The increased tempo of organizational and procedural change reflects the wider changes taking place: the revitalization of party competition, the arrival of younger, better-educated members and their growing insistence that they play a more active role, the growing volume of work to be done, the improvements in the resources available to caucuses, and a larger more specialized staff working for the legislature itself.

Technical and procedural inconsistencies have crept into the rules over the years. In 1985 the Rules Committee instructed the Clerk's Office to conduct a review of existing practices and, if time permitted, to identify procedural developments in other jurisdictions that might usefully be considered in Manitoba. The phrase 'time permitting' is revealing because it indicates that there is not at present sufficient staff resources, despite dramatic increases in the 1980s, in the Clerk's Office or elsewhere, to do a thorough review. Back in 1977 a task force on government operations observed that: 'Those who exercise authority should be held accountable to the Legislative Assembly. The Task Force believes that further action is necessary to make this maxim a reality. Because the issues involved are so fundamental to our system of government, we recommend that a special commission or a committee of the Legislature be established to review the broad question of accountability of ministers and officials to the Legislative Assembly.'[18]

Things have improved somewhat since then, but a strong case could still be made for such a review today.

It likely will not happen. This is partly because no party will wish to disturb the existing system to its potential disadvantage. Not many MLAs are prone to reflect on how they perform their representative and legislative roles. There is almost no immediate political payoff in worrying about the health of the Legislative Assembly. It is left, therefore, to a small minority of members to ensure that the institution is in good shape. For their part, the general public seems to accept the deficiencies of their legislature with a kind of stoic resignation. Their knowledge of its activities is limited to the coverage, incomplete and often sensational, provided by the mass media. The impetus for further reform will have to come from within. But change is likely to be gradual. Part of the legislative culture is a belief in evolutionary, pragmatic reforms to meet emerging needs.

FREDERICK C. ENGELMANN

ALBERTA

From one overwhelming majority to another

The story of the Alberta legislature, like that of the society itself, is one of one-party dominance and of second-party weakness. Since the Second World War there have been only four oppositions worthy of the name. The first was the Liberals under Harper Prowse, elected in 1955 with fifteen members. It did not survive its leader's resignation. The second was the six Progressive Conservatives under Peter Lougheed, elected in 1967. The third was Social Credit, saving twenty-four seats after its defeat by the Progressive Conservatives in 1971. It also failed to survive the resignation of the opposition leader. The fourth was, and is, the Alberta New Democrats, electing sixteen members in 1986 and the same number in 1989.

As Canadian provinces go, Newfoundland is, of course, the youngest province but as a European society it dates back to Cabot. Saskatchewan entered Confederation in 1905, along with Alberta, but it was more thickly settled at the time. Alberta may now be a 'province' but as a provincial society it can claim to be the youngest of the ten.

Both Saskatchewan and Alberta entered Confederation as reasonably egalitarian societies and, not surprisingly, with unicameral legislatures. The Legislative Assembly of Alberta has grown from twenty-five to eighty-three members. The number of legislators grew mostly during the Liberal regime. It was left to the Conservatives to raise sitting days mildly and indemnity spectacularly. From 1905 through 1971, all but nine years have had one session only (there were three in 1937).[1]

Since 1972 two sessions has been the norm. Over the six years from 1980 to 1985 Alberta, with sixty-five sitting days, ranked sixth in this regard among the provinces – ahead of Quebec, New Brunswick, and Prince Edward Island.

Political Culture and the Legislature

One characteristic of Alberta society has never changed. Close to one-half the population has been of neither British nor French origin. However, the rural-urban mix of the population has taken a sharp turn since the Second World War. Until then, about 70 per cent of the population was rural.[2] By 1986, 79 per cent was urban.

The reason for this radical change was Alberta's transition from an agricultural to an oil and gas economy.[3] Oil was found in the Turner Valley, south of Calgary, before the First World War. The first big find, however, came in 1947 at Leduc, south of Edmonton. It lifted Alberta's population above the 800,000 level and, after the two oil crises of the seventies, nearly trebled it. Oil was clearly the factor in urbanizing Alberta. By 1971 this urbanization was sufficiently important to enable the rejuvenated, urban Progressive Conservatives to defeat the essentially rural-based Social Credit party.

This quantum change, then, in both number and locus of the population, accounted for the third major shift in Alberta politics. It is more difficult to account for the two earlier ones.

The main reason for the shift from the Liberals to the United Farmers of Alberta was the severe agrarian discontent following the First World War, also manifested by the Progressive gains in the federal election of 1921. The main reason for the shift from the United Farmers was the dismal agricultural economy as a result of the Great Depression. William Aberhart's huge religious radio audience was of crucial use to the high-school principal once he embraced the funny-money Social Credit economic theory and organized a province-wide political movement.

In retrospect, it is possible to regard 1921 as Alberta's major political watershed. Until then the young province had a traditional two-party system; from 1921 on, Alberta's governing party has always represented Alberta not so much *in* as *against* Canada. It represented alienated Albertans, whether they felt they were worse off than central Canadians or, after 1973, that central Canadians would not permit them the full fruit of provincial prosperity. United Farmers, Social Credit, and Progressive Conservatives thus have had a common stance. It is for this reason that I maintain that, since 1921 and regardless of party, Alberta has been governed by the 'Provincial Liberation Front.'[4]

Until urbanization set in, around 1950, Alberta was, by necessity or choice, an extremely frugal province. Between the two wars expenditures hovered between $25 and 50 million. Only in 1950 did they break $100 million and in 1971, $1 billion; they have grown more than tenfold since.

How did the legislature develop in this political culture? There has never been a quantum change in the volume of legislation. Legislative activity did not rise with increased governmental activity, and official delegated legislation (orders-in-council) actually declined as the government became more active after 1970. In sum, we find a rather meagre legislative activity. Meanwhile, in terms of dollars appropriated per statutes plus orders-in-council, legislative activity, from the sixties to the eighties, grew twenty-five times. This discrepancy between legislation and expenditures cannot be explained in terms of inflation, population growth, and amount of legislation plus delegated legislation. The answer is the vast increase, since 1971, in the number of requests for decision (RFDs), a device by which a minister or a cabinet committee persuades cabinet to arrive at a favourable decision on a proposal. Funds are then appropriated by the lieutenant-governor's warrants. Usually these devices are beyond even the scrutiny of the Legislative Assembly, except by the ex post facto passage of a supplementary appropriations bill.[5] Their ample employment shows that Alberta has a substantial component of non-legislative policy-making.

It is difficult to determine to what extent the Alberta Legislative Assembly reflects the political culture of the society it serves. The culture of the Assembly has changed twice, and both changes pre-dated the urbanization of the province. The first took place when the United Farmers of Alberta replaced the Liberals in 1921. A traditional legislature was replaced by one reflecting the Farmers', and especially Henry Wise Wood's, notion of 'group government.' In theory, at least, members of the Assembly were completely subordinated to the wishes of their constituents – they even had to sign recall agreements upon election. While group government became increasingly traditional government, especially under the strong leadership of Premier John. E. Brownlee, it was reversed with the election of Social Credit in 1935. In the fifty-four years since then, Alberta has spent forty-nine of them under essentially 'executive government' by some of Canada's strongest premiers, including William Aberhart, Ernest Manning, and Peter Lougheed.

The important role of the governing caucus, instituted in 1975 by Premier Lougheed, appears to have had a buffering effect on urbanization. Constituencies are not equal; the rural-urban distribution key is about seven to four. It also appears to have had a conservatizing effect. One former minister, however, boasts that he managed to circumvent the caucus (and thus the Assembly) by liberalizing liquor regulations by ministerial order. Despite the flaunted or complained about conservatism of the PC caucus, not even urban opposition members claim that the Assembly has a 'red-neck' character.

From a limited number of interviews, it appears that there is no agreement about inter-caucus personal relations. Whether good or not so good, they are certainly civil and tend to be job-oriented. A Liberal member feels that PC cabinet members get along better with the New Democrats and PC caucus members better with the Liberals. Members seem to have good relations across party lines when they are on delegations outside Alberta. Two members were singled out to me as senior members to whom deference is shown: Ray Speaker (Representative party), the dean of the Assembly, and Neil Crawford, the former Progressive Conservative house leader.

The following unwritten rules of behaviour were mentioned: constituency offices are not to be used for party purposes, one expresses sympathy regardless of party,[6] one does not listen to other members' (usually ministers') media scrum sessions, one does not spread rumours about personal lives, one does not repeat private members' lounge talk, and one does not attack a member when that member is absent. In general, common sense and a sense of balance are expected.

Structure of the Legislature

The Legislative Assembly of Alberta derives its authority from the Legislative Assembly Act.[7] The Speaker is the presiding officer of the Assembly and heads its administrative structure. His precincts are among the most restricted in Canada: his administrative control is restricted to the legislative chamber – the remainder of the building is controlled by the premier's office. However, the relationship between Speaker David Carter and Premier Donald Getty is such that one can expect the Speaker to exercise at least de facto control over the entire legislative building in the future.

Alberta has had only nine Speakers in eighty-one years. Three have held office for short terms, while the average for the remaining five Speakers (excluding the incumbent, Dr David Carter) is close to fifteen years each. Peter Dawson served from 1937 to 1963, a total of twenty-six years. There has been considerable stability in the office, though each regime has brought in a new incumbent. Only the last three Speakers have come from the major cities, two from Calgary and one from Edmonton.

There has been more turnover in the office of Deputy Speaker and chairman of committees. During the same eighty years (1906-86), fifteen Deputy Speakers have served, for an average of more than five years; only two have served more than ten years.

The Speaker has one executive assistant and two secretaries. He has administrative control over the Alberta legislative internship program. The cost of this program is borne by the province with diminishing assistance from corporate sponsors. The universities of Alberta, Calgary, and Lethbridge participate in the selection process. The entire staff of the Legislative Assembly, however, is, at least technically, part of Alberta's (executive) public service.

Along with those of Nova Scotia and Newfoundland, the Alberta Legislative Assembly lacks control over its finances; there is no board of internal economy. Instead, the Speaker is chairman of the Special Standing Committee on Members' Services, consisting of one member of cabinet and nine private members, including, at present, two members of the official opposition (New Democrats) and one of the third party (Liberals). The committee does not have basic autonomy in that it is merely advisory to the cabinet; its estimates are received by the Priorities Committee of Cabinet. The committee's autonomy is reduced further since a member of cabinet serves as its floor leader[8] and the committee's government caucus is firmly in control.

This was shown in early 1987 when all private members' research accounts were cut by 20 per cent. The funds of the three opposition leaders were cut less, so that the reduction for each of the three opposition parties amounts to 18 per cent, a figure well above the average budget cut for executive departments. In 1988 the committee cut the number of legislative interns to four, each serving only one of the four caucuses continuously. It also abolished the legislative research service and severely cut travel allowances, except for trips to the capital. The latter two changes severely hamper opposition activities. The committee has recently adopted a number of administrative reforms, such as computerization, which should facilitate the operations of the Assembly.

In contrast to the limits on the legislature is the exalted position of the government caucus. There was nothing unusual about the government caucus in Alberta until 1975, when Premier Lougheed found himself with sixty-nine out of seventy-five members. From then on much of the activity of the *public* Legislative Assembly has been displaced by the *private* meetings of the Progressive Conservative caucus[9] (no records are kept of meetings).

The role of the caucus was institutionalized further in 1979, when the governing party had seventy-five out of seventy-nine seats. In that year the caucus committee system was developed. It is as yet too early to know whether the entry of twenty-two opposition members (sixteen New Democrats, four Liberals, and two members of the Representative party, both long-serving former Social Crediters) into the Assembly in 1986, and the retirement of Premier Peter Lougheed one year earlier, are bringing about changes in the role of the caucus.

The Progressive Conservative caucus under Lougheed met under the chairmanship of the premier. The chief whip was deputy caucus leader and the house leader usually presented the agenda. The Speaker did not attend meetings during sessions. Caucus met for forty-five minutes prior to each sitting of the Assembly; every Thursday morning during sessions, and occasionally in the evening. When the Assembly was not in session, caucus met for two days each month.

Before 1975 the Progressive Conservative caucus – and presumably other governing caucuses earlier[10] – operated by consensus. In that year Premier Lougheed felt that it would strengthen him and caucus if votes were taken, and they have been taken frequently since. Lougheed himself interpreted the votes. Normally, a two-thirds vote was required for the premier to consider the caucus committed to a policy or a course of action. There were no abstentions and attendance was compulsory; all members not ill or away on authorized business attended as a matter of course.

Cabinet members attended, but Lougheed made every effort to equalize the role of private members with that of ministers. For this reason, all members sat in alphabetical order. The premier exercised influence by determining the order of speaking. Peter Lougheed says that he used his influence beyond that only when he felt very strongly about an issue, such as the provincial relief of mortgage interest payments in 1982. To make sure every member of caucus felt a full participant, longer meetings always featured a period for open discussion, with no set agenda. Otherwise, caucus meetings agenda are highly structured.

Caucus attendance was and is restricted to members. The only others present under Lougheed were four staff members from the premier's office. Premier Lougheed was usually sufficiently briefed so that he rarely called on them for assistance. Once caucus arrived at a decision which the premier considered binding, absolute discipline was expected. Members had to clear with caucus not only dissent but even abstentions on grounds of conscience or constituency interest. Because caucus commits behaviour in the Assembly, the whip's role was and is the most important, except of course for the leader himself. The chief whip chairs the caucus in the absence of the premier.

For once, all of the present seriously contending parties have their leaders sitting in the Assembly. For many years, until 1986, this had not been the case with the Liberals. Because of the small size of the New Democratic and Liberal caucuses, they have no back-benchers; every member has the role of a critic. There seems to be fairly general agreement that the Liberals and some of the New Democrats play their role of critics as effectively as the composition of the Assembly will permit.

Who have been Alberta's legislators?[11] Relatively few of those elected between 1905 and 1967 were native Albertans (19 per cent). Ontario was the most common birthplace with 31 per cent. Of the 21 per cent foreign-born, 12 per cent were born in the United States and 9 per cent in the United Kingdom. By 1985 this situation had changed; of the members then sitting, 70 per cent were native Albertans, and Ontario (tied with Saskatchewan) had been reduced to 6 per cent, the United Kingdom to 4 per cent, and the United States to 3 per cent. Thus, there has been a considerable nativization of the Assembly over the years.

Of the 1905-67 group, 37 per cent were university graduates, 13 per cent had some kind of collegiate education, and an additional 17 per cent were high-school graduates. In 1985, 68 per cent of MLAs held university degrees. The breakdown for 1987 is 34 per cent with postgraduate education and 43 per cent with post-secondary education completion not recorded. Despite the dubious comparability of the data, there is a definite elevation of the educational level. It is of some interest that even in the 1905-67 group, 34 per cent of those with university degrees obtained their education in Alberta, 23 per cent were educated in Ontario, 15 per cent in the United States, and 7 per cent in the United Kingdom. Of the 1985 group, 54 per cent had their higher education in Alberta, 10 per cent in Ontario, 11 per cent in the United States, and 3 per cent in the United Kingdom.

Of the 1905-67 group, 33 per cent were in business, 32 per cent in farming, 12 per cent in law, and 11 per cent in teaching. In 1985, 28 per cent were in business, 25 per cent in farming, 20 per cent in teaching, and 12 per cent in law. The 1986 election did not bring major changes, though all major occupations went down slightly: business to 27 per cent, farming to 21 per cent, teaching to 19 per cent, and law to 11 per cent. Over the long haul, there is a slow move from business and farming to occupations or professions other than law. No one claiming to be a worker has ever sat in the Alberta legislature.

Religious affiliation is still known for most members of the Assembly. Here, the United Church and Presbyterians have dropped from 51 per cent in 1905-67 to 38 per cent in 1985, while Anglicans have increased from 12 per cent to 20 per cent and Roman Catholics from 10 per cent to 11 per cent (11 per cent to 14 per cent, if Ukrainian Catholics are included).

Previous legislative experience has declined from 36 per cent for the 1905-67 group to 23 per cent in 1987. Most of this experience was in municipal politics. However, as of 1988, two former MPs, Peter Elzinga and Stan Schumacher, sit in the Assembly.

In the 1905-67 group, 47 per cent sat in the Assembly less than five years, 26 per cent six to ten years, 17 per cent eleven to fifteen years, 5 per cent sixteen to twenty years, 3 per cent twenty-one to twenty-five years, and 2 per cent longer. Because of three Progressive Conservative victories, by 1985 only 24 per cent of MLAs had less than six years' experience, 30 per cent had between six and ten years' experience, and the eleven-to-fifteen year group had grown to 39 per cent. The group with sixteen to twenty years remained at 5 per cent, and only 1 per cent had served longer. The changes of the 1986 election brought some decline in longevity. By 1987, 47 per cent were newly elected members and therefore the zero-to-five-year group was up to a spectacular 61 per cent. Sixteen per cent served six to ten years, 12 per cent eleven to fifteen years, 10 per cent sixteen to twenty years, and 1 per cent (Ray Speaker) over twenty years.

Louise McKinney and Roberta McAdams were elected as early as 1917; both served one term only. In 1921 two prominent UFA women were elected, Nellie McClung and Mary Irene Parlby. Mrs Parlby was Alberta's first female cabinet member. Seven women won seats for the Social Credit (up to 1967), including Hannah Gostick and Edith Rogers, who were elected in 1935; Cornelia Wood, who was first elected in 1940 and served for twenty-three years; and Ethel Wilson, elected in 1959 and appointed to cabinet as a minister without portfolio in 1962. The Honourable Helen Hunley (member of cabinet, 1971-79) is the first woman to serve as lieutenant-governor of Alberta.

Four of the eleven women elected up to and including 1967 were housewives; two each were teachers and nurses and one each an author, a telegraph operator, and an industrial employee. None was below the age of forty when first elected, and only two had a university education.

As of 1988, there are two female house leaders – Pam Barrett (New Democrats) and Bettie Hewes (Liberals) and – five women are cabinet members. In sum, Alberta's legislators have become more educated but their occupational profile has hardly changed over the decades. While members tend to be male and well educated, they are at least somewhat representative of Alberta's population.

Routine Operations and Services to Members

As was indicated above there has been no great change in the number of sittings of the Alberta Legislative Assembly over the years. The first legislature did not sit long; the fourth legislature, the Liberals' last, almost doubled the sittings. There was a slight increase under the United Farmers, while the first Social Credit legislature, the eighth, reduced sessions sharply, especially in the evening. Their last legislature, the sixteenth, returned to about normal. The Progressive Conservatives increased the number of sittings. The level of activity of their first legislature, the seventeenth, was maintained by the two successive legislatures; but the last complete legislature, the twentieth (1983-86), showed a fairly sharp decrease of activity. We find here a confirmation of the contention that the activity of the Legislative Assembly did not keep pace with the growth of Alberta's population or government.

As in other parliamentary institutions, the business of the Assembly is dominated by the executive. Private members may feel important in caucus, but they cannot do much by themselves. While private members' bills (the official designation is a 'public Bill other than a government Bill'[12]) may be moved by any member, they need to be examined by the Speaker. As soon as a private member's bill is introduced and given first reading, it is dropped to the bottom of the list of those bills and must work its way up to second reading. They are lowest on the order of business,[13] below government motions, government bills and orders, private bills, motions other than government motions, and, finally, public bills and orders other than government bills and orders.

The time limit on speeches in the Assembly is thirty minutes.[14] Exceptions are forty minutes for a member speaking on amendments to more than one statute, and ninety minutes for the following: the premier, the leader of the opposition, the mover of the budget, and the mover of amendments to more than one statute.

In 1986 Alberta had, next to Quebec, the largest provincial press gallery.[15] As of 1988, its forty members are made up of twenty-two representatives of the print media and nine each of radio and television. The Progressive Conservatives must be given credit for giving the public most of the opportunities it has for watching its Legislative Assembly. In 1972, two revolutionary events occurred: a printed *Hansard* was introduced, and television was admitted to the Chamber.

In the late Social Credit years, proceedings of the Assembly were first taped and recorded in mimeographed form. A regular printed *Hansard*, however, was only introduced in Premier Lougheed's first year in office. The volume is not an independent phenomenon, but an artifact of the number and length of sittings.[16]

Television also came to the legislature in 1972. Alberta was once one of the few provinces to televise all proceedings; however, since 1982 only question period has been televised.[17] While cameras have always been placed behind both sides of the Chamber, the one focusing on the opposition was hardly ever used before 1986. The effect (a decision of the cable company) was that government members were shown speaking full face, while opposition members had to be satisfied with showing the back of their heads to constituents and public. Since the beginning of the twenty-first legislature (1986), the faces of the twenty-two opposition members are shown whenever they rise to speak.

Under the Progressive Conservatives, the Assembly has been fairly well funded. For the year 1986-87 Alberta's legislative budget, in excess of $15 million, was the fastest growing in Canada (29.3 per cent over the previous year).[18] The 1988-89 estimates, however, show no increase. Despite this development, caused by the oil price crisis, Alberta is not likely to lose its position; the next-ranking legislatures (British Columbia and Saskatchewan) have budgets of about $10 million. The Alberta legislative budget went above $100,000 in 1910, and above $1 million in 1972.

In addition to the Speaker's office, the Legislative Assembly contains a unit called house services, an administrative office, *Hansard*, and the legislature library. House services consists of the clerk, a clerk assistant, two law clerks (parliamentary counsel), and related staff who provide secretarial and administrative assistance to legislature committees. The administration office looks after day-to-day management of the House and is under the direction of the director of administration. The present legislative librarian also serves as assistant deputy minister of administration.

Hansard, which is unilingual[19] and printed by a commercial firm, has five full-time and sixteen sessional employees. The staff strength of the legislative library is twenty-four. The total number of salaried employees of the Legislative Assembly, as of 1988, is 144. In 1986 it ranked fourth in the country.[20]

Alberta's legislators are not particularly well paid. In 1986 they ranked eighth, above only Saskatchewan and Prince Edward Island.[21] As of 1988, their indemnity is $29,548 and their tax-free allowance, $7,833. Members receive fairly typical committee, accommodation, travel, and pension benefits.

Members have individual offices at the legislature and two members share one secretary. As of 1988, members received $26,000 to rent and staff a constituency office. The government caucus has thirty-three employees, the opposition twenty, the Liberals nine, and the Representative party four.

Accountability Mechanisms

Historically, accountability has not been writ large in an Assembly almost always under the complete domination of the governing party. It remains, two years after the 1986 elections, a question of speculation whether an opposition of twenty-two members (with sixteen belonging to the official opposition) will secure noticeably more accountability than an opposition of four members (with two belonging to the official opposition).

The central mechanism for holding government accountable to the Assembly is the oral question period. It lasts a maximum of forty-five minutes and is the tenth and last item of the Assembly's daily routine business.[22] Since 1986, with three opposition parties in the legislature, the Speaker first recognizes the leader of the opposition for two questions and then the leaders of the Liberal party and the Representative party for one question each. After these initial questions, each with three supplementaries, and one supplementary for each party, including the governing party, question period is open to all members.

From 1975 to 1986, question period was strictly a David and Goliath affair. The Goliath, of course, was the Progressive Conservative cabinet with its massive caucus. David was Grant Notley, the young NDP leader, tragically killed in an air crash in late 1984. Notley persistently asked questions, but he simply did not have the research resources to keep track of much the government was doing.

Following the 1986 election, the Conservative-dominated Members' Services Committee voted a major increase in research funds to all parties. The government members insisted that the new funding arrangements be based on caucus representation (excluding cabinet ministers). As a result, not only did the government members' office receive the lion's share of these funds, but it received substantially more funds than the previous year even though it had significantly fewer members. The following year, under a general government restraint program, which cut expenditures by approximately 3 per cent, the Members' Services Committee slashed the party research budgets by 20 per cent. The practical result was a severe limitation on opposition research while the government members returned to the pre-1986 levels. At the same time the intern program was reduced from eight to six interns and the non-partisan legislative research service was cut back from three to two researchers. In 1988 the intern program was cut back again to four interns who are restricted in their service to only one caucus each, and the legislative research service was abolished altogether. Government members can go through their ministers to receive research assistance from the entire Alberta public service, but this is not true for the opposition. Indeed, most opposition queries must be cleared through the respective minister's office.

During the long summer (post-election) session of 1986, a lot of oral questions were asked. Some were better researched than others. Answers to some of the best questions were delayed by ministers, who claimed to lack sufficient information. While this tactic is legitimate, it also means that, when the answer is given at the end of a successive question period, the opposition member has no opportunity for probing with supplementary questions.

Government back-benchers (or, as they prefer, private members) intersperse friendly questions. They may relieve a minister struggling with an opposition question, but more often questions are orchestrated with the help of a minister's executive assistant to enable that minister to make a statement or announcement. If they ask a question on their own initiative, it is usually in an ombudsman role. In all they appear to take up more time than government members elsewhere in Canada.

When the 1979 election did not yield a substantial opposition, Patrick O'Callaghan, then the publisher of the *Edmonton Journal,* pledged to serve as unofficial opposition. Unfortunately, O'Callaghan now publishes the *Calgary Herald* which, because the city is three hundred kilometres from the capital, has much less of an impact on events in government and the legislature. The *Edmonton Journal* does a fair job of covering question period, but otherwise it does little to inform on events in the Assembly. The same is true of the *Edmonton Sun,* though its columns tend to be more informative. The CBC now and then tries to inform Albertans of goings-on in the legislature, but these attempts are sporadic.

Still, there is, as a legislative intern noted, the occasional (she calls it frequent) 'feedback cycle' with respect to question period: 'Opposition members draw upon press reports as sources for questions to pose to the government; the press covers questions and answers in the House and often includes additional information and analysis; the opposition picks up on these reports for a new line of questioning; and so on.'[23] What the author of these lines fails to note is that only occasionally are there press reports for members to draw upon. At the time of writing, New Democrats complain that the Liberals receive much more press coverage than they do. A general criticism, not only by the opposition, is that the press shows no interest in sessions once question period is over.

Following Lougheed's experience in opposition (1967-71), he decided in 1971 that the Public Accounts Committee, following recent parliamentary tradition, would be headed by an opposition member. This practice has been continued; since 1986 Barry Pashak, a member of the New Democratic caucus, is chairman of the committee, which otherwise consists of fifteen Progressive Conservatives, four New Democrats, and one Liberal.

The Public Accounts Committee meets once a week, but only during sessions. Meetings are restricted to two hours, and the government members decide on the order of business. The committee can hear ministers only; no bureaucrats appear. Because of the preponderance of government members, they can severely constrain opportunities for questioning by opposition members. Because of the limited capabilities of the committee, the strengthened opposition persuaded the committee to allow full questioning, not only of ministers, but also of deputy ministers and other relevant bureaucrats, and to arrange meetings when the Assembly is not in session. All of these reforms were vetoed by the Members Services Committee and the immediate outlook is for a further ineffectual Public Accounts Committee. There is no practical public way in which the Assembly can call the bureaucracy to account, though it is possible for the Progressive Conservative caucus to do so in private.

There is no routine review of orders-in-council by the Assembly. Many of them refer to personnel, but a number deal with policy. Generally speaking, they can be effectively controlled only in camera by the Progressive Conservative caucus.

Accountability to the Assembly is clearly not the strong suit of Alberta's parliamentary system, but it would be unfair to place all the blame on Premier Lougheed or his successor Don Getty. The Social Credit regime faced too little opposition to have to concentrate on accountability. Albertans do not remember a Legislative Assembly with teeth, if there ever was one. The only thing that became worse under the Progressive Conservatives is a further emasculation of the Assembly by transferring essential policy-making functions to the caucus of the governing party. There is little enough accountability for administrative actions, except for idle post factum speeches; there is none for the policy-making process, since only the caucus has policy-oriented committees.

The Committee System

Even a cursory glance at the number of standing and special committees conveys the impression that they are not terribly important. Historically, there has been a decline in the number of standing committees and an increase in the number of select and special committees.

A look at the titles of Alberta's standing committees shows that they have very little to do with policy, and thus with the legislative process.[24] The Special Standing Committee on Members' Services is important, but it has household functions. There are six subject-matter committees. The Public Accounts Committee is, as it is elsewhere, headed by an opposition member, although the opposition has no control over its operations.

The Committee on Privileges on Elections, Standing Orders, and Printing has among its twenty-one members six members of the cabinet, four New Democrats, one Liberal, and one Representative. The Committee on Private Bills has twenty-one members, including five New Democrats and one Liberal. The Committee on Law and Regulations (which meets infrequently) has nineteen members, including three New Democrats, one Liberal, and one Representative. The Committee on Legislative Offices has nine members, including one member from each of the three opposition parties. One of the Assembly's committees has an important potential: the Committee on the Alberta Heritage Savings Trust Fund Act (fifteen members, including three New Democrats, one Liberal, and one Representative). There is, however, no evidence that this committee has had any important policy input;[25] the fund is and remains firmly in the hands of the cabinet. The Committee on Public Affairs, used only once in recent years, contains all members of the Assembly.

There being no policy-area committees, bills passing second reading can be discussed only briefly in the Committee of the Whole Assembly, which is headed by the Deputy Speaker and chairman of committees. The Committee of Supply, also a Committee of the Whole, is limited to debating budget estimates for twenty-five days and Heritage Savings Trust Fund estimates for twelve days. Before 1982 there were no limits to these debates in the standing orders. The limits were adapted to those of the House of Commons, disregarding the fact that, in Parliament, standing committees examine estimates in detail.

If the committees of the Assembly are not particularly important, the caucus committees of the Progressive Conservatives are. Caucus committees are policy-area, subject-matter committees.[26] Their areas of competence are somewhat similar to those of the Executive Council (cabinet) committees.[27] Cabinet committees are: Priorities, Finance and Coordination; Treasury Board; Economic Planning; Energy; Social Planning; Metropolitan Affairs; Agriculture and Rural Economy; Labour Relations; Management Policy;

Legislative Review; and Cultural Heritage. Agriculture, Economic Affairs, Forestry and Natural Resources, and Health and Social Services are caucus committees with clear parallels in the cabinet committee structure. The other caucus committees are Education, Irrigation, Calgary, and Edmonton. The average membership of seven of these eight committees is thirteen. Because of the Progressive Conservatives' lack of success in Edmonton in the 1986 election (four members elected), the caucus committee on Edmonton has only six members.

Caucus committees have essentially two functions. First, they react to department or cabinet policy proposals. According to Premier Lougheed, they did not always follow these proposals closely. If a committee was not unanimous in its report, chances that caucus would adopt it were only about 50 per cent. Secondly, since 1979 caucus committees (and the relevant minister) have received and heard delegates from province-wide organizations. While many of these organizations preferred to meet, as they did earlier, with cabinet or cabinet committees, the 1979 reform is, while not a beefing up of the Assembly as a whole, a strengthening of its government members. Caucus committee chairmen are important and Mr Lougheed held periodic meetings with them. They are appointed by the chief whip.

An overview of committee activity in the Assembly brings one to the conclusion that, in matters of policy-making, most activity is limited to members of the governing party. All that opposition members can do is speak in brief sessions of the Committee of the Whole, question ministers, and engage in losing plenary debates.

Because of this policy-making activity of private members of the Progressive Conservative caucus, the results of a survey of twenty-two of them, conducted by a legislative intern in 1985,[28] are interesting. They were asked to rank in importance the following roles: representative, ombudsman, legislator, and partisan. It is not surprising that, in an overwhelmingly PC legislature, the partisan role was ranked lowest (six third and sixteen fourth ranks). What is surprising is that the legislator role was a poor third (one first, three second, thirteen third and five fourth ranks). The ombudsman role was first (thirteen, seven, one, and one) and the representative role second (nine, twelve, two, and zero).[29]

Reform Process

The Alberta Legislative Assembly lacks a reform tradition. When government began to get bigger in the late Manning years, there was too much executive domination for reform. The same was true under Premier Lougheed, who did, however, elevate the Progressive Conservative caucus to its present prominent

– and reformed – position. This reform does not help the interested public and it certainly does not help opposition members, but it must be called a reform none the less. Thus, in the Progressive Conservative era, reform has been restricted to the role of the governing caucus, a printed *Hansard*, and the televising of, first, all proceedings and now only question period.

The opposition caucuses have given some thought to reform, but they claim the Conservatives will permit only government-sponsored changes. Suggested reforms include more unrestricted debate, more debate on estimates, earlier publication of government bills, review of order-in-council appointments, summoning of committee witnesses by all parties, and relinquishing of government domination of the Members Services and Public Accounts committees. A reform suggested by the Liberals would be to have much longer sessions with fewer plenary sittings per week. It is of some interest that the establishment of policy committees was not a reform proposal volunteered to the writer.

Conclusion

To someone who knows more about the House of Commons and foreign legislatures, the Legislative Assembly of Alberta seems unimportant indeed. Comparisons with other provincial legislatures indicate that the relatively modest policy presence of Alberta's Legislative Assembly is due, to an important degree, to the one-party dominance which so far has given Alberta a quasi-party system.

While the governing caucus has increased in importance, in a basic political institution no part, no matter how large, can stand for the whole. The opposition can question and debate with the government, and the public can watch question period on television. But no one who is not one of its members can know what goes on in the Progressive Conservative caucus. Policy is made by government and caucus, and opposition members can enter detailed debate only in brief discussions in the Committee of the Whole. The real legislative work will have taken place already in the private caucus of the governing party and in its committees. If one adds to this the government domination of the Public Accounts and Members Services committees, one must speak of an Assembly which – way beyond the Westminster model – is an appendage of the province's government, which is also firmly in control of any potential reform effort.

As long as the government of Alberta is backed by not only a legislative but also a popular majority, those resisting reform can claim that more than half of Albertans have the Legislative Assembly they want. Should the electoral situation change, the outlook depends on whether Alberta moves from a one-party dominant to a two- or three-party system. If we see another massive alternation – either to one of the present oppositions or to a new party – it will be up to the new government to decide whether it wants more open legislative participation or control. It is possible, however, that a more mature Albertan society will also want more political competition. Such a constellation would make the state of the Assembly more of a public issue than it is now. In such a case, it will be up to the (presumably Progressive Conservative) government to decide whether or not to change the Assembly to one that is more open and has more possibilities for public policy-making processes and for effective public control. Until this happens, Alberta's Legislative Assembly can best be characterized and defended as one that reflects Alberta's prevailing party system.

JEREMY WILSON

BRITISH COLUMBIA

A unique blend of the traditional and the modern

The government perspective on Parliament is always characterized by a certain degree of ambivalence. On the one hand most governments will, at one time or another, feel some impatience with Parliament. Indeed, this may be an understatement – the attitudes of many government members seem dominated by resentment of its 'talkshop' qualities. On the other hand all governments appreciate the symbolic importance of Parliament, and recognize that many voters will take cavalier treatment of parliamentary traditions as an indication of disdain for democracy itself. Governmental impatience may also be tempered by empathy for the position of the opposition or by a genuine belief that policy is best made in a co-operative atmosphere.

In British Columbia the second point of view has often been emphasized much less heavily in government thinking than the first. In this respect, the government perspective has mirrored the dispositions of a resource-based, frontier society. In his seminal commentary on British Columbia political culture, Ed Black argued that economic and geographical realities combined to create an 'action-oriented' electorate, one containing large numbers of people who:

have little respect for the established elites and are intolerant of their institutions. Neither do they have much cause to respect the established parties, their traditions, or the niceties of their parliamentary procedures. Such people are interested only in 'the government that gets things done' without much regard for how it is accomplished or what violence may be done to parliamentary or political procedures that are traditional in other times or places ... Because traditional procedures are restraints, action-oriented politicians have little interest in them, and neither do their constituents.[1]

These features of the society help to account for the history of the legislative reform process in British Columbia. This process has followed a peculiar trajectory. The W.A.C. Bennett era (1952-72) was marked by rigid adherence to the procedural status quo and rather rough treatment of the House. The brief NDP interlude (1972-75) represented a catch-up period, bringing extensive reform to the legislative system. The Bill Bennett years (1975-86) featured some consolidation of NDP initiatives along with some further reforms. But this period also saw some reversals. The events of the 1983 session cast into doubt the status of some of the unwritten norms of legislative practice which had seemed to take root in the 1970s. Since 1984 the process of maturation seems to have resumed.

The legislative system left in place as a result of this history of reform, reversal, and retrenchment combines traditional and modern features in a unique way.

The Traditional Legislature

The Legislature has undergone major changes since 1972. In a number of fundamental respects, however, it continues to bear the marks of the W.A.C. Bennett era. During Bennett's two-decade regime, legislative politics were marked by brief sessions, regular use of 'legislation by exhaustion' tactics, and staunch government resistance to such things as an oral question period, a full *Hansard*, or other procedural reforms.

The average length of sessions increased only marginally during these years. The House normally convened late in January, authorized the government's funding requirements in advance of the premier's rigorously enforced 1 April deadline, and prorogued shortly thereafter. Although growth in the scope of government business might have warranted longer sessions, W.A.C. Bennett clearly recognized that during sessions the opposition parties enjoyed political advantages not available to them between sessions. While he gave every sign of enjoying the House, Bennett saw no reason to give the opposition more than six or eight weeks in the limelight each year. As a consequence, the legislative theatre was dark for much of the year.

After 1958 the leader of the opposition was given a year-round office in Victoria. But other opposition members were expected to disappear at prorogation. As one opposition politician from that era says: 'In those days once the session finished you were out. Not only were you out but the Sergeant-at-Arms after three or four days would come in and put four cardboard boxes on your desks and you were, in effect, given to understand that you'd better get out of there in four days or else you'd find your cardboard boxes out in the street. ... one weekend I went home for Easter, came back and they were moving girls into our offices to work. I mean that's the kind of attitude that Bennett had towards the opposition and its works.'[2]

In the long periods between sessions, the opposition parties had a difficult time either scrutinizing the government or presenting themselves as credible 'governments in waiting.' The leader of the official opposition did maintain a watching brief between sessions; but a party forced to transform itself into a one-man operation for nine or ten months each year naturally had difficulty presenting itself as a team qualified to take power. In effect, a full-time cabinet enjoyed the luxury of a part-time opposition.

W.A.C. Bennett's attitudes towards the Legislature were also reflected in the services and accommodation provided members. As Walter Young once put it, the premier was like the Oxford fellow who protested that the undergraduates did not need bathtubs 'because they are only in the place for eight weeks at a time.'[3] Research and secretarial assistance was minimal, and neither government back-benchers nor opposition members had private offices.

During his time as premier, W.A.C. Bennett served as his own house leader. While the standing orders of the era made no reference to time limits on speeches or debates, Bennett had little difficulty maintaining close control over proceedings. He was able to do so without having to resort to the closure procedure provided for in the standing orders. What he did use on a fairly regular basis was the tactic that came to be referred to as legislation by exhaustion. Whenever Bennett perceived a need to truncate debate he would simply command the government majority to vote down attempts to have the House adjourned at the normal 11:00 p.m. adjournment hour. The House would stay in session until the opposition capitulated and allowed the measure to come to a vote. The average session between 1952 and 1972 witnessed at least three or four post-midnight sittings. Many of these sittings lasted until past dawn, and on at least one occasion carried on until the following afternoon.

Not surprisingly, this treatment of the Legislature helped produce a sour, embittered atmosphere. Walter Young's comments could stand as a general statement of the consequences of the government's attitude:

... all-night or late-night debates undermined the standards or decorum in debate and made the process of mutual agreement on legislative business and proceedings between both sides of the House problematic ... The anger expressed in these debates was less the righteous anger of any self-styled defenders of the people's interests, and more the personal anger of men and women who had been deliberately belittled and pointlessly compelled to stay up all night ... [These tactics] made those aspects of the parliamentary system that presume some joint or common purpose, extremely difficult to develop ... In such a climate agreements 'behind the Speaker's chair' or such sensible arrangements as pairing became rare events, or simply opportunities for political tricks.[4]

Although the opposition bore most of the negative consequences of Bennett's approach, it did manage to extract considerable advantage from the opportunities available. Many opposition members became skilled 'street fighters,' expert at pestering the government with dilatory tactics, and adept at procedural guerrilla warfare. But the procedural jousting skewed the opposition's focus, diverting attention towards legislative gamesmanship and away from activities that might have better served attempts to build an image as a responsible alternative government.

In its criticism of Bennett's treatment of the Legislature, the opposition was often joined by editorial writers and interest group spokesmen. For the most part, however, the premier was unmoved. He ignored arguments favouring a larger role in the legislative process for the standing committees,[5] choosing instead to restrict committees to occasional study assignments. He refused to give the chairmanship of the Public Accounts Committee to an opposition member, and ignored calls for the establishment of an auditor general's office. He rejected the idea of an oral question period, suggesting that the existing written (or 'order paper') question procedure was adequate. He refused to renounce the use of legislation by exhaustion techniques. In 1970 he did finally make a concession on the issue of a *Hansard*, but it was only made available after prorogation, and debate in Committee of the Whole House (that is, debate on committee stage of bills and in the all-important Committee of Supply which considered spending estimates) was not recorded. Except for the provision regarding *Hansard*, the standing orders in place when the Bennett government was defeated in 1972 were exactly as they had been when it was first elected.

The Bumpy Path towards Maturity

Although opposition criticism of legislative procedure had little impact on the Bennett government, this criticism did ensure that the NDP government elected in 1972 was under immediate pressure to implement the agenda of procedural reforms it had championed during its long years in the wilderness. The new Barrett government handed the job of recommending changes to the new Speaker, Gordon Dowding, a veteran of the procedural battles against W.A.C. Bennett. Under the terms of the Legislative Procedure and Practice Inquiry Act passed in the NDP's first session, Dowding was given a broad mandate to tender advice. With the assistance of subcommittees of members and technical advisers, he produced five reports.[6] Unfortunately, although these reports offered considerable guidance as to how certain changes could be implemented, they presented neither a blueprint for an integrated overhaul of procedure nor a solid foundation for an informed debate on reform. None the less, the new government moved quickly to implement significant reforms. It established a daily, fifteen-minute oral question period and instituted a full daily *Hansard*. It announced that, henceforth, opposition members would be allowed to reply to ministerial statements. It pledged to observe the 11:00 p.m. adjournment time for evening sittings, and indicated that an opposition MLA would be installed as chairman of the Public Accounts Committee.

On a more general level, the new government moved to create a busier, better-funded legislature. It began to hold both spring and fall sessions. Although the long-standing practice of using Committee of the Whole House rather than the smaller standing committees to consider supply business and committee stage examination of bills was not altered, standing committees were given a greater investigative role. With increased sitting time and committee work likely to keep members busy year-round, the MLAs were told to henceforth regard themselves as full-time members. In keeping with this new status, their salaries were more than doubled and their office facilities and research allowances upgraded.

The NDP government moved impatiently, basing most of its reform agenda on its long experience in opposition. The new government's interests, and probably the long-run interests of the Legislature, would have been better served if the NDP had proceeded in a more measured way, after some consideration of the problems it might face as a government.[7] Some reflection from the government perspective might have suggested that the tradition of processing all of the spending estimates in Committee of Supply and the absence of time limits on debate would spell trouble for a government with a large legislative agenda. Double trouble might have been predicted for a government determined to renounce use of the legislation by exhaustion tactics which had been W.A.C. Bennett's main instrument of control. In the early going, the NDP government did not appreciate its vulnerability in the face of these considerations. If it had, it might have proceeded more carefully, trying to exchange the procedural gifts it was offering the opposition in return for concessions that would have enhanced its capacity to control proceedings. That is, the time limits question might have been addressed as part of a comprehensive reform package. This bargaining approach was not adopted. Instead, the government blundered forward into a politically damaging series of traps.

After experiencing problems in getting its estimates passed in 1974, the NDP pushed through a scheme to limit the amount of time that could be devoted to supply business to 135 hours or forty-five sittings (whichever occurred last). Once this global limit was attained, all further votes would be passed automatically, without more debate. Not surprisingly, this plan acted as a red flag to the opposition parties. In the 1975 session they made sure that all the spending estimates were not passed when the 135-hour limit expired. When the government moved under the time limits plan to push through the remaining estimates, the opposition quickly donned the mantle of martyrdom. Bill Bennett, the new Social Credit leader, led the way, embarking on a province-wide crusade under the banner of 'not a dime without debate.'

This episode had far-reaching consequences. A glorious opportunity to modernize the supply process and reach some consensus on time limits was missed. The prospects for future change were undermined. The precedents and commitments left in place when the smoke cleared ensured that the Bennett government elected in 1975 was loath to tamper with the status quo. The new premier indicated as much in 1977 when he presented a motion suspending the provision limiting supply debate:

The motion I bring before this House today will prevent any government ... this government or future governments ... from repeating that sorry incident that will always characterize the former Barrett New Democratic Party government and their attitudes to democracy and the right of the Legislature to debate the spending of the public purse. That dark spot on the history of this Legislature, a reminder of that government, will be with us and will be there for future governments to guard against in their weakness or arrogance or fear of debate from ever imposing such rules again. [8]

The first two terms of the Bill Bennett regime (1975-79 and 1979-83) produced a mixture of reforms and reversals. The new government built upon the NDP changes by establishing the office of the auditor general in 1976 and the office of ombudsman in 1977. The statutes governing these two offices are noteworthy. Both provide that the person appointed must be unanimously recommended to the Legislature by a special selection committee of the legislature. Given the presumption that opposition parties are represented on these committees, this means that both government and opposition parties have veto powers. In addition, in 1977, the government introduced legislation establishing a Crown Corporations Committee. This new committee, which was to scrutinize the operations of five (later reduced to four) major crown corporations, was empowered to sit throughout the year and allotted a budget large enough to allow it to develop a reasonably sized research arm.[9]

The impact of these forward steps was, however, neutralized by certain retrograde developments. First, although the practice of allowing an opposition member to chair the Public Accounts Committee was continued, the government seemed reluctant to see the committee establish a significant, or even partially independent, role in the post-audit process. After 1976 the number of cabinet ministers on the committee was increased to five or six, and moves by government members on the committee to limit the chairman's powers became commonplace. Secondly, in 1983, the Crown Corporations Committee was eliminated. Thirdly, the government was plainly not interested in expanding or continuing the practice of assigning responsibilities to the other legislative standing committees. The Committee on Standing Orders and Private Bills continued its routine work of processing private bills, the Committee on Agriculture undertook an extensive analysis of the food industry in the 1977-79 period, and the Committee on Transportation and Communications was asked to study motor vehicle testing in 1983. But all of the other committees (Municipal Affairs and Housing; Labour and Justice; Environment and Resources; and Health, Education and Human Resources) remained moribund.

The years between 1975 and 1983 were ones of relatively calm legislative politics. The House generally opened in March or April and then, after the throne speech and budget debates, along with passage of interim supply, proceeded to debate estimates and bills into the summer months. By pushing sessions up against the vacation period, the government exerted a subtle form of control, thus reducing the need for the older and rougher control devices. By the early 1980s, legislation by exhaustion seemed to be a thing of the past.

The 1983 session proved such judgments premature.[10] After its re-election in May 1983, the Social Credit government served notice of its plans to implement a series of radical 'restraint' measures. Embodied in twenty-six bills introduced with the 7 July budget, these measures were met by intense opposition from organized labour and an array of community, women's, and human rights groups. These interests joined together in the 'Solidarity Coalition.' Amidst talk of a general strike, this extra-parliamentary opposition mounted a series of large marches and demonstrations.

While the action in the streets unfolded, the legislative adversaries warily circled one another. The government called some of the bills for debate in July and August but seemed in no hurry to push them through. The NDP opposition meanwhile served notice that it would try to delay passage of even minor bills and indicated it would resist with particular intensity the bills it labelled the 'dirty dozen.'

By mid-September the government's patience had run out. On 19 September it declared what was tantamount to a state of legislative siege. In the first four days after this declaration the House sat almost continuously, with successive all-night debates adjourning at 9:10 a.m., 1:46 p.m., 5:16 a.m., and 9:20 a.m. The House sat for more than seventy-six hours in the first week after 19 September, for more than sixty in the second and for nearly fifty in the third. It sat past midnight on eleven of twenty-two days in the siege part of the session, with seven of those sittings extending into the dawn hours or beyond. In addition to using legislation by exhaustion tactics on an unparalleled scale, the government also liberally applied the closure procedure set out in Standing Order 46. This procedure, which had not been used since 1957, allows the majority to end debate at any stage by moving 'that the question be now put.' This motion is not debatable, but the Speaker may reject it if judged 'an abuse of the Rules of the House, or an infringement on the rights of the minority.' The Bennett government invoked closure twenty times in the 1983 session.

Given the embittered atmosphere that prevailed in the House between 19 September and Premier Bennett's 21 October announcement of a cooling-off period, it was probably inevitable that the Speaker would be dragged into the fray and the impartiality of the Chair called into question. The first controversy arose over the interpretation of the standing order pertaining to time limits on speeches. Adopted in 1974, the rule allowed the leader or 'designated speaker' from each party an unlimited speaking time in the budget and throne speech debates, in second reading debate, and during 'all other proceedings ... not otherwise specifically provided for.' Under the rules in place at that time, other participants were limited to forty minutes. The meaning of this rule was called into question on 19 September when NDP leader Dave Barrett, the designated speaker on the bill under debate, rose to continue debate on an NDP amendment. Barrett's status was challenged. In response, the Speaker ruled that the unlimited time provision did not apply to debate on amendments. Thus Barrett was forced to relinquish the floor. When he protested too strenuously, he was ejected from the House.

The Chair became embroiled in another controversy on 6 October. This second episode highlighted the fact that, unlike most other jurisdictions, British Columbia had not abolished appeals to Speaker's rulings. Again the issue arose out of a government attempt to disarm the opposition. In the early part of the siege, the NDP had pestered the government by proposing periodic adjournment motions throughout the night. When these motions were disallowed by the Chair, the NDP would appeal the ruling, thus necessitating a recorded vote and forcing government members to rouse themselves from the makeshift bunks they had set up around the buildings. Starting on 27 September, the government put into effect a plan to blunt this tactic. The Speaker stated his view that in disallowing adjournment motions, the Chair was not making a ruling, but simply applying a rule. Thus the decision could not be challenged.

The government used this gambit without much protest on a couple of occasions, but on 6 October Barrett decided to challenge a 4:00 a.m. application of this interpretation by John Parks, one of the team of government back-benchers who filled in for the Speaker during the extended sittings. The ensuing imbroglio led Parks to order Barrett to withdraw from the Chamber. When the opposition leader refused, Parks ordered his removal by the sergeant-at-arms. Barrett, in full passive resistance stance, was tipped out of his chair, dragged from the House, and dumped on the corridor floor. Less than two hours later the Speaker suspended Barrett for the remainder of the session.

Both sides of the House must bear some responsibility for the sorry events of 1983. It is difficult to sustain a blanket condemnation of the government's response to an intransigent opposition. While legislation by exhaustion tactics may be difficult to justify under any circumstances, closure certainly is an accepted part of the government arsenal in most jurisdictions. What is questionable, though, is the use of closure before there has been a chance for full debate. While some of the Social Credit government's controversial bills had been extensively debated prior to the 19 September imposition of legislative war measures, others were not introduced for second reading until the second or third week of the siege. They had, that is, received no consideration during the period when calmer, more reasoned debate was possible. It is difficult to justify using closure in such instances.

In the wake of the 1983 brawl both the government and opposition sides indicated signs of contrition. The NDP house leader seemed to express the thoughts of many members when he said: 'Right now this House is ... not a house of ill repute, but a House in ill repute insofar as the general public is concerned. The public is disenchanted, disillusioned, maybe even disinterested ... not in what we are doing here but in how we are doing it.'[11] Such thoughts translated into renewed calls for reform from both sides of the House. In March 1984 the Legislature unanimously approved a government motion asking the Select Standing Committee on Standing Orders and Private Bills to review the standing orders with a view to improving proceedings.

The committee, chaired by Social Credit MLA Austin Pelton, met more than twenty-five times. The proceedings were apparently characterized by a high level of bipartisan co-operation. At one of its first meetings, the committee agreed to pursue a set of objectives defined by NDP member Mark Rose. These were :

(1) to improve public understanding of the Legislature's work, (2) to create interest by better debate, (3) to encourage more meaningful participation by more members in the House and its committees, (4) to provide opportunities for members to raise important issues other than through question period or estimates, (5) to establish a better balance between the government's right to govern and the opposition's right to oppose, (6) to make more predictable the calling of sessions and the timetabling of government business, (7) to develop means to make ministers and members more accountable for what is being said in debate, and (8) to ventilate and examine current rules and procedures and to evaluate how each contributes to or frustrates the foregoing. [12]

The committee agreed unanimously on a long series of changes to the standing orders. These in turn were unanimously approved by the Legislature. The right to challenge Speaker's rulings was eliminated. A one-hour block of time every Friday would henceforth be set aside for 'Private Members statements.' Time limits on speeches in all debates were reduced. A time limit of two hours was established for the speeches of party leaders and designated speakers, who had previously enjoyed unlimited time. The throne speech debate was reduced from a maximum of eight sitting days to six, while the budget debate was cut from ten sittings days to six. A new clause on ordinary meeting times specified a normal adjournment time of 6:00 p.m., thus ensuring that evening sittings would be held only in special circumstances. Sections referring explicitly to the possibility of referring estimates and bills to select standing committees were added to the standing orders. In order to facilitate greater use of committees, Wednesdays were to be classified as optional sitting days.

In addition to adopting these and a host of minor changes to the standing orders, the House also accepted a series of 'practice recommendations' suggested by the Pelton committee. The most significant of these were aimed at encouraging consultation between the party house leaders. The Legislature also endorsed the committee's view that the idea of broadcasting proceedings should be pursued, and approved its recommendation favouring increased expense allowances for members.

The Contemporary Legislature

The reforms of the past fifteen years leave British Columbia with a legislative system substantially different from the one prevailing in the W.A.C Bennett era. Interested members of the public now have access to a full daily *Hansard*. When the House is in session members have daily opportunities to direct oral questions at the ministers, along with weekly opportunities to present brief statements on matters of their choosing. A set of time limits, imposed in two stages (1974 and 1984), prescribe the length of the major 'set piece' debates, while limiting the length of speeches in all proceedings. Most contributions are now restricted to thirty or forty minutes. Evening sittings are no longer part of the normal routine.

Despite the scope of change, key elements of the traditional legislative system have persisted. Reforms that have been at the centre of the modernization process elsewhere have not been implemented. As a result, the British Columbia Legislature remains a unique blend of traditional and modern elements.

Most important, all of the government's spending estimates continue to be examined in the version of Committee of the Whole House known as Committee of Supply. A switch to a system that would see some or all of the estimates sent to standing committees seemed possible at a couple of junctures in the recent past. The idea was suggested to the NDP government as a way out of the 1974 impasse described above. The 1984 amendments facilitating standing committee examination seemed to indicate a general consensus in favour of the idea. But the traditional format remains intact. These supply proceedings, which see each cabinet minister take his or her turn on the hot seat for a yearly accountability session with the opposition, continue to take up a large portion of each session. In 1986, for example, nearly 60 per cent of the session was given over to Committee of Supply proceedings. After completion of the budget debate, the House turned its attention to the business of supply, devoting at least part of almost every sitting to the estimates until it adjourned for the summer over two months later. This session's preoccupation with the estimates was somewhat greater than normal, but in most sessions over the past decade at least 40 per cent of time has been devoted to this end.

Between 1975 and 1986 the only two standing committees to meet regularly were Standing Orders, Private Bills and Members' Services (which meets to consider private bills such as those required by companies and institutions operating under provincial charters) and Public Accounts (discussed below). The 1987 and 1988 sessions brought a resuscitation of the committee system. Several of the subject-area committees were directed to undertake investigative tasks, with most of these panels carrying their inquiries into the post-recess months. Several committees were permitted to acquire the services of researchers or consultants. The idea of involving committees in examination of the spending estimates or at the committee stage of deliberation on bills has been discussed, but the prevailing view seems to be that the small size of the House (currently sixty-nine members) makes such an expansion of committee functions impractical.

While its effectiveness continues to leave much to be desired, the Public Accounts Committee has begun to establish itself as a significant actor in the post-audit process. Progress has been slow. Until recently the committee continued to live up to its billing as the Legislature's 'best showcase for MLAs' worst manners,' with government and opposition members bickering over such things as the right of members to call witnesses, the scheduling of meetings, and the right of members to photocopy spending vouchers. And the committee's effectiveness oscillated radically from year to year. In the early 1980s it met about a dozen times a year and carried out a reasonable review of the auditor general's report. But the committee also experienced years like 1986, when it was able to muster less than forty-five minutes' worth of comments and questions on the auditor general's report.[13]

Since 1986 the situation has improved. The committee has met regularly while the House is in session and carried out its business in a civil atmosphere. The establishment of a stable working relationship between the committee and the auditor general has contributed to the development of audit procedures which the public service takes seriously. But the effectiveness of the Public Accounts Committee continues to be hindered by a number of factors. It does not meet when the House is in recess; it has no research assistance; members continue to experience difficulties in getting access to government spending vouchers; and the presence of cabinet ministers on the committee continues to be a source of concern.[14]

In setting forth his legislative reform priorities following Social Credit's 1986 victory, Premier Vander Zalm spoke of the need for a new atmosphere in the House: 'I want to see a new style in the House, with government listening to the opposition's point of view and consulting with it on a continuing basis. With a restored sense of purpose ... with a willingness to seek co-operation instead of confrontation ... we can make the legislature a place of pride for British Columbians ...'[15]

The first years of the Vander Zalm government have not transformed the House into a chamber of sweetness and reason. Signs of increased civility are, however, apparent. According to one close observer: 'The B.C. government and Opposition are developing the kind of professional relationship that prevails in other parliaments, by which I mean they agree to co-operate on the orderly conduct of the house while reserving the right to utterly oppose each other on more important matters, like politics and policy.'[16]

Whether such changes in atmosphere turn out to be harbingers of lasting changes in legislative culture or not, the new spirit of goodwill has had one important concrete manifestation. The 1987 session brought legislation transferring power to manage the Legislature to a new all-party committee, the Board of Internal Economy. This long-overdue step represented a clear statement of legislative autonomy and guaranteed the opposition a voice in budgetary and management decisions pertaining to the legislative precinct and member services, salaries, and accommodation. This step was extremely well received on both sides of the House, and so far the board seems to be functioning as an effective, bipartisan committee.

Conclusion

The British Columbia Legislature remains a rough-and-tumble place, its affairs indelibly coloured by the polarized climate that continues to be a hallmark feature of political life in the province. But two decades of fitfully prosecuted reform efforts have produced a Legislature which is undoubtedly more independent and more mature than the institution extant at the close of the W.A.C. Bennett era.

Viewed in the most positive light, the mix of traditional and modern features that has emerged can be said to allow for both comprehensive government control of the agenda and full opportunity for opposition criticism. Less positive evaluations might focus on various dimensions where there is still scope for improvement. To highlight just one of these in closing, we would note that the BC House does not do a particularly good job of stimulating informed public debate on critical public policy issues. Too often, it seems, policy decisions of monumental importance are not preceded by anything close to a full public discussion of costs, benefits, risks and alternatives.

This situation is not unique to British Columbia. Few political societies consistently manage to generate what might pass for a rich policy debate. And because of their size the political societies of the Canadian provinces face special problems in this regard. Because they are small societies they have difficulty sustaining a robust interest group life, or a range of groups capable of participating effectively in the policy- making process. In a sense, the problem is one of 'critical mass' – while the provinces may contain as great a diversity of interests as larger polities, many of those interests remain unarticulated.

From this perspective it can be contended that if we are concerned to foster strong democracy in the provinces, then in our deliberations about legislative reform we should give special consideration to measures with the potential to enrich political debate in the society generally. While acknowledging the deep and complex roots of the problem highlighted here, we should emphasize the important role legislatures can play in 'sponsoring' broader societal debate, and consider ways in which performance of this function could be improved. Such considerations are particularly appropriate in British Columbia, where too often, intense legislative debate fails to translate into informed public debate.

NOVA SCOTIA

The wisdom of their ancestors is its foundation

One of the oldest traditions of our parliamentary democracy is that our institutions are in a constant process of change. Yet in 1841 Charles Dickens attended the opening of the 1841 Legislative Assembly in Nova Scotia and one wonders how different his comments would have been if he attended a similar opening one hundred and forty-eight years later.

It happened to be the opening of the Legislative Council and General Assembly, at which ceremonial the forms observed on the commencement of the new session of Parliament in England were so closely copied, and so gravely presented on a small scale, that it was like looking at Westminster through the wrong end of a telescope. The Governor, as her Majesty's representative, delivered what may be called the Speech from the Throne. He said what he had to say manfully and well. The military band outside the buildings struck up 'God Save the Queen' with great vigour before his Excellency had quite finished; the people shouted; the in's rubbed their hands; the out's shook their heads; the Government party said there never was such a good speech; the opposition declared there was never such a bad one, ... and, in short, everything went on and promised to go on, just as it does at home upon like occasions.[1]

This does not mean that there have not been any changes in Nova Scotia's system of parliamentary democracy since 1841. Indeed there have been. Yet Nova Scotia's House of Assembly remains true to its British roots.[2] In 1841 Nova Scotia enjoyed representative government and had since 2 October 1758, when the first assembly of twenty-two elected representatives met in Halifax. This, the first assembly of elected representatives in Canada, was the foundation of today's House of Assembly. The Assembly did not have a permanent home until Province House was constructed in 1819. Not until seven years after Dickens's visit to Halifax was responsible government obtained. On 9 February 1848 the first responsible ministry in Canada, indeed in any British colony, was formed, with J.B. Uniacke as premier. Constitutional reform in Nova Scotia was attained not by rebellion or revolt, but through evolution and the political process.[3]

The chief architect of reform was Joseph Howe who, as publisher of the *Nova Scotian,* used the power of the press to generate public opinion in favour of responsible government. Not only did Howe's acquittal in 1835 by a Halifax jury on a charge of libel win 'freedom of the press' for Nova Scotians, but the decision became the catalyst for political reform.

The principle of responsible government was achieved in 1840 when the Assembly voted non-confidence in the Executive Council, forcing the governor, Sir Colin Campbell, to resign. Because of the delaying tactics of the Colonial Office, responsible government was not obtained officially until after the election of 1847. The Reform party made responsible government the election issue of that year. When the Assembly opened, it adopted a motion of non-confidence in the appointed Executive Council. The governor had no alternative but to call on Uniacke to form a government, 'with no restrictions upon his choice of members.'

Originally, Nova Scotia had a bicameral legislature: the elected House of Assembly and the appointed Legislative Council. Like the Canadian Senate, the Legislative Council rarely rejected legislation adopted by the Assembly, except on those rare occasions when the governing party was in a minority position in the Council. It was such a situation which ultimately led to the Council's demise. When the Conservatives assumed office in 1925 after forty-three years of continuous Liberal rule (which is still the Canadian political longevity record), they found they had only one member in the Council. The new government looked upon the Council as an anachronism with no wide public support and determined to abolish it. Twice the Council defeated bills which would have done so, although in 1925 the councillors did adopt legislation which limited the term of all new appointees to ten years, rather than for life. The premier, E. N. Rhodes, carried the battle to the courts and in 1927 the Judicial Committee of the Privy Council in London agreed with his contention that the members of the Legislative Council served at the pleasure of the crown and thus could be removed by the government of the day. The Judicial Committee also decreed that there was no limit to the number of members who could be appointed to the Council.[4] Armed with this decision, in 1928 the Conservative government was able to 'manufacture' a majority in the Council to amend the provincial constitution assuring the Council's demise. 'The

Legislative Council of Nova Scotia passed away, unwept, unhonoured and unsung.'[5]

The advent of Confederation in 1867 had a significant impact on the House of Assembly. The division of powers in the new constitution meant that many subjects of importance in Halifax would now be debated in Ottawa. The number of seats in the provincial House, which had been forty-four when Joseph Howe entered politics, had risen to fifty-one in 1867. But by 1870 there were only thirty-eight seats, and it would not be until the 1978 election that the House would surpass by one the number of seats that had existed in 1867.

An even greater change was in the composition of the House. Ottawa and the federal scene now held the spotlight, and it was to the House of Commons that many of the major political figures turned their attention. Joseph Howe and Sir Charles Tupper left almost immediately for Ottawa and the federal cabinet. They were followed later by Sir John Thompson and W.S. Fielding, both former premiers. Others, including Sir Robert Borden, George Nowlan, Robert Winters, Angus L. Macdonald (who later returned), Robert Stanfield, Clarie Gillis, Allan J. MacEachen, Gerald Regan (who returned to Ottawa), and Elmer MacKay, for one reason or another either left provincial politics for the federal scene, or entered politics immediately at the national level.

Nova Scotians are more politically attuned and politically aware than are the residents of any other province, with the possible exception of Prince Edward Island.[6] Historically, many Nova Scotians have been tethered to a subsistence economy and dependent upon government to alleviate the province's poverty, something that neither level of government has been able to do with complete satisfaction. Economic changes, such as the growth of the service sector, have offered some improvement. The sea has traditionally served as a safety value for dissatisfaction, as have the more developed economies of New England and 'Upper Canada.' There has been little infusion of new blood from immigration into Nova Scotia. However, the rise of a national media, particularly television, and the return of some Nova Scotians to the province with new ideas has brought about a liberalizing of the province's political culture.

Economic development, especially in the Halifax-Dartmouth metropolitan region, as well as 'modernization' of the economy, has also made an impact on Nova Scotia's political culture. Nevertheless, the prevailing political orientation of Nova Scotia continues to revolve around four elements: conservatism, cynicism, parochialism, and the British connection. These are the forces which have shaped and continue to shape the House of Assembly in its evolution from an independent colonial parliament to its current status as a provincial legislature within the Canadian federation.

Section 92 of the Constitution Act 1867, which lists the provincial powers, may not have the glitter or the appeal of section 91, yet an inspection of the constitutional cases adjudicated by both the Supreme Court of Canada and the Judicial Committee of the Privy Council illustrates that the provinces do indeed have considerable constitutional authority within the Canadian federal political system. The role and function of the House of Assembly, like any other provincial legislature, is important not only to the residents of the province, but also to the operation of the Canadian political system. The advent of 'interdependent federalism,' the 1982 amendments to the Constitution Act 1867, and the Meech Lake Accord, should it become part of the constitution, have given all of the provincial legislatures a more prominent role to play in the operation, maintenance, and evolution of Canadian federalism than they've had during the initial seventy years following Confederation. Many provincial politicians and their constituents have yet to grasp this fact.

Redistribution and Elections

The Assembly today, as in the days of Dickens, operates on the principle of modified representation by population. By tradition each county must have at least one seat in the House, no matter what its population. Consequently, Victoria County, with fewer than 7,000 electors, has one member. At the same time, many of the suburban Halifax-Dartmouth constituencies have double the population of Victoria County. This tradition of maintaining riding boundaries within county borders continues to exist, even though partially elected school boards now cross county lines. In 1988 several Halifax-Dartmouth suburban ridings had populations in excess of 20,000, the largest being Halifax-Bedford Basin with over 22,000. The smallest riding is Cumberland Centre with only 5,200 people; the provincial average is about 11,800 residents. It is clear from these figures that Nova Scotia requires a wholesale redistribution of all fifty-two ridings; it is not right in a democratic system that currently some individuals' voting strength is only one-fourth the voting power of certain other residents.

The system in place for the redistribution of seats in the Assembly on the surface looks to be open and democratic. A panel of three persons, usually one a supporter of each party, draws up the boundary changes and presents them to the House. Normally, the House will accept these proposals, but it may amend or even reject them and draw up its own proposals. All boundary changes must have the approval of the House using the normal legislative process. Thus the real power over redistribution lies with the premier, and secondly – and a very distant second – with the members.

There has not been a major examination of the constituencies in Nova Scotia in over thirty years and a major redistribution is long overdue. However, neither the general public nor any of the political parties appears to be particularly interested. The last redistribution took place prior to the 1978 election. As in most provinces, only the suburban growth areas, around Halifax and Dartmouth, Sydney, and Truro, were realigned and the number of seats increased from forty-six to fifty-two.[7] Little concern seems to have been expressed about the total membership of the House, and one can only surmise that this question will only arise when there is no longer room to seat all of the members in one of Canada's smaller and more beautiful legislative chambers.

Prior to the 1981 election the current government, using its legislative majority, redistributed the last two remaining dual member constituencies of Inverness and Yarmouth. This action had been considered in 1978, but at that time no consensus could be reached on how to divide these two counties into single-member ridings. The 1981 changes, particularly in Inverness, were controversial. The Liberals cried 'Gerrymander,' and an impartial inspection of the map would lead one to agree that there was at least some validity to their charge. It would appear, however, that the Conservatives' manoeuvring backfired. In 1981 they won the gerrymandered Inverness South, defeating the Liberal incumbent Bill MacEachren, who had been a thorn in their side, but lost the other three new seats. In 1984 they won all four, but they lost two of them in 1988.

Another question concerning representation is one which is common to those legislatures which, following British parliamentary tradition, use the first-past-the-post system of voting in elections. There have been many elections in Nova Scotia in which the governing party has benefited from this system when minuscule shifts in the popular vote can bring about major changes in the complexion of a small legislature. The major problem in Nova Scotia has been the domination of the House by the governing party, most often the Liberals. From 1867 to 1956 the Conservatives held office for a total of only thirteen years, and in many of those years in opposition their ranks were reduced to a corporal's guard.

Since the 1956 election of the Conservatives under Robert L. Stanfield, Nova Scotia politics has undergone a transformation. Indeed, it could be argued that 1956 was a 'realigning' election.[8] Prior to 1956 Nova Scotia had a 'one-party dominant' system, but since then the historic dominance of the Liberals has waned and Nova Scotia can now be said to enjoy a functioning three-party system. These changes are evident in popular vote tabulations in subsequent elections. The growth of the NDP from its foundation in industrial Cape Breton into a party which now obtains support province-wide is but one example of this change. The fact that the Conservatives have held office for twenty-five of the thirty-three years since 1956 is further evidence of these alterations to the political system. Furthermore, in the last ten elections the winning party has received a majority of the popular vote only three times (in 1963, 1967, and 1984). In the previous twenty-two elections the victorious party received a

majority on nineteen occasions (seventeen of these were Liberal victories). This
new party structure has led to changes in the House of Assembly. The
competition between the parties has become more intense, and the dynamics of
the current three-party House are much different from the traditional two-party
alignment.

At the same time – and perhaps it is no mere coincidence – there has been a
demise of the strong leader, or father-figure image, used so effectively by
Angus L. Macdonald and Robert Stanfield. The lack of a strong leader has
influenced the House, particularly the behaviour of the members during
question period. Members on both sides now feel they have a greater
independence than existed during the Macdonald and Stanfield eras. This
feeling of independence on the members' part has made the House into a more
important public forum and it receives a higher public profile than in the past,
though this may also be due to technological changes in the news media, and to
the growth of government and the impact of political decisions on every aspect
of Nova Scotians' daily lives.

Rules and Reform

Following the sudden death of the clerk of the House in 1976, Premier Gerald
Regan worked out an agreement whereby Michael Ryle (at the time a principal
clerk in the British House of Commons) acted as one of the table officers in
Halifax during the 1976 session. Mr Ryle was specifically requested 'to carry
out a review of the present procedures and practices of the House to see whether
they should be modified in the light of modern circumstances.'[9] The Rules of
Procedure had not been reformed, or indeed given more than a cursory glance,
since 1955.

Ryle noted that the House was well attended and went on to say:

it is alive and vigorous – much of the debate is hard-hitting and effective and yet most of
the proceedings are conducted in high good humour ... it is quickly responsive to the
problems of the day; matters which are concerning the electorate are frequently and
persistently raised on the floor of the House. My main anxiety is that some of these very
virtues are mirrored by corresponding faults. The vigorous debate is not always well
informed; the humour sometimes obscures the wisdom; instant reaction to public events
sometimes means that they are debated before the relevant problems had been fully
studied; many topics are brought before the House but many of them are not debated.[10]

In March 1977 a select committee of the House was established to examine
Mr Ryle's review. It reported in July 1978 when the House was not in session.
The Conservatives were elected to office that September and commenced their
own review of the rules. Their proposals for reform contained only minor

changes from those recommended by the select committee, but both the Liberal and the NDP opposition opposed the proposals. Any change or suspension of the rules of procedure in Nova Scotia requires the consent of at least two-thirds of the members present, and at that time, the Progressive Conservatives could not muster the required number of votes.

Consequently, the House agreed to the establishment of a three-member committee consisting of the then Deputy Speaker, Arthur Donahoe, Hugh Tinkham, the Liberal whip, and Jeremy Akerman, the leader of the New Democratic Party. The committee tabled its report on 26 May 1980 and the reforms, which bear a striking similarity to Ryle's recommendations, were adopted and came into effect shortly thereafter.[11]

The process illustrated a number of interesting aspects of parliamentary reform. First, procedural reform can be a painstaking and tedious process. Secondly, a political party's view on reform is influenced by its position in the House: members are in favour of reform until they see their own position being undermined. Thirdly, reform requires a catalyst, which, in the case of Nova Scotia, was the Ryle report.[12]

Michael Ryle proposed a number of changes to tighten up the rules surrounding question period, specifically to limit the time and to provide that, where appropriate, notice be given. In line with his recommendations, in 1980 the rules were altered. Oral questions may now be asked only on Tuesday, Wednesday, and Thursday, and a time limit of one hour and fifteen minutes is imposed. Rule 31 states that 'questions shall be concisely put and shall relate only to matters for which a minister is officially responsible.' It goes on to say, 'in putting any such question or in replying to the same no argument or opinion is to be offered nor any facts stated except so far as may be necessary to explain the same, and in answering any such question the matter to which the same refers shall not be debated.'[13]

Nevertheless, question period in Nova Scotia remains in need of further reform. The opposition parties do not take full advantage of their opportunities and all too frequently the questions are inadequately researched and poorly put. The Nova Scotia members appear to have forgotten John Diefenbaker's dictum that you do not ask a question unless you already know the answer.

There is nothing in Rule 32 concerning 'relevancy of the question.' Consequently, the Speaker has little authority to keep both the questioner and the minister from straying all over the political map. The members might insert the need for 'relevancy' into the rules, thus giving the Speaker an opportunity to bring a little more order out of what can only be classified as a chaotic and somewhat ineffective question period. In May 1986 the all-party Special Committee on the Rules and Procedures proposed having a one-hour question period on Tuesdays and Thursdays, and a one-and-a-half hour period on

Wednesday. They also suggested that all questions should be 'concisely put.'[14] These suggestions were adopted in the 1987 session.

Another idea put forward by Ryle concerned the hours that the House is in session, and the procedure to extend the hours. At present the House sits from six o'clock in the evening until ten on Mondays, from two o'clock in the afternoon until ten on Tuesday, Wednesday, and Thursday, and from eleven in the morning until two o'clock in the afternoon on Friday. With the consent of at least two-thirds of the members, the hours may be extended and include Saturday sittings. Every session the government must extend the hours, but still not all of the government's spending estimates are approved. The members are either going to have to have longer sessions (which no government desires), or find a more appropriate method of reviewing the estimates. Currently a maximum of seventy-five hours is permitted for the consideration of the estimates by the Committee of the Whole.

Occasionally during the time of the Regan government (1970-78), there would be a fall session, not to deal with parliamentary business as much as to improve the income of the members, who at that time were paid for each session. Members are now paid on an annual basis, and consequently this reason for a fall session has evaporated. The opposition parties continually demand a fall session and the government continues to reject their demand.

The government of the day will always be able to hasten the end of the session by turning up the thermostat on warm spring days to make the non-air-conditioned chamber a trifle uncomfortable for the members. As there are relatively few farm MLAs, there is not the overwhelming desire in Nova Scotia, as there may be in some other provinces, to end the session early in time for spring seeding. Currently the Nova Scotia session lasts from mid-February to approximately the last week of June. This represents a substantial expansion of the House's workload in recent years; the Forty-Ninth Legislature (1967-70) sat for a total of 129 days, whereas the Fifty-Fourth (1985-88) sat 220 days.

Ryle's proposal to give ordinary members an opportunity to raise 'matters other than government motions' has been incorporated as Rule 5. On Tuesdays and Thursdays members of the opposition parties may present such motions, while Wednesdays are reserved for members of the governing party. The so-called late show lasts for thirty minutes and no vote is taken. Speeches during this period are limited to ten minutes. It is unfortunate that Rule 23, concerning the length of speeches, was not amended in 1980. At present a member may speak for up to one hour; this is obviously too long.

Michael Ryle had an uncanny ability to foretell the future, for he recommended 'that when a roll call vote is demanded the bells should be rung and the Speaker should direct the Clerk to call the roll ... not later than fifteen minutes from the time the bell is rung.'[15] The members thought that fifteen minutes was a bit short, so Rule 38(4) states that 'in no event shall the bells be rung for longer than one hour.'

Prior to the tabling of Ryle's report, a minister frequently chaired the Public Accounts Committee. More recently the chairman has been a government back-bencher. In May 1986 the Special Committee on Rules and Procedures advocated that, starting with the 1987 session, the members of the Public Accounts Committee shall select their chairman from among those members of the committee who are members of the official opposition.[16] In 1987 this was adopted as Rule 60(3). This change might well have been implemented in 1986 except for the fact that the NDP, at least in the government's view, unduly politicized the issue and the government did not wish to be seen as caving in to NDP pressure. It is to be hoped that the suggestions for reform of the Public Accounts Committee made by Arnold Sarti, the former auditor general of the province, will also be implemented. Sarti proposed that the committee be given research assistants, that it be permitted to meet when the House is not in session, and, most important, that it report to the House annually.[17] This important parliamentary committee, at least in recent years, has been less effective than even a paper tiger. Governments do not wish to have their mistakes broadcast about and in Nova Scotia the administration has done its utmost to see that the Public Accounts Committee is ineffective. Perhaps the reforms of May 1986, plus those of Sarti, and continued public pressure will force the government to recognize the importance of the committee and permit it to carry out the customary tasks assigned to it in Westminster-style legislatures.

Ryle recommended the Speaker's authority be strengthened. Specifically, he desired that 'the rule permitting an immediate appeal against the Speaker's rulings be repealed.'[18] This proposal was adopted in 1980. Another important reform concerning the speakership was an increase in salary to equal that of a cabinet minister. At present there is no discussion in Nova Scotia of appointing a permanent Speaker. In the interests of impartiality, both the current Speaker and one of his predecessors, George Mitchell, have made it clear that they do not attend their party's caucus or other partisan events during the session.[19]

The reforms of 1980 have strengthened the position of the Speaker. He is now responsible for the administration of Province House, its staff, the legislative library, and *Hansard*. He is also chairman of the Assembly's Internal Economy Board. On most occasions since 1980 the Speaker's estimates have experienced little difficulty in Committee of the Whole, although in 1986 one item concerning the budget of the Office of Legislative Counsel did produce some debate. It would be unfortunate if this set a precedent; the Speaker, unlike a minister, should not be drawn into debate on his estimates if he is to maintain his authority over the House. With the appointment of Arthur Donahoe as Speaker in 1981, Nova Scotia, for perhaps the first time, has a Speaker who is truly interested not only in the reform of the rules and procedures of the House, but also in improving the lot of the back-bencher.

Nova Scotia, unlike many other provinces, only has two table officers, the clerk and his deputy. During the past few years neither of these positions has been considered full-time. This is unfortunate and something which must be changed if the committees are to meet when the House is not in session. There is a full-time legislative counsel; there needs to be a full-time clerk.

One of Michael Ryle's more important recommendations which was not accepted in 1980 was, 'that a rule may only be suspended on a debatable motion moved after notice by a simple majority, on a debatable motion moved without notice on a two-thirds majority, or otherwise with the unanimous consent of the House.'[20]

This proposed reform was aimed at establishing a more formal and fairer method for temporarily suspending a rule, so as to encourage government to avoid the practice of asking for the waiver of a rule without advance warning to the opposition. Instead, the members produced rule 85 which reads: 'no rule adopted by the House shall be dispensed with unless by consent of at least two-thirds of the members present.'[21]

One important reform arising from Ryle's recommendation is the new Rule 19 (1980) which permits the opposition parties to determine the order of business on Wednesdays.[22] This reform not only permits the opposition to bring forward items for debate but gives them an excellent opportunity to attack the government. This change in the rules may, in the long run, prove to be the most significant of Ryle's recommendations, provided, of course, that the opposition does its research and is adequately prepared beforehand.

Committees

In 1987 the committee structure was amended. There are now nine standing committees: Internal Affairs, Law Amendments, Private and Local Bills, Public Accounts, Economic Development, Human Resources, Community Service, Resources, and Veterans' Affairs. The Speaker is empowered to direct, without question put, to which committee a bill shall be sent;[23] however, with the exception of appropriation bills, nearly all legislation is referred either to Law Amendments or to the Private and Local Bills Committee. Appropriation bills and the estimates are handled in the Committee of the Whole. The Internal Affairs Committee was established for 'the purpose of considering rules, privileges, procedures, matters relative to the Legislative Library, and members indemnities.'[24] The Human Resources Committee considers issues concerning drug dependence and alcoholism, health, housing, human rights, and social services. The duties of the remaining committees are to carry out the functions one would expect from their titles. Obviously some committees, such as Economic Development and Resources, are busier than others. Although the size of the committees, nine members, may not be large in some circumstances, it is interesting to note that the new select committees at Westminster have only seven members, the same number recommended in the McGrath Report for the Canadian House of Commons.

The committee system in any legislature will remain under a cloud as long as the party whips continue to rigorously impose party discipline upon members. Reform of the committees in Ottawa, Toronto, and London has given the back-bencher a more meaningful role to play in the parliamentary system. Even though the Nova Scotia House is small and approximately half of the members hold a position of one kind or another, there are still others who deserve to be given a useful role in the process, and not be expected merely to be trained seals for their leaders. Since Nova Scotia does not have a system of parliamentary assistants, committees are the major outlet for any back-bencher to take any part in the policy process.

Any future reform will undoubtedly involve the function of the Law Amendments Committee. This committee, usually chaired by a cabinet minister, can and does hold public hearings. It is held in a some esteem by pressure groups and opposition members, as well as by most government members. But does the committee have an opportunity to carry out its legislative functions properly? During the early days of the session the answer is yes, but then few bills go to committee at this point. Most bills are referred to the committee late in the session at a time when the members are involved in many different endeavours. On balance, therefore, the Law Amendments Committee does not have time to perform as it should. But the debate on how to reform this committee may prove to be one of the more difficult and protracted debates over reform in recent Nova Scotia history.

The committees could be given a greater role to play in the approval of the estimates, particularly when one remembers that the allotted seventy-five hours in the Committee of the Whole expired before all of the estimates were approved in 1986, while in 1987 and 1988, although the estimates of all departments were considered, some major programs received no scrutiny whatsoever. It might be appropriate if those estimates still awaiting approval after the expiration of the time limit in the Committee of the Whole could be referred to the requisite committee. Once again, a time limit would have to be stipulated in order to prevent filibusters. Such a change would also mean that the committees would have to meet when the House was not in session.

The standing committees should be able to scrutinize crown agency and departmental reports. They should also be permitted to initiate research studies on their own. The Law Amendments Committee should not deal with every piece of legislation, but only those bills on the provincial constitution, the administration of justice, and local government; all other bills should be sent to the proper standing committee. Committees should be the bailiwick of the ordinary members. There should not be members of cabinet on any standing committee.

Since assuming the speakership and the chairmanship of the Special Committee on Rules and Procedures, Arthur Donahoe has been involved in the introduction of an internship program in 1985, has strengthened the research capabilities of the legislative library, and has improved the facilities in Province House. However, Nova Scotian members do not have adequate office space or research facilities. This is particularly true of committees.

The recognized parties do receive public funds, based upon their representation in the House, for research purposes, but these funds are often monopolized by the leader and thus not always available to the back-bencher during the heat of the session.

The House of Assembly

A further change now being considered by the special committee concerns televising the proceedings of the House and its committees. In 1987-88 the Speaker carried out a study on the costs of establishing an 'in house' television system. It was estimated that the capital costs to install television facilities would be $2 million and the annual operating expenses would be $600,000. Faced with sums of this magnitude, the committee decided that television was too expensive for Nova Scotia. In the early 1970s cameras were permitted into the Chamber on a trial basis. At that time the House was not televised 'live'; the local television stations were able to use 'footage' for newscasts and for a daily fifteen-minute program on what the television producers considered to be the day's most significant highlights. This experiment has not been repeated. Some commentators believe it was because of the heat generated by the lights in the Chamber which the Speaker of the day found to be quite uncomfortable.

At present, sound recordings, using the *Hansard* feed, which is recorded on tape rather than by hand, may be made by any member of the press gallery. At the beginning of each session, film footage may be shot for background use by the provincial television stations. There appears to be little public demand or interest in televising the House, except among the members of the press gallery. Fears have also been expressed that the installation of television equipment would seriously detract from the architectural integrity of the small, historic Chamber.

The question of members' salaries has been a problem for every popularly elected legislature, for no parliamentarian wishes to raise his own income because of the political consequences. The House of Assembly has now given this job to a two-member royal commission which reports to the Speaker each December on the amount of monies to be paid to the members for the coming year, and its report is binding. Handing over this difficult question to a royal commission could be interpreted as an abrogation of political responsibility; however, the practice now appears to be well accepted and the issue of salaries is no longer a matter of public controversy. Furthermore, by bringing members' base salaries more in line with those of other provinces, the commission has, at least indirectly, made political life a more attractive calling for many Nova Scotians. Nevertheless, a member of the House of Assembly is not exactly overpaid in comparison with other professional groups in the province. For example, the average salary for a school teacher in Nova Scotia in 1989 is $41,977, and for a deputy minister it is $80,002. In 1986 the members received an increase of 2 per cent for a base of $32,450. By 1989, the base had risen to $41,145. In addition, members residing in the Halifax-Dartmouth metropolitan region receive $28,500 for expenses and those living more that twenty-five miles from the legislature will receive an additional $1,000 plus reimbursement for fifty-two trips between their place of residence and Halifax.

In discussing the need to pay members adequately so as to attract good people to public life, the commissioners recognized the difficult lot of the elected politician, observing, 'the Member of the Assembly must act as legislator, negotiator, ombudsman, social worker, public relations officer and perform several other tasks at almost any hour of the day or night, often seven days a week and nearly 365 days a year. It is a role with no job security beyond the next election, with the members term of office subject to public endorsement or rejection at the polls every three or four years.'[25]

The question of expenses has been a recent public issue in Nova Scotia. Three former members have been charged with falsifying their expense claims; two were found guilty, and the third agreed to repay certain overpayments, but has now declared personal bankruptcy. The upshot of all of this was the 'Billy Joe MacLean bill,' or to be correct, 'An act respecting reasonable limits for membership in the House of Assembly,' which is an amendment to the House of Assembly Act. The October 1986 act was aimed directly at MacLean, who had pleaded guilty to falsifying his expense accounts but had refused to resign his seat. It stated, in part, that any person found guilty of a crime which is punishable by a prison term of more than five years cannot be nominated, or elected, or serve in the House for five years following the conclusion of the punishment.[26] According to one public opinion poll, 88.4 per cent of respondents agreed with the government's action to expel MacLean.[27] The one-day session to expel the member for Inverness South cost the taxpayers $8,000! However, the chief justice of the trial division of the Nova Scotia

Supreme Court ruled that the section of the act which prevented a person from running for elected office was unconstitutional under the Charter of Rights. MacLean was subsequently re-elected as an Independent in a February 1987 by-election, but was defeated in the 1988 general election.

Women have not fared well in Nova Scotia politics. Only six women have been elected to the Nova Scotia House and only one has served in cabinet. The largest number of women elected at one time is three, in 1984 and in 1988. The election of Alexa McDonough of the NDP in 1981 ruffled the House's club-like atmosphere. Mrs McDonough was not the first woman elected but she was the first female party leader and, at the time, the only woman in the House. In 1981 a prominent Conservative had argued successfully that his party should not run any women candidates in 1981, and they did not. McDonough found her colleagues cool, one even going so far as to say at an evening soirée that 'she was the most dangerous person in the House.' Her battle over the future of the New Democratic Party with fellow member Paul MacEwan was bitter and resented by many members of the public.[28] McDonough has from time to time broken the parliamentary club rules and the conventions of the House, particularly in public statements about salaries and the committee system. Such openness is apparently frowned upon by at least some other members.

One of the major problems confronting MLAs is their own behaviour in the House. Certainly no one expects any legislature to be as pristine as a bridge club, but no one wants it to be considered as Nova Scotia's version of Animal House either. This is not a new situation. Indeed, as Murray Beck points out, it is part of a long-standing tradition.[29]

The House has essentially no security system. There is one 'plainclothes' but armed Halifax policeman on duty in the gallery during the session. Twice, once concerning the Michelin bill in 1979 and once on the establishment of a sanitary landfill project in 1976, demonstrations forced the Speaker to adjourn the House and clear the galleries. This lack of security does not appear to concern the members, although it certainly is a concern to Speakers both past and present.

Political life in Nova Scotia can be lengthy, as Angus L. Macdonald and Robert Stanfield have illustrated. At the present time, though, the average period of service for the House is 5.9 years. The father of the House is John Buchanan who was first elected in 1967. It appears that the average age of members is decreasing over that of a generation ago; as of October 1988, it was 47.8 years. The House has been a white male bastion for many years. In 1988, among those elected there were twelve businessmen, twelve teachers, three physicians, and eight lawyers (only one of whom was in opposition). But the background of members is becoming more diversified, although it is still accurate to say that the majority of members come from the middle class. Currently there are no members who might be classified as 'hourly employed,' though none of the members can be classified as members of the establishment. The lawyers, for example, are not members of any of the large prestigious law firms. Of those elected in 1984, 23.1 per cent had been elected to a municipal council, while no one had been elected to Parliament. In 1984, 19.2 per cent had received a secondary school education, 44.2 per cent had attended a post-secondary educational institution, and 36.5 per cent had obtained post-graduate degrees (including law).

Religion has played a considerable part in Nova Scotia politics in the past. For example, Halifax-Cornwallis was always considered to be a Catholic seat until George Mitchell was elected there in 1970. Similarly, the neighbouring constituency of Halifax-Citadel was a Protestant seat, also until 1970. John Buchanan maintains that he never would have gone into politics if Halifax-Atlantic, which was created prior to the 1967 election, instead of Halifax-Chebucto had become a Catholic seat in 1967. Today, fortunately for all, religion is no longer a dominant factor in the selection of candidates.

'In Nova Scotia,' Dalton Camp has written, 'politicians are either looked up to or looked down upon ... The quality of the chieftain matters a good deal to Nova Scotians.'[30] One might say the same is true of the House of Assembly. Nova Scotians continue to respect their political institutions, but they also regard them with their native respect for tradition, and their inbred cynicism towards politics. The members are justly proud of the history of their institution.

The rise of the NDP in the Halifax-Dartmouth region has had a major impact, not only on the composition of the House but on the performance of the members. Much of the NDP's new strength has come at the expense of the Liberals. Thus, the Liberals as the official opposition are not only attempting to dislodge the Progressive Conservative government, they are also doing their utmost to keep the NDP in third place. The House of Assembly, because of its prominence in the media, is the principal ongoing forum for this struggle. The Liberals naturally use the session to promote their own ends and to attack the government. Interestingly, they have not attacked the NDP in the House as vigorously as one would have expected, given the NDP's encroachment on their urban support in recent provincial elections.

The NDP attempt to prove to the public that they are 'the real opposition,' and are the party most concerned with the major issues of the day. The current Nova Scotia situation is rather similar to that of Ontario in the 1960s and 1970s when the NDP, led by Donald C. MacDonald and Stephen Lewis, claimed to be the real opposition. On certain issues, the Nova Scotia NDP has mounted a more effective opposition to the Conservative government than have the Liberals. However, the results of the 1988 election were a devastating blow to the NDP: they did not make their cherished breakthrough and appear destined to remain the third party in the House.

The Progressive Conservatives, who in 1988 saw their majority reduced from thirty to four, can no longer act with disdain toward the opposition as they did before the election. The Tories must take the House, particularly question period, more seriously than they have in the past. One expects a more vigorous performance from the government benches in 1989.

The Cape Breton Labour Party was but a blip on the electoral map, existing from 1984 to 1988. It was Paul MacEwan's personal vehicle for continuing his war with his former colleagues in the NDP. MacEwan, who was first elected in 1970, was expelled from the NDP in 1980 for his refusal to follow party discipline and policies. His impact on the Assembly has been negative. His virulent attacks on NDP leader Alexa McDonough, though within the rules of debate, have not been well received outside the House. Although MacEwan is an excellent constituency person and was re-elected as an independent in 1988, his impact on the party structure within the Assembly will be minimal at best, unless a minority government occurs.

Although Premier John Buchanan, Vincent MacLean, the Liberal leader, and Alexa McDonough tend to dominate the House, one cannot say that the Nova Scotia Assembly is as 'leader dominated' as it was in the days of Angus L. Macdonald or Robert Stanfield. The days of the powerful leader who could, with his mere presence, control the House are a thing of the past.

The future health of the Nova Scotia House of Assembly rests upon the members' ability to reform the committee system. In order that good people be recruited to public life, it is not only important to see that they are paid well, but also necessary that they know they can have a meaningful input into the policy process. As David Black, drawing on his background as one of Nova Scotia's first interns in 1986, has stated: 'On the assumption that most Members have been elected because they are able and intelligent, it must be viewed as a great loss to the public that Members' skills are not better used. Strengthened committees with broader functions would increase the opportunities for Members to contribute their ideas and abilities to the government process.'[31]

The size of the House is one of its greatest assets; the back-bencher can have a feeling of involvement in the parliamentary process. The problem of personal disillusionment with the political process which besets back-benchers in some assemblies is not a significant issue in Nova Scotia. Of course, certain members are always going to be dissatisfied with their lot on the backbench, and no reform will change this fact.

The very nature of government in the positive state, as well as the adversarial nature of politics, means that any assembly will be dominated by the cabinet. Nova Scotia's House is no exception. Nevertheless, the members do take advantage of their opportunity to participate in the policy process. The reformed rules have given the members, especially those in opposition, an opportunity to become more effective, not only in the policy process, but also in holding the government accountable for its stewardship.

Politics is a social occupation, and, like all such undertakings, is altered whenever the actors are changed. The atmosphere and effectiveness of the Assembly will undoubtedly be altered by the results of the 1988 election, particularly the fact that the Conservatives hold no seats in Cape Breton. Changes in the media, including its increased competitive nature, will mean that the House will be given greater coverage than in the past. This increased publicity will help to improve the members' effectiveness in holding the government accountable, for all members will wish to show their constituents they are working diligently.

The party system is a positive aspect, for the warfare among the three of them keeps one and all on their toes. One suspects that the party fights will only increase in the future as the three of them are as firmly rooted in the province's tradition as is the fishery.

DAVID L.E. PETERSON

NEW BRUNSWICK

A bilingual assembly for a bilingual province

The political institutions in the Maritime provinces have much in common. Perhaps the most distinctive aspect of New Brunswick's Legislative Assembly is its bilingual nature – as befits Canada's only bilingual province. The relationship between French and English in the Assembly is all the more noteworthy because, generally speaking, the cultures live 'together, yet apart.'[1] Of course, New Brunswick became distinct in another respect following the 1987 election when the Liberal party led by Frank McKenna won all the seats in the legislature. It is, for the moment, the only province in Canada with no official opposition. Parliamentarians, political scientists, and ordinary citizens are watching with keen interest to see how the government and the unofficial opposition parties will deal with this situation.

Language and Politics in New Brunswick History

Every Legislative Assembly reflects the political and social values of its society. The political culture of a society consists of beliefs, attitudes, and opinions about the political world that are widely shared by members of that society.

Initially a part of Nova Scotia, New Brunswick was poorly represented in the government of the province at Halifax. Disaffection between the populations north and south of the Bay of Fundy prevailed until August 1784 when that area of Nova Scotia north of the bay became the province of New Brunswick.

Sir Guy Carleton was appointed governor of New Brunswick in August 1784 and chaired the first meeting of the Legislative Council. Its nine members were selected in England on the King's instructions to Carleton. Although the council represented respectability, the members were drawn from a narrow segment of society so that the common people looked upon it as an aristocratic body and it soon became unpopular. The governor held total control through his power over the purse and there was no way to check his authority.

New Brunswick entered Confederation in 1867 as a bicameral legislature with a Legislative Council as well as a House of Assembly. The province soon realized that, considering its financial difficulty, the upper house was an unnecessary appendage, and in 1892 it was abolished. The ingenious device used in this instance, since the Legislative Council could veto any bill aimed at eliminating itself, was to wait until attrition had reduced its numbers to such a point that the appointment of a group of pro-abolitionists would carry the day.[2]

The different ethnic groups have settled in separate regions of the province. The French and English are roughly divided by an imaginary line drawn from northwest to southeast.[3] The three main Acadian concentrations are in the northwest, northeast, and southeast corners of the province, the 'French' counties being Gloucester, Kent, and 'la République du Madawaska,' while Restigouche, Victoria, and Westmorland (containing Moncton) are 'mixed' English and French. The English population consists primarily of Loyalist descendants – in the southwest part of the province, Yorkshiremen, and a large number of Irish in Saint John, Moncton, Restigouche, and the Miramichi river basin.[4] Ethnic politics have played a predominant role in New Brunswick politics, certainly during the most recent elections. As Edmund Aunger has expressed it: 'The nature of elite political culture in New Brunswick is aptly summed up in one traditional expression: bonne entente.'[5]

Katherine MacNaughton, describing ethnic relations in the Legislative Assembly during the nineteenth century, noted: 'For the most part a spirit of "See how well we get along together" prevailed in the Legislature. It was perhaps not difficult for a majority group to exhibit such a spirit toward a relatively small minority sensible enough to display a pleasing combination of dignity and modesty.'[6] In 1913, when the Speaker requested an Acadian MLA to address his remarks in English, this request was overridden by a motion presented by English members, who defended the use of French in the Assembly as 'a courtesy from English-speaking gentlemen to French-speaking gentlemen.'[7] While such examples are largely representative of the tradition of bonne entente which continues to exist in New Brunswick, the pattern is not without its exceptions.[8]

The official report of the debates of the Legislative Assembly for 1885 notes that an interesting feature of the discussion on the Portland Revisor's List bill was a series of speeches in French. This was evidently unusual, for one of the speakers, who afterwards spoke in English, said he was proud that 'the language spoken by so large a proportion of the people of New Brunswick had been heard in the House.' He also thanked the members for 'their kindness towards himself and all who spoke the same language.' In 1890 three speeches in French on a bill relating to the Colonization Company of the Maritime Provinces were received 'with loud applause from both sides of the House.' As far as the legislature was concerned, the nineteenth century seems to have drawn to a close on a note of cordiality. This, of course, does not mean that the minority abandoned its claims for recognition.[9]

Until recently, Acadians had to speak in English in the legislature if they wished to be widely understood, but since 1967 the Chamber has operated on a bilingual basis with simultaneous interpretation.[10] Since about 1960, after considerable improvement of their educational system, Acadians have made their influence felt politically.

In 1981 the population consisted of 53.5 per cent British background, 36.4 per cent of French descent, and 10 per cent others, most of whom were French-English combinations. In this context, the Acadians are more capable of resisting assimilation than are French-speaking minorities in other provinces.[11]

New Brunswick's Official Languages Act, introduced in 1968 following the earlier appearance of a white paper on the subject, more or less coincided with similar developments in Ottawa. It provided that services should be available equally in English and French in schools, courts, government agencies, the public service, and the legislature. Although it was largely a statement of principle, and not all of its provisions were immediately implemented, the effect of this legislation, in addition to the program for equal opportunity, was to allow Acadians to be integrated into the mainstream of the province, something that most objective observers considered to be long overdue.[12]

Generally speaking, the move to official bilingualism in the province has been a smooth one, leaving aside a few extremists on either side, and both major parties have supported it. In 1981-82 New Brunswick was the only province to voluntarily commit itself to official bilingualism in the new constitution.[13]

Political Parties

Although twenty-four premiers led New Brunswick through its first one hundred years after Confederation, each spent only four years in office, on average, and most left little mark. Seven stand out in terms of longevity: King, Blair, Hazen, Veniot, McNair, Robichaud, and Hatfield. Of these, Blair served for thirteen years, McNair for twelve, and Robichaud for ten. Richard Hatfield, elected in 1970, served longer than any of his predecessors in New Brunswick until his crushing defeat in 1987.[14]

Political parties in New Brunswick were slow to develop into their modern, disciplined form and seven different regimes can be identified in the 1867-1960 period. Four Conservative periods alternated with three Liberal ones, the longest being the twenty-five years of Liberal rule between 1883 and 1908. It would be misleading to think of the early period in terms of a modern two-party system, however. Party discipline was not strong, so governments of the day were often coalitions of Liberals and Conservatives, and the labels usually used were those of 'Government' and 'Opposition.'[15]

After 1886, few candidates ran for office without a link either to the government or to the opposition.[16] In 1890 Premier Blair issued the first government election manifesto in the province. Not until 1899 did the opposition present a unified manifesto. As time went on there was increasing pressure for the government party to call itself Liberal and for the opposition to don the Conservative label, but this practice was not widely adopted. The provincial (Liberal) government was favoured with increased Acadian support after Wilfrid Laurier became the first French Canadian to lead a national party, and Premier Blair joined his Nova Scotian counterpart, W.S. Fielding, in the federal Laurier cabinet in 1896.[17]

Despite the results of the election of 13 October 1987, New Brunswick does possess one of Canada's purest two-party systems. Ever since Confederation there have been two major parties in the province and they have alternated in power at regular intervals, most commonly after serving two terms each.[18]

The 1944 campaign was remarkable because for the first time the opposition party explicitly used a party label (Progressive Conservative), the name adopted by the federal party shortly before.[19]

The first election to the House of Assembly in 1785 returned twenty-six members. Gradually that number has increased to the fifty-eight seats the legislature has had since 1967. Constituencies used to be linked to county boundaries and were represented by more than one member, but since 1974 each constituency has elected a single representative.

New Brunswick's two major parties, Liberal and Progressive Conservative, have been closely matched, with each receiving nearly one-half of the vote in recent years. In the 1970 election the Liberals received 48.6 per cent and the Conservatives 48.4 per cent of the total vote. Both parties received similar proportions in the elections of 1974 and 1978.[20] The 1982 election resulted in a significant change in that popular voting pattern when the Progressive Conservatives received 47.1 per cent, the Liberals 41.0 per cent, and the New Democratic party 10.1 per cent, while the Parti Acadien received less than 1 per cent of the popular vote. In 1987 the Liberal party swept to power capturing 60 per cent of the popular vote while the Progressive Conservatives received 28.4 per cent, the New Democrats 10.5 per cent, and Independents 0.5 per cent.

There is a long tradition of party discipline. 'Party votes' are promoted in each party by the whip and are to be contrasted with 'free votes.' In New Brunswick, 100 per cent of the recorded votes during the fiftieth parliament (1983-87) can be classified as 'party votes.' Premier Hatfield once stated that all votes by his or the government caucus were free votes. His definition of a free vote is rather simplistic; it is doubtful that all members of his caucus would agree that they have been totally free of party discipline in voting. The imposition of party discipline provides the government with the assurance that its legislative program will be passed intact and it is supported as a means of maintaining the viability of parties in the parliamentary system.

In New Brunswick, and probably in other legislatures as well, when a member feels obliged to cast a 'free vote' which is contrary to his party's position, and feels the pressure of party discipline not to do so, he very often exercises his free vote by absenting himself from the Chamber during the vote.

Politics in New Brunswick have been dominated by pragmatism and, as in the other Maritime provinces, one would look in vain for any consistent ideological differences between the Liberals and Conservatives.[21] Members and governments have usually run on their records, and the challengers have regularly charged them with patronage and corruption.[22]

The Legislative Assembly

Writing about New Brunswick politics in the 1950s Dalton Camp 'marvelled at the elaborate, mysterious irrelevancies of the New Brunswick legislature, the interminable hours of meaningless debate, and the dramatic, highly stylized interventions of Premier McNair.'[23] To others '... the proceedings seemed less a series of debates than a program of recitations. Members did not speak from notes, but read directly from prepared texts.'[24] Unfortunately the tradition of members reading from prepared texts continues in the 1980s.

Professor P.G. Fitzpatrick describes the behaviour in the Assembly as appearing infantile to the political scientist, but as 'the boys havin' a bit of fun,'[25] to the people of New Brunswick.

Leadership in New Brunswick politics is often not a matter of putting forth ideas or initiating well-defined policies. A visitor to the Legislative Assembly in Fredericton is more likely to hear a member advise the Assembly that maple syrup time has come to the Keswick than a debate on French Canada's role within Confederation. Even before the present one-party monopoly of seats in the legislature, question time was not used to challenge policy, but rather to query ministers about expenditures, in hopes of discovering patronage.[26]

A typical legislature is divided by partisan feelings, and occasionally events have provoked bitter actions. Personal attacks on the leadership of the government have led to judicial inquiries and trials, and resulted in irreparable damage to personal relationships between members of the Assembly. Discussion with older members leaves the impression that a more gentlemanly code of conduct between members of opposite parties existed in past years and that social interactions were more common. That is not to say that debate was not, at times, very heated, but outside the Chamber, debate did not have such significant negative effect on personal relationships.

The executive council in New Brunswick has a record of relatively low rate of turnover. Major cabinet changes – defined as the turnover of the first minister or half of his ministers – have occurred, on average, only slightly more than every five years. Often these changes have amounted only to a shuffle of the existing ministers to new posts, rather than a wholesale injection of new blood. The major mechanism for such changes has been the decision of the electorate at the polls; the electoral returns have ensured a changing cabinet by returning the opposition party to power about once each decade.[27]

Most of New Brunswick's legislators carry out their duties on a full-time basis. By profession, the 1987 Legislative Assembly was composed of approximately 34.5 per cent businessmen, 24 per cent teachers, 7 per cent lawyers, 6 per cent retired persons, and 28.5 per cent other (undertakers, executives, consultants, social workers, civil servants, technicians, security personnel, and salesmen). By contrast, the Legislative Assembly of 1948 consisted of 46 per cent businessmen, 23 per cent professional people, 21 per cent farmers, and 10 per cent tradesmen. Before the 1987 election, the average age of a legislator was 49.5 years; he or she had spent approximately 11 years in the House, and the thirty-seven Progressive Conservative members had spent an average of 5.5 years either in cabinet or as Speaker. The youngest MLA was 36 and the oldest, 74. One member was a legislative veteran of 35 years. Approximately 65.5 per cent used English only as their mother tongue, while 34.5 per cent were bilingual. Only three legislators, or 5 per cent, were female but over 90 per cent were married with children. More than half of them had university training and approximately 67 per cent had either technical training or a university degree.

Following the 1987 Liberal sweep to power, the composition of the legislature changed. The current members of the New Brunswick Legislative Assembly have spent an average of 3.9 years in the House, and the average age of a legislator is 46. Approximately 35 per cent are bilingual. Eight (14 per cent) of the legislators are women and three, or 14 per cent, of the twenty-one member cabinet are women. By profession, 24 per cent of the 1988 members of the Assembly are teachers, 22 per cent businessmen, 12 per cent lawyers, 9 per cent tradespersons, 7 per cent doctors, and the remaining 26 per cent consist of engineers, farmers, salesmen, broadcasters, public servants, and a historian.

Sixty-two per cent of our legislators have a university degree and 88 per cent graduated from either university or technical school.

In 1889 the then premier of New Brunswick foresaw with horror that, if women got the vote, someday a woman might become a member of the House. He was quoted as saying, 'She might even occupy the Speaker's chair ... Oh, no, that must never happen. No woman should have a vote.' A review of the 1913 debates illustrate members' responses to a delegation of suffragettes from Saint John who went to the legislature to lobby. Members frankly voiced their opposition but tried to convince the ladies it was only because they didn't want to bring them down to a man's level. One member said that it was because he held women in the highest admiration that he would deeply regret to see a woman dragged from the height upon which she stood and brought to the arena of politics. By 1918 women had been given a full federal franchise and in 1919 the term 'male person' was struck from the voter qualifications and replaced with the phrase 'a person whether male or woman, married or unmarried.'

Women were denied the right to run for the Assembly until 1934. On 27 June 27 1935 Frances Fish became the first woman to run in a provincial election. However, it was not until 1967 that Brenda Robertson, who is now a senator, became the first female member of the Legislative Assembly of New Brunswick. The black and native populations have not been successful in having members elected to the New Brunswick legislature.

The October 1987 general election brought to the Legislative Assembly the first Acadian female, Aldéa Landry, president of the executive council and minister responsible for intergovernmental affairs. A lawyer, she was elected for the electoral district of Shippegan-les-îles.

Administering the House

The Speaker is more than a presiding officer, more than an administrator: he is the very embodiment of parliamentary democracy. The office of Speaker in New Brunswick follows closely the Canadian model. The Speaker has been assuming a far greater responsibility for the administrative duties of his office, which have evolved from a part-time role to a position of full ministerial status. New Brunswick Speakers have yet to assert complete independence from any political allegiance as is done in Britain. Upon election, the British Speaker renounces all party affiliation, and when seeking re-election to the House, runs as the Speaker; his return is virtually assured as he is not likely to be opposed by the major parties. Since 1786, forty-nine men have occupied the Speaker's chair in New Brunswick. During that period each has brought to the Chair his own individual background and reputation, coupled with an individual style and technique by which he attempted to maintain the Chair's authority.

In the 1978 election Premier Hatfield's PCs won thirty seats compared to the Liberals' twenty-eight. He cleverly asked a Liberal member, Robert McCready, who was a former Speaker, to accept the speakership. Mr. McCready agreed, against the wishes of his leader and his party. In consequence, he had a difficult time with Liberal members during the next two sessions. At the same time, the government experienced some tense moments in the process of surviving, especially when two members were ill. Mr McCready subsequently joined the Conservatives and was eventually appointed minister of transportation.

In a 1984 by-election New Brunswickers elected Peter Trites, a teacher from East Saint John, their second New Democratic party representative. Mr Trites's adherence to the NDP was short-lived; he sat as a New Democrat during the 1985 session but joined the Liberal party before the 1986 session opened.

The clerk of the House is the chief procedural adviser to the Speaker and to the members of the Assembly. He is also the chief administrative officer or deputy head of the Office of the Legislative Assembly. In 1978 the Legislative Assembly created the Legislative Administration Committee, composed of two cabinet ministers, two opposition members, two government back-bench members, and chaired by the Speaker. The Legislative Administration Committee is responsible for the day-to-day operations of the Legislative Assembly, and the clerk of the Assembly is responsible to the committee for the administrative affairs of the Assembly. With the establishment of this committee, the Legislative Assembly began to exercise more control over its affairs, most of which had previously slipped away from its control. The board has been a very important tool in strengthening the role of the legislature against the executive branch of government. The establishment of the Legislative Administration Committee saw the beginning of a process of establishing an office of the Legislative Assembly with permanent senior staff in the form of clerk, clerk assistants, and accounting officer. Prior to 1979, clerks of the Legislative Assembly were appointed at the pleasure of the government and, understandably, were perceived as being partisan government appointments.

Reporting of parliamentary debates began long before members of the press were first admitted to the press gallery of the House of Commons in Westminster or in New Brunswick. Thomas Curson Hansard, son of Luke Hansard, the printer of the House of Commons at Westminster, purchased the *Political Register* in 1829 and began *Hansard's Parliamentary Debates*, which continued as an entirely private undertaking, compiled mainly from newspaper reports until 1855. In New Brunswick the first contract for reporting the debates was awarded in 1836. Subsequently, the contract was given to a newspaper reporter 'for whatever small compensation that the House, at the close of the session, might think fit to award.' In 1942 the custom of tendering for official reporting came to an end and the duties were assigned to the office of the clerk of the House. The first reporter, a sports reporter for a local radio station, held the part-time position of official reporter for twenty-one years.

The manner in which members are reimbursed for their work varies a great deal from one jurisdiction to the next. Members of the New Brunswick legislature share secretarial services on a nine-to-one basis. Mailing privileges are minimal and research assistants are assigned to the caucus in a ratio of about twenty to one. One of the most glaring deficiencies in support services to members is for their constituencies. New Brunswick members do not have constituency offices or staff. As reforms are introduced and as the role of the private member has been enhanced, members require increasing amounts of support to allow them to carry out their duties. In New Brunswick, for example, the committee system has been expanded. As a result, members are increasingly serving on a full-time basis and make ever greater demands on the resources of their caucus.

Committees and Accountability

The Assembly is the principal forum for the clarification of government policy and its scrutiny on behalf of the public by the opposition. The oral question period is without doubt the most interesting part of the parliamentary day as far as the public is concerned. Written questions put to ministers provide much information, as do motions for the tabling of documents and correspondence. The use of both devices has increased from an average of 53 instances per year between 1945 and 1949 to 137 per year between 1971 and 1975. In 1986, of the 108 motions introduced in the House, 74 were tabling motions.

The most intensive exploration of government activity occurs in the committees of Supply, Estimates, Public Accounts, and Crown Corporations. In Committee of Supply, detailed probing of estimates is possible but, since all are dealt with by the Committee of the Whole House, many remain undiscussed; moreover, the opposition tends to concentrate on one issue in an attempt to inflict maximum damage upon the government, and in pre-election years the exploration of policy is generally overshadowed by the search for scandal. Sessions open with leisurely debate on the speech from the throne, gain momentum through the budget speech, and culminate in the simultaneous consideration of accounts, estimates, and legislation in marathon sittings.

During the 1986 session an average of three hours was spent on the estimates of each department, although the Department of Tourism, Recreation and Heritage required five hours, while the Department of Health and Community Services required ten hours. During the 1985 session even less time was spent on each department. The average per department was slightly over one hour, with a maximum of five hours and a minimum of ten minutes spent on a department.

Quietly, almost unnoticed by many people, a major change in the committee structures took place in 1986. Gone are the old committees with large membership and minimal responsibilities. In their place, the House established a system with two types of committees. The new standing committees include those on Crown Corporations, Estimates, and the Ombudsman. The House retained its standing committees on Private Bills, Privileges, Procedure, Public Accounts, Law Amendments, and its Legislative Administration Committee. The committees were given budgets and the authority to spend the funds deemed necessary.

During the last session, the Standing Committee on Estimates was so successful that concern was expressed by both sides of the House that the estimates would be concluded too quickly. The members agreed that when the tenth department had been completed, the standing committee would no longer meet.

Recently the Standing Committee on Crown Corporations accepted the responsibility for a major review of petroleum pricing practices in New Brunswick. In addition to the standing committees, provision was made for the appointment of small select committees, composed of a maximum of five members. The House appointed five select committees with broad orders of reference, in the hopes that the committees themselves would be freer to set their own course and not be restricted or limited by narrow orders. There is now ample scope for private members to expand their parliamentary activities, if they so wish.

In the context of New Brunswick's parliamentary tradition, it is fair to say that these changes should be viewed as major advances in legislative reform. The next important reform will be the introduction of a new Legislative Assembly Act which, if approved, will improve the administrative structure to provide more efficient and professional services for members.

SUSAN MCCORQUODALE

NEWFOUNDLAND

Personality, party, and politics

The legislative history of Newfoundland is unique in at least one particular: Newfoundland is probably the only country in the world that voluntarily gave up self-government. The date was 1934 and the word 'voluntarily' should be put in quotation marks. The Great Depression really left the political leaders of the colony with little choice. The population was small and dependent on the export of a single commodity. When the world price of fish dropped sharply, it added the final straw to a debt burden inherited from the building of a railway at the turn of the century and the costs of World War I. More generally, Newfoundland was comparatively late in winning self-government. Its first Assembly was not elected until 1833, so perhaps the attachment to self-government was less secure. There had been Englishmen (and Irishmen) more or less settled on the island for one hundred years before they asked for, and the imperial power granted, first representative, and then in 1855 responsible, government. In the 1930s a poor and scattered population was in no position to resist Britain's insistence that an appointed commission to govern Newfoundland was the price of financial help.

The effects of the loss of an elected, responsible assembly for the fifteen years between 1934 and 1949 are not altogether clear. It has been suggested that the period of a 'rest from politics' allowed old quarrels to die, thereby setting the stage for the new era. Others argue that the values of the bad old days merely slept and were awakened again during the Smallwood years.[1] What is clear is that while many Newfoundlanders felt a terrible sense of betrayal for the end of their status as an independent member of the Commonwealth, others felt a sense of relief that the struggles of the past were over.

The making of this choice bitterly divided the society along denominational and regional lines and left a legacy which took the political community many years to heal. For all factions, however, it must have been a proud day when the twenty-eight members of the Newfoundland House of Assembly (twenty-two Liberals, five Progressive Conservatives, and one Independent) met on 11 July 1949 after fifteen years of silence.

In the first years after Confederation in 1948 the Liberal premier, J. R. Smallwood, dominated the inexperienced House as he dominated the government. The Progressive Conservative party was a long time emerging from its tag as anti-confederate Roman Catholic in a province two-thirds Protestant and pro-confederation.

The Study of Legislatures

Today an assessment of a provincial legislature, or any legislature for that matter, usually adopts a functional approach. It is widely recognized that the law-making role of legislatures has long since passed to executives, especially those that control disciplined parliamentary majorities. A functional approach allows us to see legislatures as adaptable institutions that do a variety of things in a political system.[2]

Let us examine the Newfoundland legislature from the point of view of three principal functions it performs: policy-making, representation, and maintaining political stability.

Policy-Making

As in other Canadian provinces, policy in Newfoundland is for the most part made by the cabinet and the bureaucracy rather than by the legislature. Yet even in legislatures foreordained to approve policies initiated by others, there is a deliberative function to be performed. Discussion of issues in the legislature serves to teach and inform the mass public as well as the political elites. Moreover, the views of parliamentarians, privately and publicly expressed, can lead governments to alter proposals before they are pushed through the assembly.

If a part-time assembly is to strengthen its hand vis-à-vis the full-time executive, then one obvious reform would be longer sessions. In the case of Newfoundland the evidence is mixed. Under Premier Smallwood the average number of sitting days per legislature never exceeded fifty-three. When Brian Peckford became premier in 1979 he introduced a regular fall sitting which increased the average to eighty sitting days between 1979 and 1985. But in 1986 the policy was reversed, and fall sessions were eliminated. As a result the number of sitting days is returning to those of the Smallwood era. In addition, the number of *hours* that the Assembly sits is also declining, as evening sessions have been discontinued, largely to make room for committee meetings. Overall, the legislature remains very much a part-time body.

The main reform designed to strengthen the policy effectiveness of the legislature has been the gradual introduction of a committee system. The aim was to allow members to be more thorough in their questioning because they would be more familiar with a particular subject-matter. In a typical year (1970) before the standing orders were amended in 1979, *Hansard* records that the overwhelming focus of interest was the government's spending estimates, which took up approximately 50 per cent of the debates compared with the next largest item, the throne speech debate, which took up only about 15 per cent of the time.

When he took office in 1979 Premier Peckford decided to streamline the rules and to involve members in more effective use of legislative time. As well as the fall session, which was to be restricted totally to legislation, he created more standing and select committees. These changes were meant to 'broaden the role of Members' and show the people that 'the Legislature was very important to their lives.'[3] The standing orders were amended to provide for a new committee system designed to review the estimates and to limit speaking time (forty-five minutes for members, ninety minutes for the premier and the leader of the opposition). This was the culmination of changes that had been first introduced in 1974. Five standing committees were provided: Government Services, Social Services, Resources, Public Accounts, and Privileges and Elections. The latter two committees had limited membership of seven and five respectively; the estimates committees had a flexible membership of between seven and seventeen.

The standing committees were to sit 'whether or not the House was in Session, adjourned or prorogued.' They would be free to set their own hours of sitting but were also enjoined not to meet when the House was sitting, except by leave of the House. They were empowered to send for persons, papers, and records (except when the House otherwise ordered).

The most significant amendment to the standing orders provided that the estimates committees were to be limited to not more than seventy-five hours of debate. What appears at first to be a generous gift turns out in fact to put strict limits on debate. Three hours were allotted for each of the eighteen departmental estimates; interim supply, debated in Committee of the Whole, was allowed ten hours; and three hours were taken up with the report stage of each of the three estimate committees. This brings the process up to about sixty-seven hours and does not leave much time for the final stage, which is a debate in Committee of the Whole for the supply requirements of the Consolidated Revenue Fund, the legislature, and the Executive Council. The final constraint on the estimates committees is SO 120, which provides that at the conclusion of fifteen sitting days following the reference of estimates to a committee, all questions needed to carry every subhead of each head of expenditure are to be put without debate. In sum, seventy-five hours works out to about three hours for each department, plus nine hours to report the work of the committees. There is to be no filibustering in committee, moreover. Fifteen days after reference to committee the estimates must be put. There were flaws in the previous system, as the chairman of one of the first meetings under the new standing orders pointed out, but the new rules have in turn produced new problems.

The principal venue for the committee meetings is the Colonial Building in downtown St John's. Built in 1850, it had provided space for the Provincial Archives when the House of Assembly moved into the Confederation Building in 1960. When the Committee on Government Services met there on 26 July 1979 the chairman noted that this was the first time since November 1959 that there had been an official legislative meeting in the building. He added that under the previous system discussion of the estimates had been known to go on for eighteen hours at a stretch and be both volatile and adversarial. He hoped that the committee system would 'detract' from this negative aspect.

How has the new committee system worked in practice? Has the Newfoundland legislature found new power to effect policy or has the government succeeded in sidetracking the opposition? There are two methods whereby we might make an assessment of the work and effectiveness of the committees: their membership and the proceedings. The membership is important for two reasons. First, if it shifts too much, if there is no continuity of either chairmen or members, if there is a lot of substitution of members, then it may indicate that very little expertise is being built up. Secondly, does the government use the committees as a testing ground for possible future cabinet ministers? If so, then it seems unlikely that the committees will become a lively forum for questioning government policy. The proceedings can tell us something about the balance of time spent, about witness, and about the importance of media reporting.

Membership of Standing Committees

We begin then with the Standing Committee on Government Services. It is responsible for five departments: Municipal Affairs and Housing, Public Works and Services, Labour and Manpower, Finance, and Transportation and Communication.

Of the twenty-one members who served on the committee between 1979 and 1986 only seven served more than one year; the average was two years. The longest time served by any chairman was three years; there have been four chairmen in six years. Remembering that since 1979 there has not been a change of government, this does not seem an adequate record of continuity, and it is doubtful whether the members of the committee have been able to build up either expertise or collegiality.

The record for the Committee on Social Services is somewhat better. The committee is responsible for the overseeing of six departments: Education, Social Services, Justice, Consumer Affairs and Environment, Health, and Culture, Recreation and Youth. In this case, of the twenty-two members who have served on the committee between 1979 and 1985 only two have served more than six years, and one of them has been chairman for each of the seven years examined. All the other members have served an average of 1.9 years. While the leadership continuity has been better, the members have rotated on and off the committee much like their colleagues on Government Services.

The Standing Committee on Resources is responsible for the scrutiny of five departments: Rural, Agriculture and Northern Development, Lands and Forests, Fisheries; Mines and Energy; and Tourism, Recreation and Youth. Twenty-one members were appointed to the committee between 1979 and 1984. Here again there is some continuity as regards the chair, which has been held by two members for three and two years respectively (the latter member had been on the committee for each of the five years examined). For the balance of the membership, however, one finds that the average length of service is 1.6 years. The record also shows that at the beginning of nearly every meeting the chairman announced substitutions, which weakens the work of the committee.

The Standing Committee on Public Accounts pre-dates the committees discussed above, meeting for the first time on 17 December 1976. Over the years there had been numerous select committees of the House, but according to the records this was the first meeting of a standing committee of the House of Assembly. The list of witnesses that first day is a roll-call of the senior ranks of the civil service and gives us a glimpse of administrative history. The deputy minister of finance, for instance, noted the changes which had taken place in his department since he was first appointed in September 1974. At that time, twenty-five years after confederation, there were only two professional accountants in the department; now there were ten. There had been in general an upgrading of staff and the regularization of procedures.

Over the eleven years between 1976 and 1986 thirty-one individuals had been appointed to the PAC. Three members had served for five years and six for four years. The balance of twenty-two members (that is 70 per cent of the total membership) had served on average for two years. The first three chairmen (all opposition members) served four, two, and three years respectively. The educational backgrounds and experience of the individuals concerned produced a strong and respected leadership. Two of the chairmen were former leaders of the provincial Liberal party. The strength of the committee chairman was, however, counterbalanced by another factor. The independence of a 'watchdog' committee is weakened if many of its members look to the government for career promotion. Over 60 per cent of the eighteen Progressive Conservatives who have served on the PAC are either current cabinet members, or parliamentary secretaries or assistants. It would appear that the committee is something of a testing ground for future cabinet ministers. Combine this with an unstable and rotating membership and you get, not a cohesive committee with a common purpose, but a ritualistic and symbolic activity.

Overall, what do we learn about the system from the membership of these three committees? Of course, in a parliamentary system a government has the authority and the means to insure that its will prevails, and there is thus in any committee system a large element of futility. Everyone present – chairman, witnesses, and members – knows that the government will not permit the estimates to be changed.[4] The standing orders mean that, regardless of what a committee says, discussion will be limited, and the estimates will be reported out and passed by the House more or less automatically. A cohesive and autonomous committee might be able to use publicity to affect policy, but the practice in Newfoundland of short-term service, coupled with constant substitution, and a highly partisan environment does not make one confident of such an outcome.

Proceedings of Standing Committees

Committees in the Newfoundland House of Assembly were intended, we must assume, to allow for detailed discussion of each department's estimates. A current cabinet minister recently interviewed pointed out that before 1979 the estimates discussions, done in Committee of the Whole, seemed to go on forever. There were no time limits and after two or three hours on any one department, whatever was to be said had been said, and what was left was seemingly endless repetition.

In 1979 when the new standing orders were being implemented, hopes were high for improved effectiveness. The premier saw the new system as an improvement over what had gone before. However, even over the brief span being examined here, disillusionment has set in. At one of the first meetings of the Standing Committee on Social Services in 1979 the chairman remarked: 'In my experience of about seven or eight years in the House of Assembly, never before has a department received such scrutiny or such detailed answers been received and it speaks well for the system.' At the same time, because of the recent change of government, discussion was enlivened when a former minister of health was able to question his successor knowledgeably. On another occasion in 1979 the minister of labour and manpower remarked to the Social Services Committee that

As a Minister who presented his Estimates to Committees and who has done so for the past two years; this is the first time that my Estimates got any scrutiny at all. I was in Municipal Affairs for two years and presented Estimates in the House of Assembly and it became a matter of discussion, for two hours, I think, the first year and three hours the second year, of the Minister's salary where somebody got up on the Opposition side and debated. I got up and debated and it became a budget debate and we did not really get any scrutiny. I think this is a worthwhile process and I hope that hon. Members concur.

As experience with the system has increased some difficulties have surfaced. In the first place, the meetings are run on a fairly tight schedule. In 1984 the Social Services Committee met eight times in about two weeks, putting a considerable strain on the opposition both in preparation time and in meetings. This pressure is compounded when up to three committees meet concurrently. Unless the government allows committees to meet outside hours when the House is in session, it can mean that members of both parties are running back and forth between committee meetings and attendance in the House. This situation does not make for careful, researched questioning of witnesses.

A second problem is press coverage, a matter essential to the work of any legislature, but one which is particularly important to the oversight or scrutiny role of a committee set apart to review the estimates. Politicians need to be seen to be about the people's business, and if there are no public awards, there are likely to be few members willing to spend the time. Often the committee proceedings make reference to the press. One chairman in 1980 ironically thanked the press for their 'sporadic' attendance but went on to acknowledge that night-time meetings were a problem for reporters. If the press are not there, members feel less inclined to come, substitution becomes more frequent, and in general the quality of scrutiny is lessened.

Members are complaining increasingly on the lack of staff support for the committees. At present, the staff of each committee consists of a clerk, whose role is limited to administrative and procedural matters. The staff resources of the library are limited and no library personnel can be assigned to any one committee on anything like a continuing basis. The political parties have research staff, but these too cannot be 'assigned' to a committee. Temporary staff, hired by the committee itself, is unknown in Newfoundland. The absence of staff support weakens the committee system and is one of the important but invisible ways in which the government limits the capacity of the Assembly to investigate policy and hold the government accountable.

The question of accommodations and services for members became a politically charged issue recently. Under pressure from members with leaking office ceilings, in October 1985 the government established a select committee to investigate and report. The committee managed to make fairly sweeping recommendations about separate offices, secretarial help, increased indemnities, and increased travel and constituency benefits without ever putting a dollar figure to the total cost of their recommendations. The report has been allowed to lie fallow for about two years, and it is likely that nothing much will be done to implement it. Perhaps the issue of accommodation will be solved when a new Chamber, still in the planning stages, is completed.

The Honourable James McGrath, chairman of the Special Committee on Reform of the House of Commons, when he appeared before the Special Committee on Accommodations and Services, made an eloquent plea for the physical autonomy of the legislature, by recommending that the Colonial Building, one of the three oldest legislative buildings in Canada, should be restored and refurbished as the site of the meetings of the House of Assembly. Mr McGrath made several other points, particularly about the committee work of any legislature. He commended in particular the rules recently adopted by the Quebec National Assembly. In the end the committee ignored his preference for unpaid work by the chairmen and members of legislative committees and chose instead to recommend a stipend.

A Representative Institution

Election to public office carries with it the implication that part of the member's job is to act on behalf of the electors. This role as intermediary between citizens and government officials (both elected and appointed) is one in which many legislators find satisfaction. In the province of Newfoundland it has historically been the most commonly noted function of an MLA. Members devote a substantial portion of their time and effort to dealing with the problems and requests of their constituents; for the most part these demands emanate from their individuals rather than from groups. For the 50 per cent of Newfoundlanders who live in rural communities (to say nothing of the 32 per cent who live in communities of less than a thousand) a member of the House of Assembly is probably seen less as a legislator than as a representative, able to intercede with the system and to bring home benefits to the district.

For an elected assembly the first questions are probably how many seats, how are the boundaries drawn up, and do they roughly mean one man, one vote? During the first twenty-three years of Confederation there were more than a few problems about this basic issue. Premier Smallwood (1949-72) increased the size of the House twice from its relatively small beginnings. It went up from twenty-eight to thirty-six seats in 1956 and forty-two in 1962. For the latter increase, public interest was less in the number of seats than in the way the boundaries were drawn. The premier made a public defence of the government-drawn boundaries by giving voice to a much-quoted proposition that what mattered in Newfoundland was not a roughly equal number of voters in each district, but a roughly equal division of seats among the province's various religious denominations. It was probably not a coincidence that the results smacked of an equally traditional value: political advantage. The largest constituencies had the unfortunate habit of voting Tory. The last voters' list prepared by Premier Smallwood in 1971 showed the unevenness of the representation. The smallest number of voters was in Labrador South with 2,238 and the largest number was St John's North with 16,879. Labrador voted Liberal; St John's, Tory.

In March 1973 the Conservative government led by Frank Moores proposed legislation, modelled on the federal statute, which established a non-partisan permanent Electoral Boundaries Commission at the same time as it increased the seats in the House from forty-one to fifty-one. The proposed commission, with a mandate to review distribution every ten years, had a chairman appointed by the chief justice of Newfoundland. The three other members were to be appointed by the Speaker. The number of voters in each district was to be roughly equal, plus or minus 25 per cent. The first boundary recommendations from the commission were accepted, with what the premier called only minor 'alterations.'[5]

Ten years later, in July 1983, a second Electoral Districts Boundaries Commission was struck. Once the quotient had been established at 10,917, it worked out that fourteen district boundaries would have to be changed. The commission held public hearings for reaction to its initial proposals and the public interest and response was quite good, both on the island and in Labrador. Amendments were made to give the rural districts smaller populations than the urban ones. The final report, submitted in March 1984, was acted upon by the government and the 1985 election was fought on the basis of the new boundaries.

A second basic issue about elections is their financing. In the immediate post-confederation years the usual way of raising money for elections was by business donation and, occasionally, money from the federal Liberal party. In an attempt to regularize the system, a Select Committee of the House of Assembly was established in June 1981 to report on the issue of 'minimal financing of candidates and parties' in aid of the democratic process. The committee drew a shade over the past and merely noted that 'the history of politics in this century yields a broad catalogue of doubtful expedients resorted to at election time as parties and candidates scramble for funds.'[6] Apart from some recommendations about who is entitled to vote (Canadian citizen, a citizen of the Commonwealth, or a citizen of the Republic of Ireland), dates

(Tuesdays preferred by election officials), or the designation of party on the ballot paper, the principal recommendation of the committee had to do with the 'recognized and registered' political party which would be eligible for public funding ($2 per voter multiplied by a formula related to popular vote). To attain this state parties had to poll a minimum of 15 per cent of the popular vote, elect either a minimum of two members, or have nominated candidates in at least 75 per cent of the districts in the province. These latter provisions were the sticking points of the NDP who until 1985 had always received less than 10 per cent of the vote. So far (1988), while a draft bill has been prepared, the legislation has never been tabled. And one must assume that old habits persist.

The Members of the House

In no Canadian legislature do the social characteristics of the members closely resemble those of the population they represent. The social composition of the Newfoundland House is a matter of some political importance. In Newfoundland a legislature without, say, Roman Catholics, would be widely seen as unrepresentative, not a reflection of the population and thus an uncertain bridge between the political executive and the general population. Is the voice of the legislature a fairly accurate expression of the 'voice of the people'? The members of the Newfoundland House of Assembly, and in particular the members of the Executive Council, are much better educated than is the general population. Moreover, the differences are increasing so far as the cabinet is concerned. An earlier study of the educational background of all cabinet ministers between 1949 and 1967 can be compared with their 1985 counterparts (see table 1).

Table 1
Education, Newfoundland cabinet ministers

	1949-67 (%)	1985 (%)
University degree	39	54
Professional or technical training	35	14
Grade eleven	21	22
Unknown	4	10

Sources: *Parliamentary Guide*, relevant years

Given that 6 per cent of the general population have university degrees, the cabinet ministers, like their counterparts in virtually every executive in the world, are not representative of the population. Starting from a higher base, the cabinet is also reflecting the general rise in educational attainment in the province.

The career patterns of cabinet ministers have shown an interesting shift as well. In the earlier group about 25 per cent of the ministers had been teachers; in 1985 the figure had risen to 36 per cent. It would appear that teaching is a well-trodden path to politics in Newfoundland, whether for Liberals or Tories. From what we know of the voters who support the Progressive Conservative party, many of them are teachers and young professionals, and likely to be urban dwellers. These characteristics are sharply different from the demographic profile of the province.

Denominational balance has been until very recently a critical factor in Newfoundland's political life. Premier Smallwood had made it a point to maintain denominational representation in certain order-in-council appointments, in electoral boundaries, and in his cabinet. In none of these decisions was there ever much of a public outcry about 'old-fashioned' ideas. Although 'Her Majesty's Outport Government' (Gwyn's term) was heavily reliant on outport and Protestant voters, the Smallwood cabinets for a period of twenty years were at least 20 to 30 per cent Roman Catholic.[7]

Times and values are changing, however. A 1985 government publication giving biographical information about cabinet ministers does not even mention religion. For Smallwood, representation from the minority denominations was important for symbolic reasons; for his successors such representation is less significant, partly because the PCs draw from a wider political base. Although the churches remain important in Newfoundland because of the denominational basis of education, the House of Assembly may not have kept pace with the population in its desire to reform the educational system.[8]

Membership in the House can be readily divided into four groups: cabinet ministers, government back-benchers, opposition members, and that small group of members who serve the House as Speaker and Deputy Speaker. Each group has a primary responsibility to stay elected, which means they must 'service and cultivate' their constituency.

For cabinet ministers their day-to-day activity and their primary focus is generally their departmental and Executive Council responsibilities. To aid in their legislative and political responsibility, each minister has authorization to hire an executive assistant (currently paid between $32,000 and $39,000 per year). Additionally, some twelve or thirteen of the current twenty-one cabinet ministers also have press secretaries, also paid about $40,000 a year. Added to this general ministerial staff is one other position: parliamentary assistants. The functions and responsibilities of the latter were spelled out in a minute of council in 1982. The minute outlines 'normal' House of Assembly and government department responsibilities, but in addition three of the parliamentary assistants can accompany 'their' cabinet minister to meetings of the Cabinet Committees on Social Policy and Resource Policy. The PA can 'present the views of the minister' in his or her absence from the meeting, but is specifically barred from any voting rights. The fourth PA is called a parliamentary assistant to the premier and has, as the member for Torngat Mountains, special responsibilities to the premier for Labrador affairs. The minute of council provides further that because of the privileged position and confidential information to which a PA may have access, the conflict of interest (ministers) guidelines may be made applicable to them.

There are in fact very few government back-benchers. The 1987-88 edition of *Canadian Legislatures* notes that 58 per cent of the members of the Newfoundland House of Assembly receive more than the basic indemnity.[9] But when you look only at the government back-benchers the percentage becomes much higher. In March 1987 of the thirty-five Conservative members, twenty-one were cabinet ministers, four were parliamentary assistants, one was Speaker and another Deputy Speaker, and one was government whip. The seven back-benchers who were left must divide themselves to serve on parliamentary committees, as caucus chairman, and so on. Thus, to a remarkable degree, the government benches are filled with members who are orientated toward the work of government, who share in fact in the exercise of power.

The role for opposition members is to attack and be critical. The official positions are few: leader, whip, spokesman for a policy area, and chairman or vice-chairman of a committee. Only some of these carry extra pay. The size of the opposition adds to its difficulties. During the Smallwood years, there were times when the opposition (in a House of thirty-six) was reduced to three members. Since the sweep of the Conservatives in 1971-72 the Liberals have twice been reduced to eight members in a House of fifty-two (1972 and 1982). Since 1972 there have been five leaders of the opposition, and the turnover rate for members is about 25 per cent, about half of what it is in Ottawa.[10] Clearly the leader of the opposition finds it almost impossible to brief a shadow cabinet and present himself to public opinion as a government in waiting.

For an opposition back-bencher, the day-to-day routine in the House can be frustrating. A member might get two questions to a minister every three days. In formal debate it might work out to half an hour every four or five days. Moreover, the tone in these debates is essentially negative, pointing out inconsistencies and neglect in government policies. Positive policy proposals are few and unimportant. Most frustrating of all, the media might or might not pick up and report an individual speech. Private member's resolutions are doomed to failure. In March 1978 some eighteen such resolutions were presented in the House, ranging from the takeover of a fish plant to live coverage of the proceedings of the House. But, as the *Evening Telegram* noted, 'to judge from the track record, nearly all would be left to die on the Order Paper and a Member would be lucky to have it debated.'[11]

When the House is not in session, which is most of the year, the representatives of the people turn to looking after the concerns of their constituents. Over the last twenty years the nature of the demands from constituents has been changing. Earlier, before the 'social net' was as wide as it is today, the bulk of the requests were for social assistance as people ran out of money. Today the emphasis is on unemployment, especially trying to find work for unemployed youth. In the Newfoundland context there is often a fair bit that a member can do to help. Frequently there are summer jobs for students, help for municipal councils, various projects which require short-term staff. In these instances, however, it helps to be on the government side. The auditor general's report for 1983-84 hinted that $25 million in road-building money was channelled, apparently at the discretion of the local member, to about thirty-three PC districts.

In Newfoundland the Speaker and Deputy Speaker stand for election as candidates of a political party. But once in office they are expected to act impartially and ensure that proceedings of the Assembly are orderly and fair. This impartial role is not enhanced if Speakers move on to cabinet. Each of the three Speakers between 1949 and 1972 served about eight years and none of them went on to cabinet. By contrast, once the Tories were in office, there have been five terms for four individuals – an average of three years in office – and each Speaker has gone into cabinet. Cabinet positions can be seen as a reward for what the government regards as a good job.

As the chief administrator of the House of Assembly, the Speaker must manage staff and a budget much like a cabinet minister. The government however controls the salaries and merit increases of the senior officers of the legislature. Early in the first Tory administration, Speaker Simms was successful in heightening the prestige of the Speaker by getting the salary upgraded to that of a cabinet minister with portfolio, plus an executive assistant. The Speaker is also involved in reform of the standing orders. During the same first term of the PC government, Mr Speaker Ottenheimer worked with a committee of five Conservatives and three Liberals to produce some important changes in the rules of the House.

Despite the acknowledged importance of the procedural side of the Speaker's responsibilities, in Newfoundland preparation for the job is often minimal. Two recent Speakers have found themselves in the Chair less than one month after being first elected to the legislature. One of them, Mr Russell (now a cabinet minister) has served twice as Speaker but the first appointment, from 1972 to 1975, he has described as 'traumatic,' adding that it took him at least a year to start feeling comfortable. In a small legislature, served by an equally small House staff, it is difficult to build up the skilled experience those in the Chair and their advisers need. A permanent Speaker may not be appropriate, but there is something distasteful about the current situation. Order-in-council appointment of both the elected and appointed staff of the House of Assembly means that the provincial premier exercises considerable control over the House to which he and his government are, in theory, accountable.

The government's control is exercised in Newfoundland, as in six other provinces, in accordance with a statute. An Act Respecting the Internal Economy of the Legislature provides for a commission of five (three of whom are cabinet ministers) appointed by the lieutenant-governor in council. The Speaker oversees the hiring of staff and the expenditure of monies. He directs the clerk of the House, who acts as his deputy minister. The actual staff of the Newfoundland House is fairly small in number, about fifty individuals, which includes about twelve secretaries in the *Hansard* office and another eighteen or twenty secretaries divided among the caucuses of each of three political parties now recognized in the House. The budget is inflated because the office of the auditor general (a staff of about seventy) and the ombudsman (staff of four) are carried under this head.

A fifth group in the House is its current female members. Forty-nine years separated the first woman elected, Lady Helena Squires in 1930, and the next two. Hazel Newhook and Lynn Verge were elected with the new Peckford administration and were immediately made cabinet ministers. A third woman member was elected from Twillingate in 1982. Today (1988) Lynn Verge, the minister of justice, is the only woman in the Newfoundland legislature.

The Legislature and Political Stability

The legislative function of promoting political stability may seem more appropriate for nations trying to create and maintain a new identity than for Newfoundland. The inhabitants of this province have pride in their long and difficult collective past, and no current doubts about their cohesion as a distinct people. Nevertheless, the concept is a useful one. There has been, as recently as the 1960s, a stated need to represent the denominational cleavages in the society in a balanced way in the legislature, the cabinet, and various public offices. Moreover, legislatures integrate, through representation, different ethnic, regional, and ideological factions into the political elite. The actions of the governors are thereby legitimized. The legitimate system will seek to meet its responsibilities with minimal disruption and maximum public support. The legislature may serve to ventilate grievances or, indeed, to reveal areas of agreement and promote consensus. In any legislature a major function continues to be the creation and mobilization of support for the regime, and this is perhaps especially important in a province that has been through three regime changes in the last fifty years.

Any approach to political legitimacy should start with the understanding that government in a Canadian provincial legislature is influenced by changes in the larger political system, and this is particularly true of a province so economically dependent on the federal authorities. It is important to stress this fact, given the population size and relative underdevelopment of Newfoundland.

One simple and obvious indicator of support for the regime is voter turnout for provincial elections (see table 2). The figures are lower than similar statistics for the other Atlantic provinces. Much the same pattern is evident for federal elections. Since confederation, Newfoundland has had the lowest rate of voter turnout in Canada.[12] Moreover, during the Smallwood years, there were sixteen district seats won by acclamation; since 1971 there has been only one. Undoubtedly, part of the explanation for this change and for the low voter turnout in both federal and provincial elections is the lack of good roads. It is better in the 1980s, but it is still not easy to get around Newfoundland to both nominate candidates and get voters to the polls. But a low general interest in participation may also be a factor.

Table 2
Voter turnout, Newfoundland provincial elections, 1949-79

Year	%	Year	%
1949	76	1971	88
1951	58	1972	79
1956	59	1975	73
1959	68	1979	74
1962	57	1982	78
1966	64	1985	78

Source: *Report of the Chief Electoral Officer*, relevant years.

It should be pointed out, however, that in terms of the vote, the opposition in Newfoundland has never been wiped out in spite of the dominance of the legislature in terms of seats by both Smallwood and Peckford. The non-government vote has increased from about 40 per cent in the first period to about 50 per cent in the Peckford years. There is, in short, good support for both political parties and, by inference, a respectable measure of support for the regime.

Another way to measure support for the regime is to look at incidents when the House of Assembly became an arena for the expression of regional discontent. Can the political system adjust to new territorial or social demands? In particular it is worthwhile to look at the question of the representation of

Labrador in the House of Assembly. Labrador had become a legal part of Newfoundland in 1927 when the Judicial Committee of the Privy Council in London drew the current boundary. Labrador got its first representation to any local assembly when it sent one delegate to the 1946 national convention. Following confederation and the re-establishment of the Newfoundland legislature, Labrador had one representative in the Assembly. This was later increased to two in 1955 and three in 1962. Between 1949 and 1962 these seats overwhelmingly voted Liberal, twice by acclamation.

The break came in 1962 when an Independent won the new Labrador West seat. For the first time the concerns of the iron ore area of Labrador found expression. Once in the House the new member warned that the ties between the island part of the province and its northern dependency were weakening rather than strengthening. Services such as air transportation, libraries, or radio were not available, and a centralized bureaucracy in St John's was either unable or unwilling to decentralize its offices and staff to the north.[13] This seat returned to the Liberals in 1968, but after two years of frustration the member concerned first decided to sit as an Independent and then in September 1969, on a wave of popular support, formed a third party, the New Labrador Party. This was the first popularly based movement turned political party in Newfoundland (if we exclude Smallwood's fight for confederation) since William Coaker built the Fishermen's Protective Union between 1908 and 1921. The NLP fielded three candidates for the 1971 election. The leader, Mr Burgess, was elected and held the balance of power when the Liberals elected twenty and the Progressive Conservatives elected twenty-one. The outcome of that particular situation is part of Newfoundland political history. Our point here is merely that the regional discontent of Labrador found concrete expression through the legislature. While the consequences for the government party were unsettling, the regime probably benefited. A separatist threat was contained, a fourth Labrador seat was established in 1979, and the first Labrador-born member, Mr J. Goudie, was made minister of a newly reorganized department of Rural, Agricultural and Northern Development. The establishment of the northern branch of the department was part of a generally better, decentralized delivery of programs and services by the provincial government.

The political system had to find a way in 1978-79 to deal with another type of problem: the peaceful removal of a party leader. The change from Liberal to Conservative in 1971-72 had been, in the Newfoundland context, a particularly nasty experience. At the end of the second Moores administration the government, in spite of a majority of seats, was losing its ability to govern. Finally, in March 1979, Brian Peckford was named as new leader of the PC party; the Newfoundland Tories had taken the first step to emulate their Ontario brothers.

A number of incidents can be cited to show how the breakdown affected the legislature. In April 1978 the Speaker had to call a precedent-setting adjournment of the House, the first such move since confederation. Later in the same month in the estimates debate the opposition successfully moved that the salary of the minister of forestry be reduced to one dollar. On 27 April the minister of justice had to announce that there would be an investigation into allegations of a payoff made to the minister of industrial development. The whole series of incidents climaxed in May when half of the twenty Liberal members of the House were expelled after an all-night sitting which had capped two weeks of increasingly bitter allegations about corruption within the government and charges that Premier Moores had misled the House. In July the premier had to adjourn the whole House to try to save his embattled government over continuing charges concerning one of his ministers and problems in the Department of Public Works.

These incidents show that if a government does not inspire confidence, the members will in turn show less and less discipline. This lack of confidence will spill over into unruly behaviour by both sides. Support for a government can be withdrawn even within the 'iron cage of party government.'

The use of Richard Rose's term the 'iron cage' of party[14] brings us to another aspect of the question of system maintenance and support. The party system in Newfoundland is not anything like as rigid as it is in the rest of Canada or in the United Kingdom. In fact, crossing the floor and joining the ranks of the other side may be more prevalent in Newfoundland than in any other Canadian jurisdiction. The explanation may say something about philosophical similarities of the two parties, seeing them as not much more than the 'ins' and the 'outs.' Alternatively, crossing the floor may just be saying something about competing values: loyalty to the party versus loyalty to the constituency. Last but not least, of course, there is the motive of personal ambition.

Observers of this Newfoundland phenomenon usually categorize the incidents into two groups. First, there is a group that in the late sixties and early seventies adjusted their allegiance largely in accordance with their feelings about Premier Smallwood. John Crosbie and a young cabinet colleague, Clyde Wells, both quit the Smallwood cabinet over the Shaheen Refinery deal. They sat first as Independents or as Reform Liberals. Then Crosbie crossed back to the Liberals to try once again to reform the party from the inside. When Smallwood chose to oppose him and Crosbie lost the subsequent leadership convention, there was nothing but a final move to the Progressive Conservatives, first as a provincial cabinet minister, and then after 1979 as a federal minister.

The second more recent group of individuals crossing the floor has involved three shifts from Liberal to the Conservative side. For each it has meant advancement: one is a cabinet minister and the other two are parliamentary secretaries, one with unofficial special responsibility for Labrador. The most famous recent crossing came in 1981 when Leo Barry, minister of mines and energy, quit the Peckford cabinet, sat first as a government back-bencher, and then crossed the floor to be elected Liberal leader in 1984. Three years later he retired from politics in the face of a caucus revolt on the issue of leadership.

Crossing the floor is probably tied to the non-ideological roots of the political parties in Newfoundland. A former cabinet minister and leader of the Liberal party has argued that the fifty-two MHAs 'would be hard put to give even an extended philosophical justification of their party belief ... I think they're attracted to a leader or an issue or series of issues.'[15] An added factor is probably what Mark Graesser has characterized as the 'desperate economic circumstances.' The stakes at issue are high, he argued, when so much of the welfare of people and their careers depends on what goes on in politics as distinct from the private sector economic processes. 'The purely pragmatic aspect of politics are much more important [in Newfoundland] than they would be in Ontario.'[16]

In terms of the issues raised by our concern about regime change and stability, we have here a legislature which in composition and possibly in attitude brings an elite perspective to decision-making. Moreover, the absence of any voice from the left (Newfoundland elected its first NDP member only in 1987) probably serves to reinforce these political attitudes. The political elite of Newfoundland has stressed provincial nationalism and the fight with Ottawa in the last three provincial elections, and this has found resonance with the voters. While generating support for the political regime, this tactic may conceal the other divisions in the society. Regional divisions found expression through the New Labrador Party, short-lived as it may have been. Likewise, we have some modest evidence that there may be value differences between the preferences of the society and those of the ruling elite on, for instance, the matter of denominational education. Finally, the incidence of crossing the floor as a part of the political culture of Newfoundland points to a pragmatic value system and careerism which does not challenge the conservative nature of the system. The House of Assembly plays its role in reinforcing the regime.

The Press Gallery

The symbiotic relationship between politicians and the media is a fact of life for any modern legislature. Few read *Hansard*; indeed, for many years during the Smallwood years *Hansard* was not even produced for public consumption.

During those years it was recorded, but nothing in print was available to the public.

Today there is a published *Hansard*, but the House does not permit direct radio or television broadcasting of its proceedings on a regular basis. Before confederation Newfoundland had its own publicly owned broadcasting system and Smallwood's skills as a radio broadcaster were an important factor in the fight for confederation; but after 1949 both radio and newspapers were in private hands. It was an uphill fight with the private broadcasters before Canadian public television was licensed for the province. For the most part the general public is dependent on the media, particularly on television, for a good part of its information. Today, it is estimated the evening news and current events broadcasts of CBC television get about 75 to 80 per cent of the audience. Television broadcasting is *the* medium for public information and attitude formation.

Politicians and journalists need each other, and they probably use one another. In the latter years of the Smallwood era, one of the two locally owned daily newspapers, the *Evening Telegram*, much to its credit, kept a job for a columnist, Ray Guy, who built a career when he taught the general public that it was possible to laugh at the premier and live to tell the tale. Guy was a part of the social changes taking place in Newfoundland. The dominance, and possibly the fear, that Smallwood inspired were whittled away by any number of factors, but one of them was surely the columns by Guy.

Those who write about the relationship between politics and the press worry about such things as ownership concentration, or about the tendency of reporters to end up in comfortable public relations jobs with government. For many years St John's was one of the few cities of its size to have two daily newspapers, both largely locally owned and operated. Today there is one daily, and it has been owned by the Thomson chain since 1970. It has become a newspaper which has gradually lost its 'bustle, resources and guts.'[17] Ironically, the author of this judgment, Michael Harris, is today editor-in-chief of a new weekly newspaper, locally owned, which has become a thorn in the side of the Peckford administration to such a degree that the government has withdrawn all public advertisements from the paper and generally attempts to deny access to its reporters. In recent years regional weeklies have appeared, generally printed by one firm with feeds from the *Telegram*. For most of the media, news originates with the press release, the press conference, or the daily sittings of the House of Assembly. Generally, owners have not made the resources available for any sort of investigative reporting, and most journalists lack training and experience.

Over the years there have been not a few instances when the government has attempted to set up its own newspaper. This was always done, of course, in the guise of trying to balance the failures of the privately owned papers to be 'fair.' Smallwood established the *Newfoundland Government Bulletin*, which was widely regarded as a propaganda organ for the government party published at public expense. Moores had his 'Action Group,' and paid its editor $50,000 a year (in 1978) to 'provide information to the people on government programmes in aid of business.'[18] There are those who see the Newfoundland Information Service (NIS) in something of the same light.

The Press Gallery Association, formed in 1968 at a meeting called by the Speaker, was intended to speak for all reporters on matters of protocol and ethics. As it also aimed at improved facilities for the press and radio arrangements in the precincts of the House of Assembly, the association came under the control of the Speaker. In a recent incident, when the association barred a non-union reporter from the facilities because he was seen as a strike-breaker, it was the Speaker who resolved the issue by declaring the association could not bar any authorized reporter from the press gallery facilities. There are today about thirty individuals accredited to the gallery and membership is dominated by CBC reporters.

As we have already noted, some twelve or thirteen of the cabinet ministers are authorized to hire press secretaries. The pay range is good, between $30,000 and $40,000. Many of them are just out of journalism schools, and a few have been attracted away from the local media. The fear is that if the links become too close, the independence of the reporters is compromised by the possibility of civil service jobs. Added to this is some concern about the balance between the skills and resources of government and those of the local media. The journalists would seem to be on the weaker side.

In general terms it is more difficult for back-benchers, both government and opposition, to get publicity. The back-bencher has an opportunity for local publicity, however, with the development of the string of weekly newspapers. This is probably the best way to get information out, especially as the daily newspaper is not widely read beyond St John's. These weekly newspapers have a need for 'fillers' of one sort or another and the government information service is only too pleased to help. The NIS has a computer printer in each newsroom in the province, about twenty to thirty sites. Publicly funded to the tune of $50,000 to $60,000 per year, the service should be open to use by all the members of the House, but one does hear complaints from the opposition about access. The independence of the NIS is called into question when one notes that the cost of the premier's press office and the NIS are grouped together in one subhead in the budget of the Department of Public Works.

Conclusions

The Newfoundland legislature is one of the oldest in Canada, and its traditions rely on accepted parliamentary practices with an overlay of local experience. Public interest in the legislature is high. In newspapers and on television Newfoundlanders see and hear political issues debated, and here again, the ratings would seem to indicate a high level of interest on the part of the electorate. Closer examination, however, seems to see interest in the legislature more as a 'spectator sport' than as civic concern. Measures show a low sense on the part of Newfoundland voters that politicians can be trusted, or that they will act in pursuit of public good rather than partisan or personal advantage.[19]

The 1979 legislative reforms were aimed at a more efficient and informed examination of the estimates, but experience over the last six or seven years is not positive. Members tend to get into discussions of trivia, and meetings are highly partisan. Ministers tend to make long department-serving responses to leading questions, and increasingly the news media judge the proceedings not to be newsworthy. However, the committees have worked under a number of specific constraints: restrictive procedural rules, membership substitution, and the lack of commitment by either members or chairmen.

It should not have been expected that changes in the rules could create a new function for the House of Assembly. The responsibility to devise estimates and programs remains the paramount responsibility of the government. The Newfoundland legislature is a highly partisan arena. Committees which behaved in an autonomous or independent fashion, which developed, for instance, a consensus about an issue different from that of the government, would put that partisanship in second place. When committees venture into policy-making they can only do so in minor areas where there are no strong partisan feelings. Anything more would be to challenge the government, a foolish and unprofitable action when the government holds all the cards.

This is not to say, however, that the committees are useless. They can be of great value to a government in ventilating issues. The committee on the new provincial flag was a case in point. The government may have had a preferred design, but the work of the select committee allowed a public consensus to build. Committee hearings can be a way of providing new ideas or groups with their chance to compete for public attention. They also provide something of a testing ground for new government members prior to appointment to cabinet.

A special case is the Public Accounts Committee. Here there is a greater chance of policy impact because of two factors: the committee has the expert 'staff' of the provincial auditor general to aid it; and the chairman is a member of the opposition. Forces within the committee are pretty well balanced: the chairman has a strong motive for criticizing the government while the and the work of the committee seemed worth while. In more recent years, however, as the government has strengthened financial procedures, the horror stories have all but disappeared. The auditor general has requested many times a new Audit Act, one which would copy the fateful words in the federal statute about an 'efficient and effective' oversight role for the auditor, but so far the government has not moved to such a change in the legislation, nor is it likely to. The PAC has been less in the media spotlight lately and has come to suffer some of the same ills as other committees: shortages of competent long-term members, frequent changes in membership and chairmanship, and excessive competing demands on members' time and energy.[20]

In short, the function of policy-making/advising by the standing committees of the House of Assembly is better now that it was, but further improvement depends a great deal on the quality of the manpower available. And no reforms should be expected that would take away from the government its ultimate responsibility for policy and administration.

The representative function for the members of a legislature is both powerful and ancient. In Newfoundland with its small, scattered population, the legitimate role of 'our Member' is widely accepted.Today, however, the member has competition for this function. There is a growing network in the province of various sector interest groups (the Fishermen's Union or the Teachers' Association, for example), local government federations, development associations, resource associations, recreational associations, all of which can legitimately claim to represent citizen interests. Party identifers with some strongly held and long-standing view of what government is for are not in a position today to broker these views to party leaders. The political party is a vehicle for winning elections on issues defined by the leader and based on his personality. Add to this the new and crucial role of the media. The newspapers and television broadcasters shape public opinion much more than do the elected members either individually or collectively.

Within the House of Assembly one-party dominance for long periods of time serves to further weaken the representative function. The opposition is weak, its numbers few, its resources limited. The House is in session only a few months each year. The essential parliamentary format of discussion and debate between nearly equal forces is absent, and the executive is allowed to proceed almost unchecked. In the forty years since confederation, the Liberals were in power for twenty-three years and the Tories for sixteen before the Liberals won the 1989 election. The result is a mentality which produces an essentially negative opposition party, not attractive to good candidates, and one which turns members into spectators and critics, lacking any coherent philosophy.[21]

The Newfoundland legislature provides a legitimate forum for the representation of interests; however, the institution is only as effective as the people in it. The government has a critical role to play domestically and as a part of the government of Canada. The easy thing for any government is to bypass the legislature while trying to husband its scare resources for the playing of its role on the larger Canadian stage. In the long term, it would be more democratic and effective if the executive could carry its legislative branch with it as partner not adversary.

PATRICK L. MICHAEL

THE YUKON

Parliamentary tradition in a small legislature

It may seem incongruous to speak of parliamentary tradition in a jurisdiction which has possessed responsible government for only a decade. A serious examination of the history of the Yukon must lead, however, to the conclusion that the territory has a long and powerful attachment to the parliamentary model as received from Britain and as adapted in the Canadian context. That attachment existed when the Yukon Territory was carved from the North-West Territories by act of the Parliament of Canada in 1898 and it has continued unabated to the present.

The struggle to obtain a representative legislative body culminated with the election of the first Wholly Elective Council of Yukon in 1909. It was not until seventy years later that the goal of responsible government was achieved.

The theme which emerges in a study of those seventy years is that of a legislature significant not for its differences but, instead, remarkable in its similarity to all other Canadian parliamentary bodies. When considering the tradition of the parliamentary institution in the Yukon it should not be a revelation to discover that the Yukon Legislative Assembly conforms to all that one would expect of the modern legislature.

History of the Yukon Legislative Assembly

The Yukon Territory was created in response to the imperatives of the Klondike gold rush. From 16 August 1896, when Skookum Jim, Tagish Charlie, and George Carmack discovered rich placer gold on a small creek flowing into the Klondike River, until 1898, some forty thousand stampeders poured into the

Yukon. Two main factors led to the creation of a separate territory, the first being the federal government's desire to create a distinct administrative area in which strong measures could be taken to control the influence of foreign stampeders, a large proportion of whom were American. The second factor was the possessive attitude exhibited by the government of the North-West Territories toward the Yukon. This attitude was, in large part, evidenced by the attempts made by that government to collect hotel and saloon licence fees in bustling Dawson City.[1]

The desire by the federal government to wield a strong hand over the territory and the aliens who populated it explains the decision not to grant any form of democratic government in 1898. The Yukon Act established a government consisting of a commissioner with virtual dictatorial powers and a council of six members, all appointed by the governor-in-council, to aid him in the administration of the territory. Demands for elected representation on this council, which sat until 2 June 1900,[2] were almost instantaneous. In response the Yukon Act was amended in 1899 to allow for two members to be elected by the 'natural-born and naturalized male British subjects' who were at least twenty-one years old and who had resided in Yukon for at least twelve months.[3] An election was conducted on 17 October 1900 to fill the seats thus created. The Yukon Act was again amended in 1902, creating a council composed of five elected members and five members to be appointed by the governor-in-council. The first such council was elected in January 1903 and met for the first time on 7 May 1903.

An early and, for future historians, most fortuitous decision of this Council was that taken to publish its *Journals*. They show a group of men, in many cases split by severe disagreements on the issues of the day, united in their desire to conduct their affairs in a manner consistent with parliamentary principles and procedures. The most clear-cut example of this is shown in the 'Rules, Orders and Form of Proceedings' adopted by the Council. On 11 May a special committee was struck to prepare a draft set of standing orders for consideration by the Council. The committee reported the next day proposing standing orders based on those of Ontario, Manitoba, and the North-West Territories.[4] These standing orders, aside from recognizing the Yukon Act requirement that the commissioner be the presiding officer, bear a close resemblance to even the most modern standing orders of any legislature. The resemblance extended to including that most ubiquitous of rules dealing with unprovided cases: 'In all unprovided cases, the Rules, usages and forms of the House of Commons of Canada shall be followed.'[5]

In 1908 the Yukon Act was again amended, this time creating a fully elected council of ten members. The commissioner, while remaining the chief executive officer of the territory, was forbidden to sit in the Council, and the House was, therefore, obliged to elect a Speaker. A fully representative legislative institution had been obtained but responsible government had not. Following the election of this first 'Wholly Elective Council' on 28 June 1909, little adaptation was needed in the rules which had governed the previous councils. In most cases the Speaker's title was substituted for that of the commissioner where it was cited in those rules and a standing order was added which made the Speaker responsible for communicating with the commissioner on behalf of the House. As before, the *Journals* of the House show a group of legislators operating under and committed to the Canadian version of British parliamentary practice.

The sad irony of the timing of this constitutional evolution was that it occurred at the same time the Yukon was on a downhill slide from the boom it had experienced in 1898. Population statistics highlight the drastic decline in the economy and prospects of the territory. In the census years of 1901, 1911, and 1921 the population is recorded as falling from 27,219 to 8,512 to 4,157. The federal government, although often unaware of a great many matters affecting the Yukon, was fully cognizant of these facts and, in 1919, the Yukon Act was amended to reduce the size of the Council to three members.

The size of the Council remained at three members through eleven elections, from 1920 to 1952. Although its sessions were brief and the situation seemed almost pathetic, the members bravely soldiered on. Parliamentary procedure must have appeared one of the few sources of stability available for they clung tenaciously, even in such small numbers, to the traditions handed down from earlier councils. The results were at times almost comic. The *Journal* for 8 April 1920 records the election of the Speaker in the first meeting of a three member council :

Mr Fowlie, thereupon addressing himself to the Clerk, proposed to the Council for their Speaker, Robert Lowe, Esquire, Member from Whitehorse, and moved that he now take the chair of this Council as Speaker, which resolution was seconded by Mr. Hogan.

The question being put by the Clerk, it was resolved that Robert Lowe, Esquire, do take the Chair of this Council as Speaker, and the Clerk having declared Robert Lowe, Esquire, duly elected, he was conducted by Messrs. Fowlie and Hogan to the chair, where he then thanked the Members of the Council for having honoured him by electing him as their Speaker.[6]

This theme of a tiny legislative institution with members firmly committed to parliamentary practice within the British and Canadian context continued through the next five decades. The size of the Council had increased to only seven members by 1961, at which time the first step was taken that would eventually lead to responsible government. That step was the appointment of three members to a body called the Advisory Committee on Finance. This committee had no executive responsibilities other than to participate in the preparation of the budget, and its record in that exercise must be viewed as a chequered one.[7]

Although, in a strictly legal sense the Advisory Committee continues to exist even today, in practice it was replaced by an Executive Committee in 1970. The Executive Committee can be considered the embryo of the current cabinet as it brought elected representatives into the day-to-day sphere of executive activity, including the assumption of certain portfolio responsibilities. This first Executive Committee consisted of the commissioner, two assistant commissioners (all three being federal government appointees), and two elected councillors appointed after recommendation by resolution of the Council.

In 1974 the Council was expanded to twelve members and began calling itself the Yukon Legislative Assembly. Over the next three years the composition of the Executive Committee was gradually altered, with the deletion of one of the appointed members and the addition of two members of the Assembly, giving the elected members a majority on the executive. The commissioner, however, continued to chair meetings of the Executive Committee and held the power of a veto over the other members of that body.

The general election of 1978, the first in Yukon history to be formally conducted along party lines, returned sixteen members to an expanded Assembly. Following the election, the federal minister of Indian and northern affairs, Hugh Faulkner, issued instructions, pursuant to section 4 of the Yukon Act, to the commissioner, Ione Christensen, which brought the territory one step closer to responsible government.[8] He broke the commissioner's responsibilities into three categories and directed her to consider herself bound by the advice of the Executive Committee on those matters falling within the first category. Unfortunately, he did not make clear what he considered as belonging in this category, and the all-encompassing description of the remaining two categories, where the commissioner was not to be bound by the advice of the Executive Committee, left a great deal of doubt as to what, if any, additional power had been granted to the elected members. The minister did recognize the impact of the introduction of party politics and instructed the commissioner to appoint to the Executive Committee those members recommended to her by the majority leader in the House. The majority leader, or government leader as he was to become known, was also to be given the right to decide the number of members who would be appointed, with the limitation that they not constitute a majority in the House.

Following the 1979 federal general election Mr Jake Epp became minister of Indian affairs and northern development. On 9 October 1979 he issued a new set of instructions to the commissioner which had the effect of providing responsible government to the Yukon.[9] The commissioner was told that there was to be a cabinet appointed and portfolios assigned on the advice of the government leader, that she was not to be a member of the cabinet or to participate in its affairs, and that she was to accept the advice of cabinet in all matters. A lesser point was that the government leader was to be permitted to use the term 'Premier' to describe his office. The government leader of the day, Chris Pearson, chose not to adopt that title and subsequent government leaders have followed his example.

Responsible government has been accepted as naturally as though it had always existed. The only upheaval occurred when Ione Christensen resigned from her position as commissioner because it was her view that, although responsible government was a desirable goal in the long term, the 'Epp letter' had been a precipitous action and had not allowed the Yukon sufficient time to adjust to such a major constitutional change. Her successor, Doug Bell, had no such qualms and dedicated himself to transforming the role of the commissioner from that of a chief executive officer to that of a lieutenant-governor in all but name. Upon Mr Bell's retirement in 1986 there was little doubt that he had reached his goal; in the space of his term of office the commissioner had come to be, in Yukoners' minds, a respected 'head of state' without partisan attachment or interest and possessed of the duties and prerogative powers held by his provincial counterparts.

Perhaps the most significant change is the one which has taken place in the attitudes of the citizens of Yukon towards the Legislative Assembly and the elected government. Prior to 1979 and the achievement of responsible government there was a tendency for every issue to be placed, both by members of the Assembly and by the public, in the lap of the federal government. Since that time the focus of attention has swung to the territorial level and the members of the Yukon Legislative Assembly and, in particular, those who are in cabinet must now be prepared to answer for themselves. It is no longer acceptable to use the federal government and the commissioner, its proxy in Yukon, as whipping boys for all of the Yukon's problems. Rather, Yukoners now look to their own elected representatives for leadership in territorial affairs and, if those representatives are found wanting, they can be assured the price will be paid at the ballot box.

Political Context

The introduction of political parties and their ways to the Yukon Legislative Assembly occurred in 1978. In the general election which took place on 20 November of that year the parties finally took the plunge and each of them (Liberal party, New Democratic party, Progressive Conservative party) ran close to a full slate of candidates. Although there was some residue of support

(14.2 per cent of the popular vote) for the old system of independent candidates, there were only two independents elected and it was clear that the die for the future had been cast. There have been three general elections and four by-elections since 1978 and only once has an independent won a seat (the result of a split vote caused by internecine strife in a Progressive Conservative constituency organization). In the general elections of 1982 and 1985 there were only four independents in the running, and the popular vote for candidates without party affiliation had dropped to less than 5 per cent; in the 1989 election there were no independent candidates.

Even though party politics have been present for only a decade, the Yukon has gone through very nearly every experience that can be imagined. The 1978 election produced a large majority for the Progressive Conservatives, who won eleven seats on only 37 per cent of the vote. Though they had won the election the Conservatives lost their leader when Hilda Watson was unable to take her own electoral district. Some thought was given to having one of their members resign to open a place for her, but she declined the offer before it was seriously made and the Tory caucus selected Chris Pearson as the leader of the party. The opposition was splintered between two Liberals, one New Democrat, and two independents. Prior to the 1982 election the New Democrats became the official opposition through attracting one of the independents to the fold and winning a by-election for a seat previously held by the Progressive Conservatives. The government side was not weakened, however, as it convinced the other independent to cross the floor.

The 1982 general election was the first ever called on the advice of a government leader, and the Progressive Conservatives won again. This time, however, the results were much closer, with the Conservatives winning only nine seats, the Liberals being shut out, and the NDP forming a much more unified, and therefore formidable, opposition with six seats. The remaining seat was won by an independent, Don Taylor. Mr Taylor had been the Speaker of the House since 1974 and the Conservatives, facing some numerical problems and blessed with the acquiescence of the NDP members, placed him in the Chair once again.

The political scene was fairly stable for the next few years; there were no by-elections and members resisted any hidden urges to cross the floor and try their hand on the other side of the House. Late in 1984, however, Chris Pearson announced his intention to resign and the Progressive Conservative party was obliged to hold a leadership convention in March 1985. When Willard Phelps, who was not a member of the Assembly, emerged as a strong candidate for the leadership, questions were raised as to whether he could be appointed as government leader, since the 'Epp letter' of 1979 had stated quite clearly that the Executive Council should be composed of members of the majority party in the Assembly. To remove any doubt the minister of Indian affairs and northern development, David Crombie, issued instructions to the commissioner which were 'to ensure that no candidates are unfairly prejudiced ... in relation to others and in comparison with their fellow Canadians in the federal and provincial political systems.'[10] Mr Crombie went on to say:

Accordingly, I instruct you to regard the letter of October 9th, 1979 and any other relevant instructions as being subject to the following provision: – 'The person you ask to serve as government leader need not be a member of the Legislative Assembly at the time of your request. Any such person not then a member of the Legislative Assembly would be expected to seek election to it within a reasonable time of becoming government leader. Until elected, he or she would not, of course, sit in the Assembly. However, he or she could fulfill the other duties of the position of government leader, including forming a government and being a member of the Executive Council.'[11]

Mr Phelps did win the leadership and in early April he and his cabinet were sworn in as the new government.

Rather than face a by-election and a general election in the space of a year (the Yukon Act requires that a general election be held every four years), Mr Phelps decided to call a snap general election for 13 May 1985. It turned out to be a poor decision as the NDP, winning two seats by a combined margin of fifteen votes, returned to the House with eight members. The Progressive Conservatives won in only six electoral districts and the Liberals, although their popular vote had withered to less than 8 per cent, took the remaining two ridings. There was some brief speculation about the possibility of the Liberals playing off the other two parties against each other in order to obtain the highest bidder for their support. That, however, was essentially a 'non-starter' since supporting the Tories would have created a deadlock at the point the House met to elect a Speaker and the obvious result would have been the dissolution of the House and the call of a new election. Also, the leader of the Liberal party, Roger Coles, had experienced a bitter battle with his Conservative opponent and was not much inclined to side with the Tories in any circumstances. Following on the example set for them in Ontario, the Liberals and the NDP came to some 'understanding,' which, contrary to the Ontario experience, was not in written form and was not made public. The transfer of power, although not something anyone had done much planning for and which, consequently had its awkward moments, took place relatively easily and the new government leader, Tony Penikett, and his cabinet took office in June. The twenty-sixth Legislative Assembly met for the first time on 15 July 1985, elected a Speaker, and hustled through a quick four-day session in which the government survived the few votes of confidence that it faced.

The composition of the House was tragically changed on 13 September when a vehicle accident claimed the life of Andy Philipsen, one of the Progressive Conservative members. The by-election to fill the vacancy was not held until February 1986, at which time the Progressive Conservatives reclaimed the riding represented by Mr Philipsen. During the 1985 fall sitting, however, the seat was vacant, creating a tie in voting strength between the NDP and the opposing parties in the legislature (the NDP, of course, did have a majority of the members but it must be remembered that the Speaker was from their ranks). The government realized that a tie was not of much practical value and that Liberal support was still required, so there was little change in the existing situation.

The need for another by-election was caused by the resignation of Roger Coles on 30 October 1986 (he would plead guilty to a charge of cocaine trafficking on the following day). Once again a tie was created in the House, but the difficult part for the government was that there was now only one Liberal from whom it could hope to gain support. The by-election was held on 2 February 1987, and it was won by Danny Joe, the NDP candidate, thus giving the NDP government a working majority in the Assembly. In the general election of February 1989, the NDP was returned with a narrow majority, winning nine seats to the Conservatives' seven (the Liberals were shut out).

Aside from presenting a picture of the current political context in the Yukon Legislative Assembly, this outline illustrates the essential point that the parliamentary system has served the Yukon well. There were innumerable sceptics, particularly in the federal civil service but also among the local citizenry, who voiced the opinion that the Yukon could handle neither party politics nor the coming of responsible government and that the combination of the two was a recipe for disaster. If it had been known in 1978 that responsible government was only a year away and that during the course of the next eight years there would be three government leaders, the defeat of a government, and the election of a minority government which would obtain a majority during its time in office, the people making those predictions would have been doubly certain of the outcome. Within all of that apparent upheaval, however, the system has worked and it has worked well. There are, and have been since 1978, disputes extant in the political arena as to whether the correct policies are being pursued by the government of the day and as to the wisdom it brings to the management of the human and financial resources available to it, but those are normal and healthy signs in a democratic society. It cannot be doubted that the government and the Legislative Assembly continue to function in the manner expected.

This happy result would not have obtained in the absence of a tradition of commitment to the parliamentary institution. Even though, for some seventy years, it may have had a small legislative body fulfilling only the principle of representative government and to which the executive was not responsible, there was always in evidence a firm commitment to the parliamentary form. This lay a solid and enduring foundation from which to face the tumultuous events of the past decade. That foundation imbued the actors on the political scene with a common view of the direction to be taken in any of the particular circumstances of the times. Certainty about the proper reaction to any given event is the source of stability in every political system. The activities of the Yukon Legislative Assembly and its members during the 1980s have demonstrated, in ample degree, the strength and stability of the system. For that, they and all their fellow citizens owe much to the heritage of the legislative institution in Yukon.

The Nature of a Small Legislature

Before embarking on a description of the activities of the Yukon Legislative Assembly it is necessary to describe the impact that certain factors, including most particularly size, have on its daily operations.

There are only sixteen members in the Yukon Legislative Assembly. Although the number of members in cabinet has varied, the norm is that there will be five ministers including the government leader. Each of those ministers has responsibility, on average, for slightly more than two portfolios and three of them sit on Management Board (equivalent to the Treasury Board in most jurisdictions). The ministers almost always outnumber the private members on the government side of the House and that imbalance is heightened by the election of the Speaker and the Deputy Speaker, who is also the chairman of the Committee of the Whole.

The official opposition has been composed of six members for the two most recent Assemblies and each of those members is normally assigned critic duties covering two portfolios. When a third party is represented in the House it has tended to be composed of only one member and that member, although not troubled by any acrimony in caucus meetings, is saddled with all-encompassing critic responsibilities.

The attendance record of members of the Yukon Legislative Assembly is exemplary. The quorum requirement is high in comparison with other legislatures, as nine of the sixteen members must be present in order for the Assembly to conduct its business. Only once since 1979 has attention been called to the lack of a quorum. That occurred in the Committee of the Whole and, when the Speaker was called back to the Chair, a quorum had already been re-established so the House again resolved into Committee. Pairing is not a common practice, nor is it likely to become so as long as the government does not possess a large majority. It is, therefore, quite normal for all members to be present at all times that the House is sitting. The imperatives of the quorum requirement and the lack of a significant majority deserve emphasis, but an explanation of the solid attendance record of members of the Yukon Legislative Assembly would not be complete without acknowledging the presence of a strictly upheld ethic that members are letting down both their constituents and the House when they are absent.

The House sits from 1:30 to 5:30 p.m. on every day but Friday, and sits from 7:30 to 9:30 p.m. on Monday and Wednesday evenings. It does not sit on Fridays. During sessions caucuses tend to meet from 9:30 to 10:30 a.m. every morning and the house leaders then meet to haggle about the order of business for the day. On Fridays the caucuses often meet for the better part of the morning. Attendance at caucus meetings is viewed as obligatory and members absent without reasonable explanation (e.g., struck by large speeding vehicle, plumbing backed up) can expect to hear from their colleagues.

The combination of these factors leads, obviously, to severe demands and constraints on the time of members. Ministers in particular are placed in a very difficult situation as they are expected to find time to spend twenty-four hours of every week in the House, to prepare themselves to answer for their departments, and to attend caucus. Once that has been done, they must address themselves to their executive responsibilities. The work load and consequent stress during sessions have reached such a point that individual ministers and the cabinet as a whole are loath to deal with anything that is not related to the Assembly unless it has reached the proportions of a crisis.

Opposition members, too, are affected. The time spent in the House and caucus is the same for them as it is for the ministers. Outside of those hours, they are subject to demands for meetings with constituents, interest groups, and the disaffected. There are then the requirements to prepare for the daily question period, to draft speeches on the motions brought forward under private members' business every Wednesday afternoon, and to critically examine government initiatives found in legislation and budget proposals which often require a response on very short notice. Only a decade ago the job of the MLA was considered to be a part-time proposition and it was common for members to continue business or professional activities even when the House was in session. In 1989 and with the growth in demands on MLAs it is a rare member indeed who is able to burn that candle at both ends.

The theme of the 'small legislature' should be kept in mind through the remainder of this chapter since it is an essential backdrop to the operational description of the business of the Yukon Legislative Assembly. In nearly every instance the vagaries or unusual aspects of this Assembly can be explained by reference to its size.

Sessions

Since 1978 the Yukon Legislative Assembly has averaged thirty-nine sitting days each year. Taking into account the fact that the House does not sit on Fridays, this equates to ten weeks per annum. The usual practice is for the Assembly to open a session in mid to late March with the speech from the throne. This spring sitting is occupied with consideration of the operations and maintenance budget and legislation of a housekeeping nature. Once that business has been dealt with, the House adjourns to the call of the Chair upon request from the government leader. The session is reconvened for a fall sitting sometime around Remembrance Day. Business before the House at this sitting includes the capital budget for the forthcoming fiscal year and the major legislative initiatives of the government. Depending on the nature of legislation brought forward, the Assembly normally wraps up a week or two prior to Christmas. It then is adjourned to the call of the Chair. The formal act of prorogation is delayed until a few hours before the opening of the next session.

The practice of having the Assembly continually in session deserves explanation. It began prior to the introduction of responsible government during the time that the commissioner was under no obligation to heed the advice of an elected executive on the question of whether the House should be in session. By adjourning for indefinite periods to the Speaker's call, the Assembly was able to assure itself that it could sit whenever desired by the elected members. The commissioner still possessed the power to unilaterally prorogue a session; but to act upon that power would have appeared undemocratic and would have provoked a battle with the Assembly which would have been of little political advantage to the commissioner.

The practice was retained after 1979 for a different reason. As will be seen below, the appointment of standing and special committees came into vogue in the Yukon Legislative Assembly during the mid 1970s. Doubts were raised about the ability of those committees to sit or even exist during periods when the House was not in session. If those committees were, in fact, sitting without proper authority, it followed that they were then devoid of the powers and privileges associated with the House. To ensure that no questions could be raised about the validity of the committees' actions and that privileges such as freedom of speech were protected for the members, it was decided to hang onto the already established practice of keeping the House in session at all times.

Government Business

The standing orders of the Yukon Legislative Assembly assign all the time of the House with the exception of the daily routine and Wednesday afternoons to government business. It is rare for government to introduce motions, so most of that business is in the form of bills. This includes budgetary items which do not flow through the process of Committee of Supply and Committee of Ways and Means found in most other jurisdictions. In the Yukon, appropriation bills are not treated as formalities; rather, their introduction signals the beginning of the budget debate. A unique rule allows second reading of a bill containing the main estimates to take place immediately after introduction and first reading, and it is at this point that the minister of finance delivers his budget speech. The leader of the official opposition then moves, always successfully, adjournment of the debate and speaks in response on the next sitting day. Budget debates are usually concluded within the space of one to two days and the bill is then sent to the Committee of the Whole, where it and the estimates accompanying it are subjected to detailed scrutiny in the same manner as for any other legislation.

There are, on average, forty-four government bills brought before the Assembly each year and a majority of those are given second reading, or approval in principle, in short order. Even contentious bills will tend to pass the second reading stage after a few days' debate. This state of affairs is not hard to comprehend when consideration is given to the simple statistical fact that, barring the introduction of debatable dilatory motions such as the 'six months' hoist,' the maximum number of speakers to a motion for second reading is sixteen (including a closing speech by the mover of the motion). Of those, only the mover and the member speaking first in response are allowed unlimited speaking time; the remainder of the participants in the debate are given a maximum speaking time of forty minutes. Most speeches are concluded well before the arbitrary limit and a rough guess would place the length of speeches, depending on the issue before the House, in the range of ten to twenty minutes. This may seem a bit low in comparison to other legislatures but, again, recognition must be given to the size of the Yukon Legislative Assembly. There are so few members that anyone desiring to speak will be provided an opportunity so to do. In fact, there is such limited competition to gain the floor that the Speaker is rarely obliged to make a decision on which member first caught his eye. Instead, when two members realize they have risen at the same time it is common practice for one, in the full knowledge that his time will come, to defer to the other by taking his seat. This results in a situation where members do not feel the necessity to unburden themselves of all that troubles them when they finally get their brief moment in the spotlight. As well, the size of the legislature does not allow members to specialize in individual issues; rather, they must all be generalists capable of speaking to a broad range of issues. As a consequence and because of the time constraints outlined above, it is rare for any member to be possessed of sufficient time to prepare extensive speech notes on individual subjects.

Another factor enters here and that involves the place of the Committee of the Whole in the business of the Assembly. After second reading all bills are automatically referred to the Committee of the Whole unless the House takes specific action to refer them to a standing or select committee. This second option has been exercised only three times in the past decade and, in two of those cases, the bill in question has eventually found its way to the Committee of the Whole. In Committee of the Whole the rules on the number of times a member may speak do not apply, allowing a member to gain the floor innumerable times subject only to the constraint that he not speak for more than thirty minutes each time. When the first clause of a bill is called, general debate is permitted, and members often use this as an opportunity to enlarge upon points they may have felt were not sufficiently covered at the second-reading stage. Debate, in the sense that that word implies discussion and response to argument, is far more likely to occur at this time than at second reading, when members are more involved in expressions of opinion than in rebuttal of the points made by other members. There is no provision within the rules of the Yukon Legislative Assembly to invoke closure at the committee stage (and only the use of the previous question exists when the Speaker is in the Chair), so the activities of the Committee of the Whole can tend, especially when on general debate during consideration of the first clause, to be a bit undisciplined. Members will simply continue to participate in the debate until such time as they are talked out, and silence, rather than a boisterous voice vote, is often the signal that a clause has finally received approval.

It should not be surprising to learn that the Assembly spends a large percentage, perhaps as much as 50 to 60 per cent, of its time in Committee of the Whole. As stated, debates at second reading are not usually very time-consuming and, when a bill has passed through Committee, it is not uncommon for it to receive third reading without debate.

Private Members' Business

When considering the time available for private members' business and the resultant ability for private members to bring their own initiatives before the House, it must be concluded that private members in the Yukon Legislative Assembly fare very well. On Wednesdays, following the completion of the daily routine (which includes question period), the House proceeds to motions other than government motions. Motions standing in the name of opposition members are given priority on the first Wednesday and every other Wednesday of a session; on the second Wednesday and every other Wednesday priority is given to motions standing in the name of government private members. If there are no private members' bills on the order paper, debate on these motions will take place until 5:30 p.m., which, in the absence of any untoward events taking place under the daily routine, means that they are allotted about three hours per week.

Of note are the number of private members' motions debated and, of special note, the number that are passed. For example, during the seventy-six days on which the Assembly sat between 13 March 1986 and 12 February 1987 there were eighteen Wednesdays when private members' business was called. On those days a total of sixty-nine private members' motions were debated and came to a vote. The breakdown of the results is as shown in the table.

Private members' motions, 1986-87

	Agreed without amendment	Agreed with amendment	Defeated	Totals
Opposition motions	31	15	9	55
Government back-benchers' motions	12	2	0	14
Totals	43	17	9	69

It is, of course, the size of the Assembly which leads to these rather remarkable statistics. In larger legislatures it is a fairly easy task to talk out private members' motions, an assignment usually given to government back-benchers. In the Yukon Legislative Assembly, with its limited ranks of government back-benchers and, indeed, of government members, this strategy will not work. The government faces four alternatives in its approach to an opposition motion: to argue that it is acceptable and vote for it without reservation; to argue that it is acceptable with certain qualifications being understood and vote for it; to argue that it is not acceptable in its present form and move an amendment which, if passed, would lead the government to support the motion; and finally, to argue that it is not acceptable and vote against it. Since 83 per cent of the opposition motions are agreed to and, of those, fully two-thirds in unamended form, it is obvious which of the above options is preferred.

Private members' bills are not as common nor are they subject to the same kind fate. From 1979 to 1984 there was an average of four private members' bills introduced per year and, of those, none progressed beyond second reading. It is far easier to talk out a private member's bill since there is only one hour per week provided for debate on such bills. Also, the Legislative Assembly does not have a law clerk and private members' bills are normally drafted by the clerk of the Assembly. This circumstance, as might be expected, allows the government to express enthusiasm for the general policy direction of a bill but to refuse support for it on the basis that it contains drafting deficiencies. As a result, the demand for the clerk to don his drafting hat has decreased in drastic fashion and only one private member's bill has been introduced since 1984.

Question Period

With the exception of the opening day of a session, there is an oral question period every day that the House sits. It takes place at the end of the daily routine and is subject to a forty-minute time limit. Question period in the Yukon Legislative Assembly receives an emphasis comparable with that of most jurisdictions in the country. Opposition members devote a great part of their energy to researching and drafting questions and cabinet ministers exercise an equal effort in preparing themselves for this daily ordeal.

The standing orders of the Assembly contain, as an appendix, a set of guidelines for the conduct of oral question period which begins with the general statement that a question is to seek 'information about a matter which falls within the administrative responsibility of the Government of Yukon.' The search for 'information' does take place on the odd occasion but, far more commonly, the goal of questions is to expose government mismanagement of the territory's affairs and to demonstrate policy differences between the opposing parties. Answers, in the words of the general statement, are to provide information sought through a question. That, too, happens on occasion, but it is far more likely that an answer will take the form of a rebuttal to the preamble to the question and will cast government policy in the most glowing terms.

Question period is subject to some structure. The rules grant a member the right to two supplementaries to every question. The leader of the official opposition is always recognized for the first two questions and the leader of a third party for the next one. After that, members are recognized in an order strictly tied to the strength of their party in the legislature. During the past two years the number of questions asked in each question period has consistently averaged out at twelve per day and, equally consistently, the full forty minutes allotted to question period have been used.

If the opposition so desires, it is possible for every member to receive at least one question. It is not, however, unusual to see two or three opposition members ask all the questions; this occurs most frequently when the opposition feels the government is vulnerable on one particular issue and it wishes to see that issue pursued for maximum political gain. When this interrogative strategy is adopted it is common for an opposition caucus to ask as many as five consecutive questions on the same subject. Since, with the two supplementaries per question, this really adds up to a total of fifteen questions, a minister who is the subject of opposition attention may view this as a most unpleasant experience.

These sessions might more accurately be described as mini-debates and they are often the most lively exchanges of the day between the two sides of the House. Emotions, real and synthetic, run high with the level of partisanship at its most extreme and the Speaker is often obliged to constrain members from straying to personal and unparliamentary language.

Committee System

It is only since 1974 that the Yukon Legislative Assembly has had a moderately active committee system. From 1961 to 1974, when the Assembly, or Territorial Council as it was then known, consisted of only seven members, there were only three committee reports presented to the House. In the period since 1974 and the expansion of the Assembly to twelve and then sixteen members, there has been an average of four committee reports presented each year. The small size of the Assembly simply does not permit the House to appoint a substantial number of committees. When the standings in the House are close this point is made particularly clear. With the government side normally entitled to two or three members on each committee (on average, there is a total of five members on a committee), and there only being two to three back-benchers available for appointment, it is obvious that the creation of a new committee is not proposed without some serious thought.

In larger jurisdictions committees are often created to satisfy the demand of private members for a greater opportunity to participate in a meaningful way in legislative activities. In the Yukon there is no such demand since members are fully satisfied with the opportunities for participation afforded them in the normal course of events. As has been shown, a member of the Yukon Legislative Assembly has substantial scope to make his views known and to undertake the scrutiny of government actions and initiatives.

A second rationale for the reference of business to committees in some jurisdictions is that there is not sufficient time available for the Assembly to deal with all matters in the Committee of the Whole. Although Yukon members, and cabinet ministers in particular, are subject to significant time constraints, it is clear that the length of sessions (average of thirty-nine sitting days per year since 1979) does not justify the appointment of committees on the basis that the Assembly is unable to complete its business within a reasonable period of time. A practical point worth noting here is that the existing committees of the Assembly are not able to meet during the time that the House is sitting because members are too busy with the business of the House to allow the scheduling of committee meetings.

The Yukon Legislative Assembly utilizes committees for three separate functions. The Standing Committee on Rules, Elections and Privileges, the

Standing Committee on Public Accounts, and the Standing Committee on Statutory Instruments are required by the standing orders and members are appointed for the life of a legislature. The first of these is used primarily for reviews of the rules of the House and of the pay and other benefits of members. The other two are appointed to ensure accountability on behalf of government for its use of public funds and delegated legislation and are assigned the duties normally associated with such committees in all jurisdictions. The Public Accounts Committee, which was first established in 1979, comes very close to meeting the criteria for a model public accounts committee as defined in a report published by the Canadian Comprehensive Auditing Foundation.[12]

The third function committees cover is that of obtaining public input on controversial bills or issues. Committees created for this purpose are called select committees and exist only until their reports are tabled in the House. Examples, in 1986, of such committees were the Select Committee on Human Rights, which held public hearings on the government's proposed Human Rights Act, and the Select Committee on Renewable Resources, which travelled the Yukon in search of public response to a green paper on renewable resources.

The Assembly takes committees and their reports very seriously. With few exceptions committees have been marked by a non-partisan consensual approach, solid attendance, and attention to duty by members and timely reporting to the Assembly. Once a committee has reported it is expected that an opportunity will be afforded for a debate on the report and that the government will provide, at that time, a full response to the recommendations found in the report. Since most reports are the product of all-party agreement at the committee level, governments find it almost impossible to reject outright the recommendations of committees; rather, the tendency is to indicate support tempered by extensive qualifications.

Until there is a growth in the number of members in the Assembly it is unlikely that there will be a significant change in the committee system. In the foreseeable future committees will continue primarily to serve to obtain public input and as accountability mechanisms and, if they follow past practice, will fulfil those functions in an effective and responsible way.

Reform in the Yukon Legislative Assembly

The Special Committee on the Reform of the House of Commons (the McGrath Committee) introduced its third report with the following statement: 'The purpose of reform of the House of Commons in 1985 is to restore to private members an effective legislative function, to give them a meaningful role in the formation of public policy and, in so doing, to restore the House of Commons to its rightful place in the Canadian political process.'[13]

The grievances which led to the appointment of that special committee do not exist in the Yukon Legislative Assembly. As this paper shows, members do have an 'effective legislative function' and do play a 'meaningful role in the formation of public policy.' Also, the issue of the Assembly attaining its 'rightful place in the political process' was addressed to the satisfaction of all members when responsible government was granted in 1979.

The only times that the subject of reform is raised are those occasions on which the government is possessed of the notion that the opposition is unreasonably obstructing the government in its efforts to get its business through the House. The opposition viewpoint in such cases, of course, is that it is not obstructing the government but, rather, is doing its duty in attempting to convince the government of the error of its policies. This stress-point raises the dilemma familiar to all legislatures as to when the right of the minority to have its say infringes on the right of the majority to have its way. Fortunately, the Yukon Legislative Assembly has been able to weather these brief storms without serious consideration being given to amending the rules to allow closure in Committee of the Whole or to impose time allocation procedures on the House. Such 'reforms' weaken a legislature because they remove the power of the members to resist a government which needs resisting and to force it to the ultimate test of confidence, an election. The concept of 'checks and balances' may seem more American than Canadian but we, too, have constitutional safeguards within the parliamentary system and we should be mindful that we not discard them without due regard for the effects on our legislative institutions.

KEVIN O'KEEFE

NORTHWEST TERRITORIES

Accommodating the future

Changes in the political and geographical definition of Canada since Confederation have had a tremendous impact on the nature of government in the Northwest Territories. Most of the western provinces trace their history back to Rupert's Land and the original North-Western Territory, a vast tract of land more than two million square miles in size. Although these provinces evolved with traditional parliamentary institutions and as partners in Confederation, the modern-day Northwest Territories took a much different route.

Occupying over one million square miles, a full third of Canada, the Northwest Territories has a population of only fifty-two thousand. The majority of these people belong to either the Inuit, Dene, or Métis cultures. In comparison to southern Canada, European contact has been relatively recent, especially among the Inuit of the eastern Arctic. Traditional life-styles are a living memory for the older generation and still practised to a certain extent by younger generations. Most Native northerners claim an Aboriginal language as their mother tongue and many of the older people do not speak English at all. The bulk of the non-Native population (approximately 35 per cent of total NWT population) lives in larger communities in the western Arctic. The first Territorial electoral districts were created in 1951, but it wasn't until the 1970s that all regions were represented. Since 1979 Aboriginal MLAs have held a majority of seats in the legislature.

Basic Structure

The most interesting feature of the Legislative Assembly of the NWT is the absence of political parties. During the past few years the system of government has been described in many ways. In the north 'consensus government' is a term often used, but in the south 'non-partisan government' or 'one-party system' has become more popular lately. Whatever labels are used, there can be no doubt that the style of government is distinctly different.

Candidates for all twenty-four electoral districts run as independents, and although some of these may express agreement with the principles and platforms of a political party, partisan politics plays almost no role in Territorial elections at the present time.[1] After the election, successful candidates meet in caucus to select an executive and a Speaker, and to decide on membership for various House committees. The process for selecting an executive is not fixed, and each new Assembly is free to use any method that can be agreed upon. For example, the current Assembly chose to accept a recommendation from the previous Assembly and elect the government leader first from among all twenty-four members, rather than choose the leader from among eight duly elected executive members, as had been done in the past. Caucus did not accept the previous Assembly's recommendation to give the government leader powers of cabinet selection and conducted a second secret ballot to fill the seven remaining seats on the executive. The practice of choosing four members from the eastern Arctic and four from the west was carried over from the last Assembly.[2]

Almost without exception all House committees are composed of non-executive members.[3] The current Assembly has established committees for, among others, Finance; Public Accounts; Agencies, Boards and Commissions; Rules, Procedures and Privileges; Legislation; and a Special Committee on the Northern Economy. Relations between the executive and House committees are exceptional relative to partisan governments, and proponents of the NWT system often cite these relations as proof that consensus can work. The executive provides budget documents, bills, and other information prior to session and has been known to make changes based on committee review even before items were formally introduced into the House. Because the executive, or 'government side,' is always in a minority, the influence of House committees composed exclusively of non-executive members is significant.

Despite the absence of political parties, or perhaps because of it, House divisions regularly reveal splits between the east and west, small and large communities, and regions, and to a limited extent, along cultural and linguistic lines. However, the dynamics of these relationships are not overtly apparent and the results of many votes are unpredictable. Generally speaking, members are not bound to any particular political philosophy and vote according to conscience or the wishes of their constituents. The executive usually demonstrates 'cabinet solidarity,' but there have been a few notable exceptions in recent years.[4]

Up to seven Native languages and dialects are used in the House with simultaneous interpretation, allowing unilingual MLAs full participation. Most House documents are available in English and Inuktitut; French will be in use as an official language by 1990. A blind MLA entered the House in the 1987 election and a special service to produce House documents in braille has been implemented.

Government by Consensus or by Consent?

The operation of the government of the Northwest Territories at the political level reflects many of the unique historical and cultural characteristics of its people. The notion of consensus government is often compared with the leadership patterns and decision-making of traditional Native society. Survival in the harsh northern environment meant that decisions had to be made in the best interests of the group as a whole. Co-operative sharing of skills and resources was a concept central to social organization and produced different leaders at different times, depending on the nature of the task at hand. The interests of the group always took precedence over individual concerns. Achieving a consensus of opinion through conciliation and compromise was more practical than confrontation because it preserved the harmony of group relationships. In this context, leaders did not command, but rather 'by means of example and instruction, they reminded the people of their individual and collective responsibilities, and clearly pointed out the choices which would favour ... continued survival.'[5]

These traditions persist today, especially in the attitudes towards government at the community and regional level.[6] Nevertheless, there are obvious complexities in modern society that make traditional consensus decision-making virtually impossible for the day-to-day administration of government policies, programs, and services. These duties are relegated to an executive body. Whether or not the practices of the Northwest Territories' government can be accurately described as consensus is certainly open to question.[7]

The current Executive Council has unofficially adopted the term 'cabinet' and has increasingly referred to its 'mandate' from the other members of the House to run government and make decisions. The non-executive members have formed a committee called 'ajauqtit,' with designated critic responsibilities.[8] The current Assembly has been marked by an increasing friction between the executive and ordinary MLAs in the House. Accessibility to information and input from non-executive members into policy formulation have been the major sources of conflict. These issues are not really contentious in partisan systems, but in the NWT system there is an underlying assumption that the consensus tradition puts everyone on the same side; there is an expectation of openness and equal participation. In its quest for responsible government and political legitimacy, it may well be that the government of the Northwest Territories has imported elements of confrontation and opposition from southern models along with terms such as 'cabinet' and 'mandate.' As one MLA recently observed:

I would like to express to the acting Government Leader my concern as a new Member of this House about the workings of consensus government in this Assembly. Since November, the Executive Council has referred to itself as a 'cabinet'. Members on this side have tended to retain the old name of Executive Council. I believe, Mr. Speaker, that the words of 'Executive Council' fit in far better with the concept of consensus government. It fits in far better with the concept of a smaller Executive carrying out the wishes of this large Assembly. The word 'cabinet', on the other hand, conveys the flavour of secretiveness and mystery because that is the origin of the word; it refers to the little apartment to which the King's advisors were set aside in order to advise him; people who were chosen by him. These Members were chosen by all 24. They were not chosen by one person. Therefore they have no right to call themselves a cabinet ...

... Mr. Speaker, we are not trying to be like other people that we are not similar to when the whole thrust of this government has been to operate a completely different kind of government from what exists in southern jurisdictions? And we keep on wanting to use words like cabinet and premier and Legislative Assembly. All these words, when really the whole move over the last 15 years has been to develop something unique in the Territories.[9]

During the 1988 budget session a motion was introduced to force the government to make public a report it had commissioned on government decentralization. Although the motion was defeated, excerpts from the debate illustrate some of the real limits to consensus in the NWT legislature:

Hon. Dennis Patterson: Well, Mr. Speaker, there is a motion on the floor of the House today and I was planning to speak on it at that time. Basically, the reason I am concerned about this report being provided to the House is that, first of all, the cabinet did not accept the recommendations in that report. Now if we were to have a precedent whereby every report that was made to this government, even reports whose advice was not recommended, was made public, then we would be basically allocating cabinet decision-making functions to this Legislature and to the public process ...[10]

Mr. Richard: ... Mr. Speaker, on the issue of disclosure of these documents – quite apart from the Cotterill document – there are some days when the Government Leader, in particular, talks eloquently about consensus government; that we are different from everywhere else. There are other days when the Government Leader, like today, speaks other words. He says that once we delegate to the group of eight, we are no longer to participate in the decision-making process. This larger issue of documents and providing them to the Assembly, Mr. Speaker, to me is not one of non-confidence in this group of eight or the past group of eight. It is an issue that if the Government Leader and his colleagues believe in the consensus that they often speak eloquently about, the issue is providing this Assembly, this group of 24, with the information and documents that will enable us, assist us, to give direction to the group of eight ...[11]

Hon. Michael Ballantyne: ... I think the point has been made many times in this House – what does consensus government mean? To me there have been a number of different interpretations put on the term. But one way to look at it, and Members may not agree with me, is that, as I see it, what we have here is a consensus Legislative Assembly. But that Legislative Assembly by legislation, by the will of the Members over the years, is divided into an Executive component and a legislative component. So I think there is no doubt that by precedent, by law, and by the will of the Members, we do have an Executive branch of this Legislative Assembly. That Executive branch needs to have the tools and the trust, I guess, to do their job ...[12]

Mr. Nerysoo: ... I rise to express concern about the method and manner in which ordinary Members are being dealt with in the development or direction of the government. Ordinary Members are not being involved in the process of devolution; we are not party to discussions or the negotiations. This, despite the fact that representatives of communities are involved, despite the fact that even staff of Native organizations are involved in confidential discussions. I do not oppose the involvement of these people but what I am concerned about is the unwillingness of the Executive Council to make ordinary MLAs aware of even general principles, or to debate and receive direction from MLAs regarding the very important issues and responsibilities being negotiated by the Government of the NWT.

Mr. Speaker, I also do not agree or appreciate it when ordinary MLAs ask for information or introduce specific motions and are threatened with resignations[13] by the Executive Council. I am not an MLA who is easily manipulated but I can and have shown that I am prepared to listen to pragmatic and reasonable arguments, including why issues should not be dealt with or discussed in a public forum, but not to threats of resignation or Executive Council Members arguing privately with my intentions or the actions of responsible Members in this House. This is the forum for public debate and this is where we are accountable to the public, not in the privacy of the caucus rooms.[14]

Despite the frustration that ordinary MLAs may feel with the executive from time to time, it should be noted that ministers sit at the pleasure of the House; their fate is not linked to the fate of a political party or the wishes of the government leader. For example, during the 1987 budget session, a minister sent a note to an ordinary MLA, implying that he might not be able to support economic development projects in that member's constituency if he did not receive support against a motion under debate. The member, feeling unfairly intimidated, tabled the note in the Assembly the next day and introduced a motion to have the minister removed from the executive. The motion carried and the minister was removed. A new minister was selected by all MLAs in caucus to fill the vacant seat. All these events were beyond the control of the government leader or the executive as a whole. In fact, the government leader made a point of stating that he had instructed all ministers to vote freely on the issue, and that the rules of cabinet solidarity did not apply.[15]

During the same session several motions were introduced in Committee of the Whole to delete or reduce funding allocations for various government programs. Elsewhere in Canada this might have precipitated the fall of an entire government and a subsequent general election, but not in the NWT. Although all the motions could be interpreted as non-confidence motions, there is nothing in the existing rules and practices of the legislature that would require the executive to resign, much less cause a general election. All the motions were defeated, so the real impact remains a matter of speculation. There would likely have been an expectation for the executive to resign, and if this happened, all twenty-four members would retreat to caucus to select a new executive.[16] A report recently prepared for the Rules and Procedures Committee of the last Assembly recommended formalization of these procedures by acknowledging motions of censure and non-confidence in the rules of the Assembly.[17] Although accepted by the last Assembly, the current Assembly has not yet addressed the matter and the rules have not been changed.

The pragmatic view seems to be that when these twenty-four MLAs choose an executive, they also consent to the authority and leadership that the executive must exercise in order to properly run the government. However, if a majority of these members are dissatisfied with the performance of the executive, for whatever reason, this consent can be revoked and power will change hands. By this definition, consensus exists not so much in the day-to-day administration of government, but rather as a fail-safe mechanism to keep the government on the right track. To date, ordinary MLAs have been hesitant to use the power available to them to force the hand of government.[18] If the friction between the executive and ordinary MLAs continues to increase, it is probably just a matter of time before a vote of non-confidence is carried. It is somewhat ironic that if ordinary members passed such a motion they would be operating more like a unified opposition than members of a consensus government.

The consensus system of government in the NWT is not embraced by all politicians. Some have claimed that an absence of political parties makes for a disorderly approach to government policies and programs; that a government brought to power is not accountable because it has not been elected on the basis of commitments to a specific platform or political philosophy. One MLA commented recently on the potential for abuse of ministerial power in the consensus system. The issue was a controversial reversal of a decision on the location of a young offender's facility:

Mr. Richard: Mr. Speaker, it is the veterans on the Executive Council that I am most disappointed in. I can understand, in all seriousness, a new Minister, a new MLA, being zealous, or overzealous, having, like all of us, promised her constituents the world during the recent election, wanting to deliver something for her home community. But the others, Mr. Speaker, my point is the others should have said, 'No, the decision has been made. It was well thought out decision based on sound factors for good reasons.'... Mr. Speaker, I am trying to make the point about the precedent. What about the next new Minister, and the next new Minister after that? What sort of expectations are we building up for potential Ministers and their constituents?

There was a suspicion, Mr. Speaker, while I was in attendance during the last Assembly, that with our system of Executive and ordinary Members that the Executive was able to go and make promises individually to individual MLAs and sort of keep enough votes on side that they were able to continue as a group in office. I know there is a give and take there in the system that we have, where there are no party or team allegiances, but I ask Members to to keep these points in mind when addressing this principle of whether we are going to allow this kind of practice to be the guideline for the next four years. And I ask Members to keep these things in mind regardless of what you might be concerned about in your own constituencies.[19]

Proponents of consensus submit that the confrontational element of party politics is diametrically opposed to the traditions of Native people and is not, therefore, an appropriate method of political expression in the NWT. There is also concern, especially among Native MLAs, that embracing all the trappings of southern political models will restrict and even prevent the establishment of new forms of government suitable to the circumstances and needs of northerners. These arguments take on added meaning with the spectre of comprehensive land claim settlements in the north and a possible division of the NWT into two new jurisdictions. Arguments on both sides continue.

These examples show how the political system in the Northwest Territories has evolved in a manner completely different from in other Canadian jurisdictions. Strong regional and cultural contrasts in the Northwest Territories have inevitably led to the creation of parliamentary traditions that are significantly flexible and accommodating.

The Struggle for Responsible Government

Unlike provincial governments, the powers of the government of the Northwest Territories are not rooted in the British North America Act and the Canadian constitution, but in the North West Territories Act. The Northwest Territories has always been so vast, remote, and thinly populated that it evolved more as a colony of the federal government than as a partner in Confederation. From 1905 until 1951 the legislature was a council composed of appointed civil servants, serving primarily as an advisory body to the federal authorities.

Canada obtained title to Rupert's Land and the North-Western Territory from Britain in 1870. It was a huge territorial acquisition – over two million square miles covering the present-day Northwest Territories, Yukon Territory, Alberta, Saskatchewan, most of Manitoba, and the northern parts of Ontario and Quebec. The Arctic Islands were transferred ten years later in 1880.[20] The drive for ownership of all this territory was an attempt both to unify the existing provinces and to thwart possible American expansion into the area.[21] The sovereignty issue has persisted to the present day and offers another explanation for a strong federal presence in the north.

The first form of government was established in 1869 with passage of the Act for the Temporary Government of Rupert's Land and the North-western Territory when United with Canada.[22] In 1875 this legislation was replaced with the North West Territories Act which authorized a lieutenant-governor and appointed council, and included provisions for the gradual replacement of appointed councillors with elected representatives. The legislation allowed the lieutenant-governor to establish one electoral district for every one thousand people. When the number of elected members reached twenty-one the council would automatically become a legislative assembly. The first fully elected Legislative Assembly of twenty-two members came to power in 1888. An Executive Council was established in 1897, bringing the NWT Legislative Assembly very close to full responsible government. However, it could still not amend its own constitution and was not empowered to borrow money. The federal government also retained control over revenues from lands and resources.[23] In effect, the Territories still had no real control over its destiny.

Not long after, a drive for provincial status began, fuelled by the Klondike gold rush and rapid population growth in the prairies as rail links were established. The Yukon Territory was created in 1898, and under sustained pressure from the NWT legislature, the provinces of Saskatchewan and Alberta were carved out of the NWT in 1905. In 1912 the boundaries of Quebec, Ontario, Manitoba, and Saskatchewan were extended north, defining the boundaries in existence today.[24]

The newly created provinces achieved full responsible government and joined the Canadian confederation, but the thinly populated land left over was doomed once again to become a ward of the federal government. The period between 1905 and 1921 was a very stagnant time for the Northwest Territories. Amendments to the North West Territories Act replaced elected representatives with a commissioner and four appointed councillors (although none were appointed until 1921) and the seat of government was moved to Ottawa, where it remained until 1967. From 1905 to 1919 the head of the Royal North-West Mounted Police was automatically appointed commissioner of the NWT. In 1919 the deputy minister of the federal Department of the Interior (at that time the department responsible for the north) was appointed commissioner, a practice that lasted until 1963. Although the size of the appointed Council increased during the period 1921-51, all members were senior federal civil servants and it operated more like a departmental committee than a legislature.

The year 1951 was a landmark in the Northwest Territories' second march towards responsible government; three electoral districts were created in the western Arctic. Native people were entitled to vote pursuant to federal legislation passed in 1950, although until 1960 status Indians were required to waive taxation exemptions provided under the Indian Act to acquire franchise rights.[25] A fourth electoral seat was added in 1954, and the Council composition of five appointed and four elected members remained unchanged until 1966. The creation of electoral districts for the eastern Arctic began in the late 1960s and all regions were represented by the 1970s. During these years more and more appointed members were chosen from the private sector.

In the 1950s the Council of the Northwest Territories was given the power to authorize the commissioner to enter into agreements with the federal government. Major sections of the North West Territories Act dealing with provincial-type responsibilities were repealed so that they could be replaced with Territorial ordinances. A separate NWT Revenue Account was created in the federal Consolidated Revenue Fund and the commissioner was given the power to appropriate funds and borrow money. In 1962 provision was made for the election of a federal MP to represent the Northwest Territories.[26]

The Modern Era

Although much growth and development had taken place in the north by the early 1960s, full responsible government was still a long way away. The eastern Arctic was still relatively untouched by the modern world and lacked elected representation. In response to requests from the Council of the Northwest Territories and the many constitutional questions raised by the possibility of dividing the NWT into separate jurisdictions, the federal government established the Advisory Committee on the Development of the Government in the Northwest Territories in 1965. The Carrothers Commission, as it later became known, recommended a completely new structure for the government, which included moving the seat of government from Ottawa to the Northwest Territories, the creation of a Territorial civil service, and devolution of executive authority to the commissioner. Despite the disparity of development between the eastern and western Arctic, the report recommended against division of the NWT, citing isolation of Inuit in the east and domination of Indians in the west as prejudicial to the political interests of Native people.[27]

Many of these recommendations were acted upon immediately. In 1967 the seat of government was moved from Ottawa to Yellowknife and in 1969 the federal government began transferring responsibility for certain programs to the government of the Northwest Territories via the commissioner. The more important of these included education, welfare, economic development, and municipal affairs. A House committee system began in 1970 with the creation of Finance, Legislation, Rules and Procedures, and Indemnities and Allowances committees.

The first fully elected Council of the Northwest Territories was brought into being in 1975. Shortly after, the term Legislative Assembly was adopted and three members were chosen to sit on the Executive Council, which had until that time been controlled exclusively by the commissioner, deputy commissioner, and assistant commissioner. By this time there were fifteen seats in the Legislative Assembly, representing all regions in the NWT, and the House was authorized to elect a Speaker. The Northwest Territories legislature was finally beginning to take on the familiar appearance of a modern parliament.

Amendments to the North West Territories Act in 1979 allowed the commissioner-in-council to set the number of seats between fifteen and twenty-five. Following a boundary commission which created seven new seats, twenty-two members were brought to power in the 1979 election. Five of these members were chosen to sit on the executive, and one of these took on the role of spokesman, and eventually the title of government leader. For the first time Aboriginal members held a majority in the House, and many of them had close connections with Native organizations. During this term the number of ministers was increased to seven, and among these was a minister responsible for finance, indicating the Territorial government's increased fiscal responsibilities.

The number of electoral districts was increased to twenty-four prior to the 1983 election. All elected members participated in the selection of eight ministers and a Speaker. The NWT Legislative Assembly became the first jurisdiction in Canada to choose an Aboriginal government leader. He shared the chairmanship of the Executive Council with the commissioner of the NWT.

The accomplishments of the Assembly in recent years have made further contributions to the development of responsible government. A formula-financing arrangement not unlike federal transfer payments to provinces has been successfully negotiated. The commissioner's role has become very much like that of a provincial lieutenant-governor; in 1979 he ceased sitting in the House during formal session and in 1984 he removed himself from Committee of the Whole. In 1986 the government leader took sole chairmanship of the Executive Council. Devolution of government programs and services still under federal control continues at a steady pace and the responsibilities of the executive continue to grow. As in the Northwest Territories of 1897, however, certain key elements of full responsible government have not yet been granted. Constitutional powers and control of resources still reside with the federal government.

Constitutional Development

During the 1970s residents of the NWT were becoming increasingly dissatisfied with their government. Generally, it had all the appearances of responsibility but in fact was little more than 'a complex amalgam of administrative and political institutions, which tend to hide "real" authority and diffuse accountability.'[28] Ultimate authority still belonged to appointed officials and the federal cabinet, a fact which critics claimed resulted in a colonial approach to government. As well, comprehensive land claims had been filed by all Native organizations and each included proposals for Aboriginal self-government and division of the NWT. In fact, the Dene Nation had boycotted the Assembly elected in 1975 to publicize their belief in its illegitimacy. The political will of the people was clearly not reflected by existing government structures and practices.

In response the federal government appointed in 1977 a special representative to examine various constitutional questions in the Northwest Territories. The report of the representative, *Constitutional Development in the Northwest Territories*, or the Drury Report,[29] as it is commonly known, was released in 1980. The report acknowledged that the basic constitutional framework in the NWT was very much in question, and made numerous recommendations for change. Overall, the report favoured the establishment of government structures more relevant to the traditions and circumstances of the north, including increased political powers for communities and regions. Although not in favour of division, the report recommended that a forum be established to examine the issue and assess the will of the people. The special representative concluded that a more responsible and responsive system of government in the north could not be created without further devolution of federal powers. The increased role of Native people in the administration of this power was seen as essential. The report was a signal to northern people that the door of constitutional change was open.

In southern Canada the concept of Indian or Aboriginal self-government is defined primarily as a replacement of the Indian Act with legislation that would allow Indian bands full control over their own affairs. This authority would be limited to reserve lands or lands acquired by way of modern-day land claim settlements. Native populations in the south are a minority and the influence of non-Native populations is overwhelming. In the NWT, however, reserves are virtually non-existent and many communities have Native populations greater than 90 per cent. This characteristic of the northern population gives a whole new meaning to Aboriginal self-government. Indeed, there are those who argue that the NWT already has Aboriginal self-government by virtue of a Native majority in its legislature. This may be partially correct, but a fundamental requirement for Aboriginal self-government in the eyes of Native leaders today is a land base fully controlled by Native people. Resolution of this land base aspiration will, sooner or later, have to be accommodated by the government of the Northwest Territories. The implications for a future territorial or provincial constitution are profound.

Division of the Northwest Territories is not a new issue; it first rose in the early sixties, promoted primarily by non-Native people of the western Arctic who felt the relatively undeveloped eastern Arctic was slowing down progress in the public and private sectors. Legislation actually made it to the House of Commons in 1963 but it died on the order paper.[30] The federal government chose instead to set up the Carrothers Commission (described above) to examine the many questions associated with the development of government in the NWT.

The question gained momentum again in the late seventies, this time supported mainly by the Inuit of the eastern Arctic. The concept of 'Nunavut,' an Inuit homeland, had achieved widespread popularity as a concept central to the Inuit land claims proposal.[31] The Dene and Métis of the western Arctic had their own version of a new jurisdiction in what became known as 'Denedeh.'[32] As recommended in the Drury Report, the legislature struck a special committee to examine the division issue, and in 1982 a plebiscite was held to determine the wishes of the people. Although not strongly supported in the western Arctic, the plebiscite confirmed that a majority of NWT residents were in favour of division.[33]

At about the same time and in concert with the growing movement towards constitutional reform, an organization now known as the Constitutional Alliance was formed, composed of representatives of all the Native organizations and four members of the Legislative Assembly. The Alliance was further subdivided into the Western Constitutional Forum and the Nunavut Constitutional Forum, and with funding from the federal government, they began the task of devising constitutional frameworks and boundaries for the two new jurisdictions.

Constitutional development efforts undertaken since 1980 have been historic in nature. A plethora of studies has been produced to date, exploring such subjects as: guaranteed representation, residency requirements, protection of aboriginal rights, equality, principles of traditional Native government, principles of democratic government, regional government, and many more. Both forums were essentially trying to work out what has been succinctly described as 'the best match between social patterns and governmental structure.'[34] The difficulty of this task cannot be underestimated, owing to fundamental cultural and political differences between the north's Native and non-Native inhabitants. Whereas the traditional western democratic processes are oriented around the rights of the individual, Native society has always placed the strongest emphasis on the group as a whole.[35] A synthesis of these two approaches will be dynamic in the least. Final recommendations on future government structures will likely not come before the legislature until division becomes a reality.

A boundary agreement presented to the Assembly in 1985 met with some opposition and did not receive clear support. The walk-out of all eastern members during debate, including half the executive, demonstrated the forceful influence that the division issue had gained since 1982. It also indicated the extent to which constitutional development had become bound up in the operation of the legislature. A second agreement was presented to the Assembly two years later. A corridor for the boundary was proposed in this revised agreement, with the final line dependent on the resolution of the Dene/Métis and Inuit land claims overlap. The new agreement was endorsed by the legislature and a plebiscite on the boundary line was to be held if the land claims overlap could be resolved within a specified time limit. Unfortunately, the overlap issue was not resolved and the whole process has stalled for the moment. Native organizations and the current government have both agreed that a settlement of comprehensive land claims should precede any further action on division.

The provisions of the Meech Lake Accord present additional constitutional problems to the government of the NWT. The legislature has condemned the Accord because it will prohibit northerners from nominating Supreme Court judges and Senate appointees. As well, the Accord places the power to create new provinces or to extend provincial boundaries northward firmly into the hands of the provinces under a new amending formula which, like the old, will operate to the exclusion of representatives of the Yukon or the NWT. The Accord was legally challenged under the Charter of Rights by leaders in the NWT and the Yukon, but a recent Supreme Court decision closed this avenue of protest. The Northwest Territories government is still engaged in a struggle to assert its right as legitimate heir to powers of self-determination.

Rapid change during the past several decades has produced in the north a society unlike that anywhere in the country. Inherent in the struggle for responsible government and political power is a focus inward to discover this unique society and the potential wealth it holds for political expression. Resolution of the many complex and unique issues facing the Northwest Territories promises to completely change the face of government form and practice. The legislature is still very young and it must grapple with cultural and constitutional questions for which there are no precedents and no clear answers. It cannot be known for sure if a familiar modern parliament, a unique form of Aboriginal self-government, or a combination of the two will emerge in the end. In any case, the parliamentary traditions of the NWT have not yet congealed into a fixed form, nor can they if government is to accommodate the many changes the future holds. The dynamic nature of the present system has been described as follows: '... the opportunity exists to write a set of rules which are not immutable and which can be adapted. If an unforeseen circumstance arises, the Assembly members, in effect sitting as a constituent assembly in their caucus, can decide what to do in light of those rules, and their spirit, or to overturn them altogether. Such opportunity is unique.'[36]

NOTES

Introduction

1 Beyond a few articles comparing members' behaviour or procedures in two or three legislatures, the principal studies covering all provincial assemblies are few indeed: Harold D. Clarke, Richard G. Price, and Robert Krause, 'Backbenchers' and Philip Laundy, 'Legislatures' in David J. Bellamy, Jon. H. Pammett, and Donald C. Rowat, eds., *The Provincial Political Systems: Comparative Essays* (Toronto: Methuen, 1976); Harold D. Clarke, Richard G. Price, and Robert Krause, 'Constituency Service among Canadian Provincial Legislators: Basic Findings and a Test of Three Hypotheses,' *Canadian Journal of Political Science* 8 (December 1975), 520-42; Simon McInnes, 'Improving Legislative Surveillance of Provincial Public Expenditures: The Performance of the Public Accounts Committees and Auditors General,' *Canadian Public Administration* 20 (Spring 1977), 36-86; John Kelly and Hugh Hanson, *Improving Accountability: Canadian Public Accounts Committees and Legislative Auditors* (Ottawa: Canadian Comprehensive Auditing Foundation, 1981); Marsha A. Chandler and William M. Chandler, *Public Policy and Provincial Politics* (Toronto: McGraw-Hill Ryerson, 1979), 114-21; Michael M. Atkinson and Graham White, 'The Development of Provincial Legislatures' in Harold D. Clarke et al., eds., *Parliament Policy and Representation* (Toronto: Methuen, 1980); Allan Kornberg, William Mishler, and Harold D. Clarke, *Representative Democracy in the Canadian Provinces* (Scarborough: Prentice-Hall, 1982); Robert J. Fleming, ed., *Canadian Legislatures 1987-88* (Ottawa: Ampersand Communication Services Inc., 1988) and its annual predecessors published by the Ontario Legislative Assembly; Christopher Dunn, 'The Budget Process in Western Canadian Legislative Assemblies,' *Canadian Parliamentary Review* 10 (Winter 1987-88), 6-13.

2 Michael Ryle, 'The Procedures and Practices of the House of Assembly,' mimeo, Nova Scotia House of Assembly, 1976, 8.

3 Alistair Fraser, G.A. Birch, and W.F. Dawson, *Beauchesne's Rules and Forms of the House of Commons,* 5th ed. (Toronto: Carswell, 1978) .

4 Charles Gordon, ed., *Erskine May's Parliamentary Practice,* 20th ed. (London: Butterworths, 1983).

5 For the latter view, see Gurston Dacks, 'Politics on the Last Frontier: Consociationalism in the Northwest Territories,' *Canadian Journal of Political Science* 19 (June 1986), 350-3.

6 Even if one were to argue that, given the three-party system, a minority government was inevitable sooner or later, this does not take into account the fact that the *timing* of the minority was critical for legislative developments in Ontario in that it occurred just as the Camp Commission had completed its task of setting the stage for thoroughgoing reform.

7 Ryle, 'Procedures and Practices,' 4-5.

8 Atkinson and White, 'Development of Provincial Legislatures,' 272.

9 Figures from Rand Dyck, *Provincial Politics in Canada* (Scarborough: Prentice-Hall, 1986), 574; the ratio of constituents to members in British Columbia is about 48,000 to 1 but the government's general unwillingness to grant services to MLAs has withstood the pressure of number.

10 See, for example, Philip Norton, 'Behavioural Changes: Back-bench Independence in the 1980's' in Philip Norton, ed., *Parliament in the 1980's* (Oxford: Basil Blackwell, 1984), 36-55.

11 For more extensive discussion of the speakership in the provinces, see Robert J. Fleming and Thomas Mitchinson, 'The Speakership in Canada' in Robert J. Fleming and Thomas Mitchinson, eds., *Canadian Legislatures: The 1982 Comparative Study* (Toronto: Office of the Assembly, 1982), 25-36; and Philip Laundy, *Office of the Speaker in the Parliaments of the Commonwealth* (London: Quiller Press, 1984), 136-9.

12 Graham White, 'The Powers of Public Accounts Committees' in Canadian Council of Public Accounts Committees, *Proceedings of Fifth Annual Meeting* (Toronto, 1983), 155-91.

Prince Edward Island

1 See Wayne E. Mackinnon, *The Life of the Party* (Summerside: Prince Edward Island Liberal Party, 1973), 7.

2 Gabriel A. Almond and Sidney Verba, *The Civic Culture* (Boston: Little, Brown, 1963), 20, 22.

3 *Ibid.,* 134.

4 John H. Redekop, 'Canadian Political Institutions' in John H. Redekop, ed., *Approaches to Canadian Politics,* 2nd ed. (Scarborough: Prentice-Hall, 1983),

156; Michael S. Whittington, 'Political Culture: Attitudes and Values as the Determinants of Politics' in *ibid.*, 141. See also Michael L. Mezey, *Comparative Legislatures* (Durham: Duke University Press, 1979), 284.

5 Gerhard Loewenberg and Samuel C. Patterson, *Comparing Legislatures* (Boston: Little, Brown, 1979), 283-91.

6 Prince Edward Island Public Archives, Accession No. 2491, Item No. 1.

7 Hans Daalder and Jerrold G. Rusk, 'Perceptions of Party in the Dutch Parliament,' in Samuel C. Patterson and John C. Wahlke eds., *Comparative Legislative Behavior: Frontiers of Research* (New York: Wiley 1972), 168.

8 Dankwart Rustow, *The Politics of Compromise* (Princeton: Princeton University Press, 1955), Ch. 6-7.

9 Peter Gerlick, 'Orientations to Decision-Making in the Vienna City Council,' in Patterson and Wahlke, 105-5.

10 Ronald D. Hedlund, 'Organizational Attributes of Legislatures: Structure, Rules, Norms, and Resources,' *Legislative Studies Quarterly* 9 (February 1984), 66-7.

11 Alan Rosenthal, *Legislative Life: People, Process, and Performance in the States* (New York 1981), 111-15. Other observers of American state legislatures echo Rosenthal's findings. See, for example, John J. Carroll and Arthur English, 'Rules of the Game in Ephemeral Institutions: U.S. States Constitutional Conventions,' *Legislative Studies Quarterly* 6 (May 1981), 310-11; John J. Pitney, Jr., 'Leaders and Rules in the New York State Senate', *Legislative Studies Quarterly* 7 (1982), 497; E. Lee Bernick and Charles W. Wiggins, Legislative Norms in Eleven States, *Legislative Studies Quarterly* 8 (May 1983), 198.

12 David J. Bellamy, 'The Atlantic Provinces' in David J. Bellamy, Jon H. Pammett, and Donald C. Rowat, eds., *The Provincial Political Systems: Comparative Essays* (Toronto: Methuen, 1976), 11.

13 Richard Simeon and Donald E. Blake, 'Regional Preferences: Citizens' Views of Public Policy' in David J. Elkins and Richard Simeon, eds., *Small Worlds: Provinces and Parties in Canadian Political Life* (Toronto: Methuen, 1980), 84-103.

14 Survey by the author.

15 See, for example, Norman Ward, *The Canadian House of Commons: Representation* (Toronto: University of Toronto Press, 1950), 120.

16 See, for example, Gary C. Jacobson, 'Incumbents' Advantages in the 1978 U.S. Congressional Elections,' *Legislative Studies Quarterly* 6 (1981), 183-200; Lyn Ragsdale, 'Incumbent Popularity, Challenger Invisibility, and Congressional Voters,' *ibid.*, 201-18; J. Blondel, *Comparative Legislatures* (Englewood Cliffs: Prentice-Hall, 1973), 85-7; Loewenberg and Patterson, *Comparing Legislatures*, 106-11.

17 Occasionally, there will be a second legislative session in a year to deal with pressing matters. Hence, budgetary concerns obliged the government to reconvene the legislature for two days in 1916 and one day in 1935, and the railway strike of 1950

necessitated a one-day session in that year. See Frank Mackinnon, *The Government of Prince Edward Island* (Toronto: University of Toronto Press, 1951), 229.

18   Hugh Gordon MacNiven, 'The Legislative Assemblies of the Canadian Provinces' (Ann Arbor: University Microfilms, 1976), 184-6.

19   Norman H. Carruthers, *Report of the Commissioner Appointed Pursuant to the Legislative Assembly Act to Inquire Into the Adequacy of the Indemnities, Salaries and Allowances for Members and Officers of the Legislative Assembly and the Adequacy of the Salaries Fixed for Members of the Executive Council* (Charlottetown: Legislative Assembly of Prince Edward Island, December 1986), 15, 34.

20   Leone Bagnall, interview with the author, Charlottetown, 8 January 1987.

21   Michael Breaugh, 'Parliamentary Reform in Ontario,' *Canadian Parliamentary Review* 8 (Autumn 1985), 2. Breaugh's comments are no longer applicable to the Ontario legislature since MPPs now have full-time staffs of three or four members.

22   D.V. Smiley, *Canada in Question: Federalism in the Eighties*, 3rd ed. (Toronto: McGraw-Hill Ryerson, 1980), 136.

23   F. Mackinnon, *Government of Prince Edward Island*, 178.

24   *Ibid.*, 44-85.

25   For a discussion of British influence on this matter in Nova Scotia, see J. Murray Beck, *Politics of Nova Scotia*, I: *1710-1896* (Tantallon: Far East Publications, 1985), 209, 259.

26   F. Mackinnon, *Government of Prince Edward Island*, 99-104.

27   *Ibid.*, 216-20.

28   'Changing Perspectives: Interviews with Patrick Binns, Raymond Garneau, and Michael Cassidy,' *Canadian Parliamentary Review* 8 (Spring 1985), 21.

29   J.R. Mallory, 'Can Parliament Control the Regulatory Process?' *Canadian Parliamentary Review* 6 (Autumn 1983), 6-9. For a British perspective on this question, see Alan Beith, 'Prayers Unanswered: A Jaundiced View of the Parliamentary Scrutiny of Statutory Instruments,' *Parliamentary Affairs* 34 (1981), 165-73.

30   Thomas D'Aquino, G. Bruce Doern, and Cassandra Blair, *Parliamentary Democracy in Canada: Issues for Reform* (Toronto: Methuen, 1983), 97.

31   Fred Driscoll, interview with the author, Charlottetown, 9 January 1987.

32   Allison Ellis, interview with the author, Charlottetown, 9 January 1987.

33   Fred Driscoll, interview; Edward Clark, interview with the author, Charlottetown, 9 January 1987. For a perceptive view of the schizophrenia with which many parliamentarians regard the office of the ombudsman, see Robert Runciman, 'Ombudsmen and Legislatures: Allies or Adversaries?' *Canadian Parliamentary Review* 7 (Autumn 1984), 15-17.

34   Robert J. Fleming and Thomas Mitchison, eds., *Canadian Legislatures: The 1984 Comparative Study* (Toronto: Office of the Assembly, 1984), 75.

35   Marion Reid, interview with the author, Charlottetown, 9 January 1987.

36   Fred Driscoll, interview.

37   Philip Laundy, 'Legislatures' in Bellamy, Pammett, and Rowat, eds., *The Provincial Political Systems,* 285-6, is mistaken on this matter.

38   Until recently Nova Scotia also constituted an exception to the norm. See John Feehan and Ronald G. Landes, 'The Parliamentary Tradition in Nova Scotia,' *Canadian Parliamentary Review* 7 (Summer 1984), 6.

39   Fred Driscoll, interview.

40   Ron MacKinley, interview with the author, Charlottetown, 8 January 1987.

41   Bryan Gould, 'Televise Parliament to Revive the Chamber,' *Parliamentary Affairs* 37 (1984), 248.

42   See, for example, Bob Franklin, 'A Leap in the Dark: MP's Objectives Televising Parliament,' *Parliamentary Affairs* 39 (1986), 295, and Timothy E. Cook, 'House Members as Newsmakers: The Effects of Televising Congress,' *Legislative Studies Quarterly* 11 (May 1986), 223.

43   Leone Bagnall, Allison Ellis, Marion Reid interviews. To be fair, one should note that similar concerns have been voiced in other Canadian provincial legislatures.

44   Frank Mackinnon, 'Prince Edward Island: Big Engine, Little Body' in Martin C. Robin, ed., *Canadian Provincial Politics: The Party Systems of the Ten Provinces* (Scarborough: Prentice-Hall, 1972), 245.

45   Edward Clark, interview.

46   Marion Reid, interview.

47   Stavert Heustis, interview with the author, Charlottetown, 8 January 1987.

48   Leone Bagnall, interview.

49   F. Mackinnon, *Government of Prince Edward Island,* 237.

50   Leone Bagnall, interview.

51   Allan Kornberg, William Mishler, and Harold D. Clarke, *Representative Democracy in the Canadian Provinces* (Scarborough: Prentice-Hall, 1982), 181.

52   Leone Bagnall, interview.

53   Edward Clark, interview.

54   F. Mackinnon, *Government of Prince Edward Island* , 169.

55   See Peter Swenson, 'The Influence of Recruitment on the Structure of Power in the U.S. House, 1870-1940,' *Legislative Studies Quarterly* 7 (1982), 7-36, and David W. Brady, Joseph Cooper, and Patricia A. Hurley, 'The Decline of Party in the U.S. House of Representatives, 1887- 1968,' *ibid.,* (1979), 381-407, for discussions of how changing modes of electoral politics and, especially, of recruitment patterns at the local level affected the extent of party discipline in the legislature.

56   W. Mackinnon, *The Life of the Party,* 55-61.

57   Harold D. Clarke, Jane Jenson, Lawrence LeDuc, and Jon H. Pammett, *Political Choice in Canada,* abr. ed. (Toronto: McGraw-Hill Ryerson, 1980), 97.

58   F. Mackinnon, *Government of Prince Edward Island,* 245.

Ontario

I wish to record my appreciation of John Eichmanis of the Ontario Information and Privacy Commission, whose perceptive comments on an earlier draft of this paper forced me to rethink many parts that were woolly, wrong-headed, and outrageous. That I rethought them doesn't necessarily mean that I changed them.

1 For a thorough account of the Ontario Legislature in the mid 1960s, see F.F. Schindeler, *Responsible Government in Ontario* (Toronto: University of Toronto Press, 1969).

2 For an analysis of the impact of minority government, see Vaughan Lyon, 'Minority Government in Ontario, 1975-81: An Assessment,' *Canadian Journal of Political Science* 17 (December 1984), 685-706.

3 The text of the accord may be found in Rand Dyck, *Provincial Politics in Canada* (Scarborough: Prentice-Hall, 1986), 325-7.

4 Nelson Polsby, 'Legislatures' in Fred Greenstein and Nelson Polsby, eds., *Handbook of Political Science* 5 (Reading, Mass: Addison-Wesley, 1975), 277.

5 The accord was, to say the least, very much in the Liberals' interest since it brought them to power, but in this paper I am concerned only with its impact on the operation and nature of the legislature, rather than with its larger political ramifications.

6 See Walter White and Lawrence Leduc, 'The Role of Opposition in a One-Party Dominant System: The Case of Ontario,' *Canadian Journal of Political Science* 6 (March 1974), 86-100; and Frederick J. Fletcher and Arthur Goddard, 'Government and Opposition: Structural Influences on Provincial Legislatures,' *Legislative Studies Quarterly* 3 (November 1978), 647-69.

7 On Ontario political culture see, inter alia, John Wilson, 'The Red Tory Province: Reflections on the Character of Ontario Political Culture' in Donald C. MacDonald, ed., *Government and Politics of Ontario,* 2nd ed. (Toronto: Van Nostrand Reinhold, 1980), 208-26; S.F. Wise, 'Ontario's Political Culture,' in *ibid.*, 3rd ed. (Toronto: Nelson, 1985), 159-73; J.T. Morley, *Secular Socialists: The CCF/NDP in Ontario – A Biography* (Kingston and Montreal: McGill-Queen's University Press, 1984), ch. 1.

8 See, for example, the data presented in David J. Elkins, 'The Sense of Place' in David J. Elkins and Richard Simeon, eds. *Small Worlds: Provinces and Parties in Canadian Political Life* (Toronto: Methuen, 1980), 16-21, and Jon H. Pammett, 'Public Orientation to Regions and Provinces' in David J. Bellamy, Jon H. Pammett, and Donald C. Rowat, eds., *The Provincial Political Systems: Comparative Essays* (Toronto: Methuen, 1976), 94-8.

9 Detailed data are presented in my *The Ontario Legislature: A Political Analysis* (Toronto: University of Toronto Press, 1989), ch. 2; the data cover the 125 MPPs elected in May 1985.

10   Data on the proportion of members of various Canadian legislatures who had previously served in municipal government may be found in Robert J. Fleming, ed., *Canadian Legislatures 1987-88* (Ottawa: Ampersand Communication Services Inc., 1988); Robert J. Fleming and Patrick Fafard, eds., *Canadian Legislatures: The 1986 Comparative Study* (Toronto: Office of the Assembly, 1986), and Robert J. Fleming and Michael Wiebe, eds., *Canadian Legislatures: The 1985 Comparative Study* (Toronto: Office of the Assembly, 1985).

11   The data were collected through reference to the time notations incorporated into *Hansard*.

12   Schindeler, *Responsible Government*, 156.

13   Ontario Commission on the Legislature, *Fourth Report* (September 1975), 30.

14   The competition was even more pronounced before the 1986 rule changes, for each opposition party was permitted to ask (and usually did) a supplementary question to the other party's original question.

15   Data were compiled on sources and targets of all oral questions in the 1986-87 session.

16   Patrick Weller, *First among Equals* (London: Faber, 1985), 171.

17   Each non-cabinet member is assigned a priority by ballot (with separate lists for each party) for bringing forward one bill or resolution for debate. In practice this means that each MPP can expect to have an item come up for debate every two or three years. Members are free to introduce as many bills and resolutions as they wish but only one may be designated for debate.

18   It is technically possible for 20 MPPs to prevent a vote being held, but for practical political purposes this is equivalent to a vote.

19   Legislative Assembly of Ontario, *Debates*, 15 January 1987, 4581.

20   Ontario Commission on the Legislature, *First Report* (May 1973), 16.

21   Legislative Assembly of Ontario, Standing Committee on Procedural Affairs and Agencies, Boards and Commissions, *Report on Standing Orders and Procedure (No. 4)* (November 1985), 74-9; see also Ministry of Treasury and Economics, *Reforming the Budget Process: A Discussion Paper* (October 1985), 9.

22   See my 'Ontario's Select Committee on the Ombudsman,' *The Table* 50 (1982), 52-61.

23   Standing Order 35 (a), (c).

24   Not all such public hearing processes necessarily enhance legitimacy. It might well be supposed that the extensive committee hearings in 1985-86 on the bill to extend separate school financing, which saw hundreds of groups come forward to argue against full financing only to learn that their views would have little or no influence on the policy-makers, resulted in a reduction of legitimacy.

25   Standing Committee on the Legislative Assembly, *Report on Proposals for the Restoration of Ontario's Parliament* (January 1987).

26   On the reforms of the 1970s see my 'Teaching the Mongrel Dog New Tricks: Sources and Directions of Reform in the Ontario Legislature,' *Journal of Canadian Studies* 14 (Summer 1979), 117-32; and 'The Life and Times of the Camp Commission,' *Canadian Journal of Political Science* 13 (June 1980), 357-76.

27   Cabinet Office, 'Government Response to the Report of the Standing Committee on the Legislative Assembly on Appointments in the Public Sector,' 27 October 1986, 7.

28   In the spring of 1988 an informal, all-party working group recommended a package of substantial reforms, including a radical revamping of the estimates process. As of early 1989, it was unclear whether the proposed reforms would come to pass.

29   See, for example, the *Report of the Special Committee on Reform of the House of Commons* [the McGrath Report] (Ottawa, June 1985), and Philip Norton, 'Backbench Independence in the 1980s' in Norton, ed., *Parliament in the 1980s* (Oxford: Basil Blackwell, 1985), 22-47.

Saskatchewan

1   Saskatchewan Archives Board (SAB) interview with Tom Johnston, CCF MLA for Touchwood (1938-56) and Speaker of the Legislative Assembly (1944-56), by Chris Higginbotham, 1963.

2   In addition to the report of the chief electoral officer following each provincial election, the most complete compendium of Saskatchewan electoral data is *Provincial Elections in Saskatchewan, 1905-1983*, 2nd ed. (Chief Electoral Office, Province of Saskatchewan, 1983).

3   With respect to the nomenclature of the CCF/NDP, the term CCF is used for the period up to 1961 and NDP for the later period. In fact, the party kept the name CCF until 1967 and then called itself the New Democratic Party – Saskatchewan Section for some time thereafter.

4   SAB, Papers of the Rt. Hon. James G. Gardiner, Gardiner to Dr Charles Endicott, 28 May 1937, 42686.

5   J. Castell Hopkins, *Canadian Annual Review of Public Affairs for 1907 (CAR)* (Toronto: The Annual Review Publishing Co., 1908), 592.

6   *Ibid.*, 561.

7   See V.C. Fowke, 'Royal Commissions and Canadian Agricultural Policy,' *Canadian Journal of Economics and Political Science* 14 (May 1948), 163-75.

8   *CAR.*, 549.

9   Seymour Martin Lipset, *Agrarian Socialism* (Garden City: Doubleday Anchor, 1968), ch. 3.

10   K.A. Bradshaw, 'Saskatchewan-Westminster: An Exchange of Clerks,' *The Table* 35 (1966), 37.

11   Elgin to Lord Grey (Colonial Secretary), 25 May 1847 in Sir Arthur G. Doughty, *The Elgin-Grey Papers, 1846-1852*, 4 vols. (Ottawa: King's Printer, 1937), 46.

12   John C. Courtney, 'The Size of Canada's Parliament: An Assessment of the Implications of a Larger House of Commons,' in Peter Aucoin, ed., *Institutional Reforms for Representative Government* (published by University of Toronto Press in co-operation with the Royal Commission on the Economic Union and Development Prospects for Canada and the Canadian Government Publishing Centre, 1985), 1-39.

13   See, for example, *CAR: 1906*, 451; *1911*, 566; *1912*, 543-4; Saskatchewan, *Journals of the Legislative Assembly: 1952*, 142-3; *1953*, 93; *1957*, 167.

14   Saskatchewan, *Journals of the Legislative Assembly 1953*, 93.

15   *Ibid. 1954*, 143-4.

16   *CAR*, 533.

17   SAB, Papers of Walter Scott, Scott to J. Jameson, 5 June 1913, 39733-4.

18   Interview with Tom Johnston by Chris Higginbotham, 1963.

19   Gordon Barnhart, 'Efficiency, Not Speed: Parliamentary Reform in the Saskatchewan Legislature, 1969-1981,' *The Table* 50 (1982), 85.

20   *Canadian Parliamentary Review* 8 (Autumn 1985), 13-15.

21   'Westminster-Saskatchewan: A Further Exchange of Clerks,' *The Table* 38 (1968), 57.

22   Gordon Barnhart, 'Saskatchewan: Orientation Seminars for Members,' *The Table* 51 (1983), 102.

23   Legislative Assembly of Saskatchewan, *Public Accounts Committee Minutes and Verbatim Report*, 3 (13 October 1982), 40-1.

24   Evelyn Eager, *Saskatchewan Government: Politics and Pragmatism* (Saskatoon: Western Producer Prairie Books, 1980), 78.

25   Marilyn Domagalski, 'The Role of Women in Federal and Provincial Politics,' in Robert J. Fleming, ed., *Canadian Legislatures, the 1986 Comparative Study* (Toronto: Office of the Assembly, 1986), 39-43.

26   George Stephen, 'Machine-Made *Hansard:* Saskatchewan,' *The Table* 15 (1946), 171-5.

27   Gordon Barnhart, 'Television in the Legislative Assembly of Saskatchewan,' *The Table* 51 (1983), 80-5.

28   Clerk of the Legislative Assembly, 'Saskatchewan (Revision of Standing Orders): A Select Special Committee of the Legislative Assembly,' *The Table* 27 (1958), 162.

29   Gordon Barnhart, 'Efficiency, Not Speed,' 83. In the period leading up to and immediately following the 1986 election, the numbers of written questions increased markedly. It is too soon to tell whether the reversal in recent practice represents a permanent change or only a temporary 'blip' in the long-term trend away from the use of this legislative mechanism.

30   Gordon Barnhart, 'Administration: A Threat or a Challenge?' *The Table* 49 (1981), 53.

31   'The Legislature and Responsible Government,' in Norman Ward and Duff Spafford, eds., *Politics in Saskatchewan* (Toronto: Longmans Canada Ltd., 1968), 30.

32 'Crown Corporation Procedure: The Saskatchewan Legislature's Practice,' *The Table* 19 (1950), 191.

33 *Ibid.,* 187.

34 Franks, 'The Legislature and Responsible Government,' 37.

35 Christopher Dunn, 'Responsible Government and the Budgetary Process in Western Canada' (study prepared for the Royal Commission on the Economic Union and Development Prospects for Canada, November 1984), 42-3, 45 and appendices.

36 The quotations in this paragraph are from Saskatchewan, *Public Accounts Committee Minutes and Verbatim Report,* 1 (24 June 1982), 10; and 3 (13 October 1982), 119.

37 Legislative Assembly of Saskatchewan, *Debates and Proceedings 30,* 19 December 1986, 415. See also 18 December 1986, 355 and 358, and 22 December 1986, 446.

38 *Ibid.,* 22 December 1986, 444.

39 *Ibid.,* 19 December 1986, 393.

40 Barnhart, 'Efficiency, Not Speed,' 85.

41 Dale H. Poel, 'The Diffusion of Legislation among the Canadian Provinces: A Statistical Analysis,' *Canadian Journal of Political Science* 9 (December 1976), 605-26.

Quebec

1 See Edmond Orban, *Le Conseil législatif de Québec 1867-1967* (Montreal: Bellarmin, 1967).

2 Though all members elected in both the 1981 and the 1985 general elections belonged to the two major parties, some sat as independents within a few years of their election. None was re-elected.

3 See L. Massicotte and A. Bernard, *Le scrutin au Québec: un miroir déformant* (Montreal: Hurtubise HMH, 1985).

4 P. Charbonneau, 'La Couronne. Essai sur les Canadiens français et la démocratie,' *Écrits du Canada français* 8 (1961), 11-53; P.E. Trudeau, 'Some Obstacles to Democracy in Québec,' *Canadian Journal of Economics and Political Science* 24 (1958), 197-211.

5 Some members of the Council were elected between 1657 and 1663, as were *syndics* between 1647 and 1674. On these very limited experience, see G. Lanctôt, *L'administration de la Nouvelle-France* (Paris: Champion, 1929).

6 The basic source on the period is Henri Brun, *La formation des institutions parlementaires québécoises, 1791-1838* (Quebec: Presses de l'Université Laval, 1970). On the Cité Libristes see M.D. Behiels, *Prelude to Quebec's Quiet Revolution: Liberalism versus Neo-nationalism 1945-1960* (Kingston and Montreal: McGill-Queen's University Press, 1985).

7 See Paul Benoît, 'Remembering the Monarch,' *Canadian Journal of Political Science* 15 (September 1982), 575-87.

8 For Professor Walter Tarnopolsky, 'The only value of a monarchy is to be a unifying force and it certainly isn't as far as Québec is concerned,' quoted by J. Amernic, 'Long to Reign Over Us?' *Quest*, December 1986, 42.

9 J. Proulx, *Le Panier de crabes* (Montreal: Parti Pris, 1971), 155. Proulx was a member of the Assembly in 1966-70 and 1976-85, first as a Union Nationale, and thereafter as a Parti Québécois MNA.

10 R. Boily, 'Les hommes politiques du Québec,' *Revue d'histoire de l'Amérique française* 21, no. 3A (1967), 599-634; M.-A. Bédard, 'La profession des députés (1867-1980),' *Bulletin de la Bibliothèque* 11, no. 1 (1981), 31-54; G. Deschênes, *Le député québécois* (Quebec: l'Assemblée nationale du Québec, 1979).

11 On the importance of the legal professions, see Yoland Sénécal, 'Les professions juridiques chez les parlementaires québécois 1867-1982,' *Revue du Barreau* 44, no. 3 (1984), 545-67; Charles A. Roberge, 'Le notaire législateur,' *Revue du notariat* 87, nos. 1-2 (1984), 89-94.

12 Useful data can be found in R. Pelletier, 'Le personnel politique,' *Recherches sociographiques* 25, no. 1 (1984), 83-102; G. Deschênes, 'Portrait socio-politique de l'Assemblée nationale,' *Bulletin de la Bibliothèque de l'Assemblée nationale du Québec* 16, no. 1, (March 1986), 2-7.

13 Deschênes, *Le député québécois*, 18 (my translation).

14 M. Hamelin, *Les premières années du parlementarisme québécois* (Quebec: Presses de l'Université Laval, 1974), 329.

15 For more detail, see Louis Massicotte, 'Le Parlement du Québec en transition,' *Canadian Public Administration* 28 (Winter 1985), 550-74.

16 For the years 1867-97, the average Rice Index (a measure of cohesion, with 100 indicating perfect cohesion) of the government caucus was 98 on confidence votes, 93 on supply votes, 91 on government bills, 55 on private members' public bills, and 59 on private bills.

17 T.J.J. Loranger, *Rapport de la Commission de révision et refonte des status* (Quebec, 1881), 71-3.

18 On this, see Denis Vaugeois, *L'Assemblée nationale en devenir. Pour un meilleur équilibre des institutions* (Quebec: mimeo, 1982).

19 See the report of the House Committee on the Parliamentary Control of Delegated Legislation, *Le Contrôle parlementaire de la législation déléguée* (Quebec, July 1983).

20 A. Bernard, 'Parliamentary Control of Public Finance in Québec' (Ph.D. thesis, McGill University, Montreal, 1964).

21 M. Massé-Tardif, 'Le contrôle parlementaire des dépenses gouvernementales,' *Les Cahiers de l'ENAP* 6 (September 1982), 38-9 (my translation).

22 See the papers included in *Le contrôle de l'administration et la réforme parlementaire* (Ste-Foy: École nationale d'administration publique, 1984). See also the older work

of A. Gélinas, *Les parlementaires et l'administration au Québec* (Quebec: Presses de l'Université Laval, 1969).

23 See Louis Bernard, *Réflexions sur l'art de se gouverner*, (Montreal: Québec-Amérique, 1987).

Manitoba

1 Gordon H.A. Mackintosh, 'The Parliamentary Tradition in Manitoba,' *Canadian Parliamentary Review* 6 (Summer 1983), 2.
2 M.S. Donnelly, *The Government of Manitoba* (Toronto: University of Toronto Press, 1963), 109.
3 W.L. Morton, *Manitoba: A History* (Toronto: University of Toronto Press, 1957), 149.
4 See Donnelly, *Government of Manitoba*, 103-7.
5 John Kendle, *John Bracken: A Political Biography* (Toronto: University of Toronto Press, 1979), 141.
6 Donnelly, *Government of Manitoba*, 6.
7 Kendle, *Bracken*, 141.
8 On the evolution of the party system during this period, see Rand Dyck, *Provincial Politics in Canada* (Scarborough: Prentice-Hall, 1986), ch. 7; James A. McAllister, *The Government of Edward Schreyer* (Montreal: McGill-Queen's University Press, 1984), and Thomas Peterson, 'Manitoba: Ethnic and Class Politics' in Martin Robin, ed., *Canadian Provincial Politics*, 2nd ed. (Scarborough: Prentice-Hall, 1978).
9 Donnelly, *Government of Manitoba*, 75-8. In 1976 the Manitoba Law Reform Commission, Working Paper on Electoral Systems (Winnipeg, 1976) recommended a return to multi-member ridings and a transferable vote system, but the proposals went nowhere.
10 Report of the Electoral Boundaries Commission – 1978 (Winnipeg, 1978), 11-12.
11 Robert J. Fleming, ed., *Canadian Legislatures: The 1986 Comparative Study* (Toronto: Office of the Assembly, 1987), 75.
12 Randy M. Colwell, 'Order Please – The Speakership in Manitoba' (Paper prepared for the Manitoba Legislative Internship Program), 25-6.
13 Gordon H.A. Mackintosh, 'Heading off Bilodeau: Attempting Constitutional Amendment,' *Manitoba Law Journal* 15, no. 3 (1986), 284-6; and Tom McMahon, 'Bell-ringing Revisited: A Lack of Leadership from the Speaker,' *The Table* 55 (1987), 51-85.
14 The standing committees were as follows: Agriculture, Economic Development, Industrial Relations, Law Amendments, Municipal Affairs, Private Bills, Privileges and Elections, Public Accounts, Public Utilities and Natural Resources, Rules, and Statutory Regulations and Other Orders.

15 For a fuller discussion, see Donna A. Miller, 'Regulatory Reform in Manitoba: A Blueprint for Change,' *Manitoba Law Journal* 15, no. 2 (1986), 223-4.
16 The total number of crown corporations is somewhat open to debate since Manitoba does not have a crown corporations act and there is no single, official definition of what constitutes a crown corporation. If all 'crown agencies' were included the total would be substantially higher.
17 See the Standing Committee on Public Utilities and Natural Resources, *First Report*, 2 June 1986.
18 Task Force on Government Organization and Economy, I (Winnipeg: Queen's Printer, April 1978), 37.

Alberta

The writer would like to thank those who were interviewed. Thanks are also due John McDonough, former director, Legislative Research Service, for materials, criticism, and help; to Cynthia Alexander for help in updating; and to Caryn I.L. Duncan for most competent assistance. The writer assumes full responsibility for all undocumented passages, many but by no means all of which were inspired by interviews.
1 For much of the information about the Alberta legislature, see John McDonough, *Selected Statistical Measures Pertaining to the Work of the Alberta Legislative Assembly* (Edmonton: Legislative Research Services, 1986).
2 Howard and Tamara Palmer, 'The Alberta Experience,' *Journal of Canadian Studies* 17 (Spring 1982), 21.
3 John Richards and Larry Pratt, *Prairie Capitalism: Power and Influence in the New West* (Toronto: McClelland and Stewart, 1979), esp. chs. 3, 4, 7.
4 F.C. Engelmann, 'Grant Notley and Democracy in Alberta' in Larry Pratt, ed., *Socialism and Democracy in Alberta: Essays in Honour of Grant Notley* (Edmonton: NeWest Press, 1986), 173. The most current manifestation of this phenomenon is the demand for a 'Triple-E' Senate – elected, equal, effective.
5 RFDs were an innovation of the Lougheed government. The appropriations described here are authorized by the Financial Administration Act, first passed by Social Credit in 1968.
6 This was made very clear to the writer when many Progressive Conservative members and former members contributed to the memorial fund, at the University of Alberta, for Grant Notley, the young NDP leader killed in an air crash in 1984.
7 Statutes of Alberta, 1983, L-10.1.
8 There used to be no cabinet representative on the committee. The present situation dates from the time, less than a decade ago, when a committee member received a cabinet appointment.
9 Information on the Progressive Conservative caucus is taken from Peter McCormick, 'Politics after the Landslide,' *Parliamentary Government* 4 (1983), 8-10, and from a lecture delivered by the Hon. Peter Lougheed at the University of Alberta, 11

February 1987. Some caucus members claim there have been changes since 1985, but these have not been specified to the writer.

10 According to a former member, Premier Manning and his house leader discharged most of the present caucus functions in the late sixties.

11 I am fortunate to have available data from 1905 until past the election of 1967, collected by Dr H.L. Malliah of the University of Mysore, who assembled them in 1970 while working for his doctorate under my supervision. Comparisons will be made with legislators sitting just prior to the election of 1986, in some cases after the last election; the former will be designated '1985' and the latter '1987'. H.L. Malliah, 'A Socio-historical Study of the Legislature of Alberta, 1905-1967' (Ph.D. thesis, University of Alberta, 1970); data for 1985 are taken from *Canadian Parliamentary Guide 1986* (Ottawa: Normandin, 1986); data for 1987 are taken from Robert J. Fleming and Patrick Fafard, eds., *Canadian Legislatures: The 1986 Comparative Study* (Toronto: Office of the Assembly, 1986), 77.

12 Standing Orders of the Legislative Assembly of Alberta, No. 69.

13 *Ibid.*, No. 8.

14 *Ibid.*, No. 29.

15 Fleming and Fafard, *Canadian Legislatures*, 125-126.

16 For numbers of pages, see McDonough, *Selected Statistics*, Table C-9.

17 In April 1987, TV cameramen were ejected by the Speaker for continuing to broadcast past the question period. A compromise was reached and blanket permission was given to televise any public part of the 1987 session; it is not used much.

18 Fleming and Fafard, *Canadian Legislatures*, 117.

19 The use of French in the Legislative Assembly is not settled. In 1987, Speaker Carter disallowed the questioning of a (bilingual) minister in French. While prominent witnesses at subsequent hearings overwhelmingly favoured the use of French, the temporary rule (pending statutory settlement) is permission of the use of *any* language other than English, provided there is notice and a prepared translation into English.

20 Fleming and Fafard, *Canadian Legislatures*, 119-20.

21 *Ibid.*, 87.

22 Standing Order No. 7.

23 Priscilla Schmidt, 'Government-Press Relations in Alberta,' unpublished paper, Alberta legislative internship program, 1985.

24 Alberta *Hansard*, Twenty-First Legislature, First Session, 26 June 26 1986, 1-2.

25 Nothing of significance known to the writer has happened since his colleagues Larry Pratt and Allan Tupper wrote in 1980: 'the record of the government-dominated committee has certainly not been impressive to date' ('The Politics of Accountability: Executive Discretion and Control,' *Canadian Public Policy* 6, 1980 Supplement, 263).

26 Alberta Teachers' Association, *A Guide to Alberta's Twenty-First Legislature* (Edmonton: Alberta Teachers' Association, 1986), 32-3.
27 *Ibid.*, 20-3.
28 Jean Munn, 'Government Private Members in Alberta,' unpublished paper, Alberta legislative internship program, 1985, 4.

British Columbia

This paper draws on the author's other writing on the British Columbia Legislature: 'Continuity Despite Change: Reform of the British Columbia Legislature,' in *The Parliamentarian* 53 (January 1981); 'The Legislature' in J.T. Morley, et al., *The Reins of Power: Governing British Columbia* (Vancouver: Douglas and McIntyre, 1983); and 'The Legislature under Siege' in Warren Magnussen et al., eds., *The New Reality* (Vancouver: New Star, 1984).
1 Edwin R. Black, 'British Columbia: The Politics of Exploitation' in Ronald A. Shearer, ed., *Exploiting Our Economic Potential: Public Policy and the British Columbia Economy* (Toronto: Holt, Rinehart and Winston, 1968).
2 Interview with Ernest Hall, 30 January 1979.
3 Walter D. Young, 'The Legislature under W.A.C. Bennett,' (B.C. Project Working Paper, 1983), 37.
4 *Ibid.*, 17-18.
5 For reasons that are obscure, the B.C. committees have always been referred to as 'Select Standing Committees.'
6 Hon. Gordon Hudson Dowding, *Reports under Terms of the Legislative Procedure and Practice Inquiry Act* (five reports) (Victoria: Legislative Assembly, 1973-75).
7 See Wilson, 'Continuity Despite Change.'
8 Legislative Assembly of British Columbia, *Debates*, 16 June 1977: 2780.
9 See R.S. Milne and N.A. Swainson, 'The Crown Corporations Committee of the British Columbia Legislature,' *Parliamentary Government* 3 (Spring 1982); and R.S. Milne, 'The British Columbia Crown Corporations Committee: Comparisons and Implications,' *B.C. Studies* 68 (Winter 1985-86).
10 For a full account of the 1983 session, see Wilson, 'The Legislature under Siege.'
11 Frank Howard, in *Debates*, 23 March 1984: 4032.
12 As quoted by Austin Pelton, *Debates*, 12 February 1985: 4914.
13 See Vaughn Palmer, 'A fine public servant's not-so-fond farewell,' *Vancouver Sun*, 27 September 1986.
14 For a full discussion of the current situation, see 'The Public Accounts in British Columbia' (interview conducted by Craig James with the chairman of the committee, the auditor general, and the comptroller general), *Canadian Parliamentary Review* 11 (Spring 1988).
15 Press release, 6 November 1986.
16 Vaughn Palmer, 'All hail a new spririt of co-operation,' *Vancouver Sun*, 15 May 1987.

Nova Scotia

1 Charles Dickens, *American Notes,* 21; as quoted by J. Murray Beck, *The Government of Nova Scotia* (Toronto: University of Toronto Press, 1957), 100.
2 Michael Ryle, T*he Procedures and Practices of the House of Assembly,* mimeo, Nova Scotia House of Assembly, 1976, 3.
3 See Public Archives of Canada, letters of Stewart Derbishire to Lord Durham from Halifax; also, J. Murray Beck's two-volume biography of Joseph Howe, *Jospeh Howe Volume I: The Conservative Reformer 1804-1848; Joseph Howe Volume II: The Briton Becomes Canadian 1848-1873* (Montreal: McGill-Queens University Press, 1983). By 1841 Cape Breton was once again part of Nova Scotia; in 1758 it had been a separate colony.
4 Beck, *Government of Nova Scotia,* 251.
5 *Ibid.,* 252.
6 Rand Dyck, *Provincial Politics in Canada* (Scarborough: Prentice-Hall, 1986), 108-9.
7 Premier Gerald Regan was forced into this action by public pressure. Privately, he did not wish to create any new seats, as he feared he would lose them. His political antenna was correct, for his party lost all but one of the new seats in 1978.
8 For a vivid description of the 1956 campaign, see Dalton Camp, *Gentlemen, Players and Politicians* (Toronto: McClelland and Stewart, 1970).
9 Ryle, *Procedures and Practices,* 1.
10 *Ibid.,* 7.
11 See Arthur Donahoe, 'Procedural Change in the Nova Scotia House of Assembly,' *Canadian Parliamentary Review* 4, no. 2, (1981), 8-10.
12 See Michael Atkinson, 'Reform and Inertia in the Nova Scotia Assembly,' *Journal of Canadian Studies* 14 (Summer 1979), 117-32.
13 Province of Nova Scotia, *Rules and Forms of Procedure of the House of Assembly* (Halifax, 1987), Rule 31(2).
14 *Interim Report to the House of Assembly of the Special Committee on Rules and Procedures of the House of Assembly* (Halifax, 1986), 10.
15 Ryle, *Procedures and Practices,* 10.
16 *Report,* 11.
17 See Agar Adamson, 'Politics Without Policy,' *Policy Options* 6, no. 6 (1985).
18 Ryle, *Procedures and Practices,* 32.
19 In interviews with the author.
20 Ryle, *Procedures and Practices,* 33.
21 *Rules and Forms.*
22 Ryle, *Procedures and Practices,* 13-14.
23 *Rules and Forms,* Rule 46.
24 *Ibid.,* Rule 60(2)a.
25 *Halifax Chronicle-Herald,* 2 December 1986, 1.

26   *Ibid.*, 30 October 1986, 4.
27   *Ibid.*, 31 October, 27.
28   For details of the split in the NDP, see Agar Adamson, 'Does MacEwan's Real Ale Give the NDP Heartburn,' 1986 APPSA Papers, Wolfville, 1985.
29   Beck, *Government of Nova Scotia*, 273.
30   Camp, *Gentlemen, Players and Politicians, 213*.
31   David Black, 'The Committee System in the Nova Scotia Legislature: Problems, Potential, and Possibilities for Reform,' unpublished internship essay, Halifax, 1986.

New Brunswick

1   H.G. Thorburn, *Politics in New Brunswick* (Toronto: University of Toronto Press, 1961), 186.
2   Rand Dyck, *Provincial Politics in Canada* (Scarborough: Prentice-Hall, 1986), 144.
3   Edmund Aunger, *In Search of Political Stability: A Comparative Study of New Brunswick and Northern Ireland* (Montreal: McGill-Queen's University Press, 1981), 20.
4   Thorburn, *Politics in New Brunswick*.
5   Aunger, *In Search of Political Stability*, 153.
6   Katherine MacNaughton, *The Development of Theory and Practice of Education in New Brunswick, 1784-1900* (Fredericton: University of New Brunswick Historical Studies No. 1, 1946), 228.
7   *Ibid.*, 229.
8   Aunger, *In Search of Political Stability*, 153-4.
9   MacNaughton, *Education in New Brunswick*, 228-9.
10   Dyck, *Provincial Politics*, 144.
11   *Ibid.*, 140.
12   *Ibid.*, 156.
13   *Ibid.*, 141.
14   *Ibid.*, 166.
15   *Ibid.*, 146.
16   Calvin A. Woodward, *The History of New Brunswick Provincial Election Campaigns and Platforms, 1866-1974* (Fredericton: Micromedia, 1976), 20-1.
17   Dyck, *Provincial Politics*, 148-9.
18   *Ibid.*, 164.
19   Woodward, *Election Campaigns*, 53.
20   Aunger, *In Search of Political Stability*, 22.
21   Thorburn, *Politics in New Brunswick*, 181.
22   Dyck, *Provincial Politics*, 167.
23   Dalton Camp, *Gentlemen, Players and Politicians* (Toronto: McClelland and Stewart, 1970), 10, 18.

24 P.J. Fitzpatrick, 'New Brunswick: The Politics of Pragmatism' in Martin Robin, ed., *Canadian Provincial Politics*, 2nd ed. (Scarborough: Prentice-Hall, 1978), 135.
25 *Ibid.,* 120.
26 Aunger, *In Search of Political Stability*, 50-2.

Newfoundland

1 S.J.R. Noel, *Politics in Newfoundland* (Toronto: University of Toronto Press, 1971), 275.
2 K.C. Wheare, *Legislatures* (London: Oxford University Press, 1963); A. Kornberg, 'Parliament in Canadian Society' in A. Kornberg, ed., *Legislatures in Developmental Perspective* (Durham: Duke University Press, 1970); Michael Mezey, *Comparative Legislatures* (Durham: Duke University Press, 1979).
3 'The Premiers' in Robert Fleming and Thomas Mitchinson, eds., *Canadian Legislatures: The 1983 Comparative Study* (Toronto: Office of the Assembly, 1983), 11.
4 C.E.S. Franks, *The Parliament of Canada* (Toronto: University of Toronto Press, 1987), 171.
5 *Evening Telegram*, 30 November 1974.
6 Select Committee of the House of Assembly, *Report*, 1983, 1.
7 Susan McCorquodale, 'Newfoundland' in Martin Robin, ed., *Canadian Provincial Politics*, 2nd ed. (Scarborough: Prentice-Hall, 1978), 162.
8 Mark W. Graesser, 'Public Opinion on Denominational Education: the Majority Rule?' in William McKim, ed., *The Vexed Question: Denominational Education in a Secular Age* (St John's: Breakwater Books, 1988).
9 Robert J. Fleming, ed., *Canadian Legislatures 1987-1988* (Ottawa: Ampersand Communications Services, 1988), 100.
10 Franks, *The Parliament of Canada*, 23.
11 *Evening Telegram*, 7 March 1978.
12 Alan Frizzell and Anthony Westell, *The Canadian General Election of 1984* (Ottawa: Carleton University Press, 1985), 91.
13 *Evening Telegram*, editorial, 25 April 1963.
14 Richard Rose, 'British MPs: More Bark than Bite?' in Ezra N. Suleiman, ed., *Parliaments and Parliamentarians in Democratic Politics* (New York: Holmes and Meier, 1986), 9.
15 *Sunday Express*, 13 March 1988, 21.
16 Graesser, 'Public Opinion,' 30.
17 Michael Harris in *Atlantic Insight*, 8 November 1979.
18 *Evening Telegram*, 6 August 1979.
19 Richard Simeon and David Elkins, *Small Worlds: Provinces and Parties in Canadian Political Life* (Toronto: Methuen, 1980), 37-40.
20 Franks, *The Parliament of Canada*, 244.

21   George Perlin, *The Tory Syndrome: Leadership Politics in the Progressive Conservative Party* (Montreal: McGill-Queen's University Press, 1980), 198-200.

Yukon

1   J.D. Hillson, 'Constitutional Develohpment of the Yukon Territory, 1960-1970' (MA thesis, University of Saskatchewan, 1973), 6.
2   *Klondike Nugget*, 2 June 1900, 5.
3   62-63 Victoria (Canada) RSC 1899, c. 11.
4   *Dawson Daily News*, 3 July 1903, in D.R. Morrison, *The Politics of the Yukon Territory, 1898-1909* (Toronto: University of Toronto Press, 1968), 52.
5   Council of the Yukon Territory, *Journals*, 1903: 22.
6   *Ibid.*, 1920: 6.
7   Hillson, 'Constitutional Development,' 84-100.
8   Yukon Legislative Assembly, Sessional Paper No. 79-2-8, 7 March 1979.
9   Hon. Jake Epp to Ione Christensen, 9 October 1979.
10   Hon. David Crombie to Doug Bell, 14 February 1985.
11   *Ibid.*
12   H.R. Hanson and J.J. Kelly, *Improving Accountability: Canadian Public Accounts Committees and Legislative Auditors* (Ottawa: Canadian Comprehensive Auditing Foundation, 1981), 108-10.
13   Canada, House of Commons, Special Committee on Reform of the House of Commons, *Third Report,* June 1985, 1.

Northwest Territories

1   Some MLAs openly express their affiliation with one of the three major political parties, and party associations are established in the north. Party politics was a minor issue in the 1987 territorial election, and proponents predict that candidates may be running under party colours by the 1990s. However, party politics is strongly opposed by most Native MLAs, who have been in the majority since 1979, and it would appear that changes to legislation and House practices will not be formally considered in the foreseeable future.
2   Procedure described by David M. Hamilton, clerk of the NWT Legislative Assembly.
3   The government house leader is a member of the Standing Committee on Rules, Procedures and Privileges.
4   During debate on the 1985 proposed boundary agreement for division of the NWT, all eastern members, including four ministers, walked out of the House in protest and refused to come back to vote on the document. Western MLAs were able to muster a quorum and pass a motion approving the document. (See Tenth Legislative Assembly of the Northwest Territories, *Debates*, Fourth Session, 25 February 1985: 462-4.) In 1986 on a motion to remove a minister from the executive, the

government leader stated that he did not see the motion as non-confidence in the executive as a whole. He instructed all ministers that there was to be a free vote on the issue and that the rules of cabinet solidarity did not apply. Three ministers abstained from the vote. (See Tenth Legislative Assembly *Debates*, Ninth Session, 16 March 1987: 918-40.)

5 Leslie Malloch, *Dene Government: Past and Future*, a paper prepared for the Western Constitutional Forum, (Altona, Manitoba: Freisen and Sons, 1984), 14-15.

6 Delegates and observers to meetings of the Baffin Regional Council have commented that discussions are often very protracted until a consensus becomes apparent. As well, the strongest dissent in any vote is usually abstention.

7 A strong argument against using the word consensus in the NWT system is found in Gurston Dacks, 'Politics on the Last Frontier: Consociationalism in the Northwest Territories,' *Canadian Journal of Political Science* 19 (June 1986), 348.

8 Ajauqtit is an Inuit word meaning 'people who push,' referring to those people who help push a sled that bogs down in the snow. Also called the Ordinary Members' Committee, the group has consciously avoided using the word opposition.

9 Eleventh Legislative Assembly, *Debates*, Second Session, 26 February 1988: 443-5.

10 *Ibid.*, 22 February 1988: 276.

11 *Ibid.*, 285.

12 *Ibid.*, 286.

13 This comment refers to a rumour that the executive threatened to resign if the Assembly forced them to release the document on decentralization.

14 Eleventh Legislative Assembly, *Debates*, Second Session, 17 February 1988: 152.

15 Tenth Legislative Assembly, *Debates*, Ninth Session, 16 March 1987: 918.

16 Procedural opinion from David M. Hamilton, clerk of the NWT Legislative Assembly.

17 Legislative Assembly, Special Committee on Rules, Procedures and Privileges, *Fourth Report*, 1987, 6.

18 The 1987 motion to remove a minister from the executive was not perceived by the government leader as non-confidence in the executive as a whole, but rather as censure of an individual.

19 Eleventh Legislative Assembly, *Debates*, Second Session, 24 March 1988: 913.

20 Morris Zaslow, ed., *A Century of Canada's Arctic Islands: 1880-1980* (Ottawa: Royal Society of Canada, 1981), xiii.

21 Shirley Milligan with Walter Kupsch, 'Road to Responsible Government: The Evolution of the Territorial Council' in *Council in Transition: Government of the N.W.T. Annual Report* (Yellowknife: Department of Information, 1976), 8.

22 32-33 Victoria, c.3 (Canada); RSC 1870, App II, 243.

23 Milligan and Kupsch, 'Road to Responsible Government,' 9.

24 Canada, Advisory Commission on the Development of Government in the Northwest Territories, (Chairman, A.W.R. Carrothers), *Report to the Minister of Northern Affairs and National Resources* (Ottawa, 1966), 24.

25 Richard H. Bartlett, *Indians and Taxation in Canada* (Regina: University of Saskatchewan Native Law Centre, 1980), 8-10.

26 The Yukon/Mackenzie area of the western Arctic had been represented since 1949; the entire NWT was represented as of 1962.

27 Advisory Commission, *Report to the Minister of Northern Affairs and National Resources.*

28 C.M. Drury, *Constitutional Development in the Northwest Territories: Report of the Special Representative* (Ottawa: Supply and Services Canada, 1980), 29.

29 *Ibid.*, no page.

30 Bills C-83 and C-84 to establish the Western and Nunatsiaq Territories respectively.

31 Inuit Tapirisat of Canada, *Nunavut: A Proposal for the Settlement of Inuit Lands in the Northwest Territories*, Proposed agreement in principle, 27 February 27 1976.

32 Dene Nation, *Agreement in Principle [proposed] between the Dene Nation and Her Majesty the Queen, in Right of Canada*, October 1976. See also, Dene Nation/Métis Association of the NWT, *Public Government for the People of the N.W.T.*, Draft, Yellowknife, 9 November 9 1981.

33 Northwest Territories, *Report of the Chief Plebiscite Officer On the Plebiscite on Division of the Northwest Territories*, 1982.

34 Gurston Dacks, 'Liberal-Democratic Government: Principles and Practices,' a paper prepared for the Western Constitutional Forum, Edmonton, 16 May 1983.

35 Michael S. Whittington, ed., *The North* (Toronto: University of Toronto Press, 1985), 65.

36 C.G. Eglington, 'A Question of Confidence in the Northwest Territories Legislative Assembly' in Special Committee on Rules Procedures and Privileges, *Third Report* (Yellowknife: Legislative Assembly of the Northwest Territories, 14 October 1986), 92.

CONTRIBUTORS

Agar Adamson is a member of the Political Science Department at Acadia University where he teaches courses on Canadian and comparative politics. He is the first director of the Nova Scotia legislative intern program.

Andy Anstett graduated in political science from the University of Waterloo and served as deputy clerk of the Manitoba legislature from 1973 to 1979. He was subsequently elected to the legislature in 1981 and served as minister of municipal affairs and government house leader. He is a public policy consultant in Winnipeg.

Frederick C. Engelmann studied at UCLA and Yale. He taught in the United States from 1950 to 1962 and later at the University of Alberta. Co-author of *Canadian Party Systems* and *Canadian Political Parties: Origin, Character, Impact*, he is a past president of the Canadian Political Science Association and, in 1986, was named Professor Emeritus at the University of Alberta in Edmonton.

Gary Levy is editor of the *Canadian Parliamentary Review* and an occasional lecturer in political science at the University of Ottawa. He was 1988-89 Visiting Fellow with the Americas Societies/Canadian Affairs in New York.

Louis Massicotte is a research officer with the Library of Parliament and has lectured at Laval University and the University of Ottawa. He is completing doctoral studies at Carleton University in Ottawa.

Susan McCorquodale is a graduate of Queen's University and Manchester University in England. She teaches in the Department of Political Science at Memorial University and has written many articles about Newfoundland politics.

Patrick L. Michael is a graduate of the University of Alberta and after a year as an intern with the Alberta Legislative Assembly became executive assistant to the leader of the opposition. Appointed clerk of the Yukon Legislative Assembly in 1978 and chief electoral officer in 1983, he was president of the Association of Clerks-at-the-Table in 1985-86.

Kevin O'Keefe studied at Trent University. He was head of the Northwest Territories Legislative Assembly's Research Service from 1983 to 1988, and is currently co-ordinator of the Legislation and House Planning Committee of the NWT cabinet.

David L. E. Peterson is a lawyer and graduate of the University of New Brunswick. He was appointed clerk of the New Brunswick Legislative Assembly in 1979. He is a former president of the Association of Clerks-at-the-Table.

David E. Smith is a member of the Department of Political Science at the University of Saskatchewan and author of *Prairie Liberalism: The Liberal Party in Saskatchewan* and *The Regional Decline of a National Party*.

Ian Stewart is associate professor in the Political Science Department at Acadia University. He teaches courses in Canadian politics and has focused his recent research on Atlantic Canada. He is a past president of the Atlantic Provincial Political Studies Association.

Paul G. Thomas is professor of Political Studies at the University of Manitoba and co-ordinator of the Joint Masters Program in Public Affairs. A former intern in the House of Commons, he was the first director of the Manitoba legislature's intern program.

Graham White is a former intern with the Ontario Legislative Assembly. He was assistant clerk with the Assembly from 1978 to 1984 and now teaches political science at the University of Toronto. He is director of the Ontario legislative intern program, co-editor of *Politics: Canada* (6th ed.), and author of *The Ontario Legislature: A Political Analysis*.

Jeremy Wilson teaches in the Department of Political Science at the University of Victoria where he specializes in Canadian and provincial politics. He was a member the BC Studies project and co-author of *The Reins of Power*.